OECD
Economic Surveys

United Kingdom

2007

OECD

ORGANISATION FOR ECONOMIC CO-OPERATION AND DEVELOPMENT

The OECD is a unique forum where the governments of 30 democracies work together to address the economic, social and environmental challenges of globalisation. The OECD is also at the forefront of efforts to understand and to help governments respond to new developments and concerns, such as corporate governance, the information economy and the challenges of an ageing population. The Organisation provides a setting where governments can compare policy experiences, seek answers to common problems, identify good practice and work to co-ordinate domestic and international policies.

The OECD member countries are: Australia, Austria, Belgium, Canada, the Czech Republic, Denmark, Finland, France, Germany, Greece, Hungary, Iceland, Ireland, Italy, Japan, Korea, Luxembourg, Mexico, the Netherlands, New Zealand, Norway, Poland, Portugal, the Slovak Republic, Spain, Sweden, Switzerland, Turkey, the United Kingdom and the United States. The Commission of the European Communities takes part in the work of the OECD.

OECD Publishing disseminates widely the results of the Organisation's statistics gathering and research on economic, social and environmental issues, as well as the conventions, guidelines and standards agreed by its members.

This survey is published on the responsibility of the Economic and Development Review Committee of the OECD, which is charged with the examination of the economic situation of member countries.

Also available in French

Table of contents

Figures

This Survey is published on the responsibility of the Economic and Development Review Committee of the OECD, which is charged with the examination of the economic situation of member countries.

The economic situation and policies of the United Kingdom were reviewed by the Committee on 5 September 2007. The draft report was then revised in the light of the discussions and given final approval as the agreed report of the whole Committee on 14 September 2007.

The Secretariat's draft report was prepared for the Committee by Anne-Marie Brook, Åsa Johansson, Petar Vujanovic and Marte Sollie under the supervision of Peter Hoeller. Research assistance was provided by Desney Erb.

The previous Survey of the United Kingdom was issued in November 2005.

This book has...

StatLinks

A service that delivers Excel® files from the printed page!

Look for the *StatLinks* at the bottom right-hand corner of the tables or graphs in this book. To download the matching Excel® spreadsheet, just type the link into your Internet browser, starting with the *http://dx.doi.org* prefix.
If you're reading the PDF e-book edition, and your PC is connected to the Internet, simply click on the link. You'll find *StatLinks* appearing in more OECD books.

BASIC STATISTICS OF THE UNITED KINGDOM (2006)

THE LAND

Area (2005, 1 000 km^2)		Major cities (2005, thousand inhabitants)	
Total	242	Greater London	7 518
Agricultural	185	Birmingham	1 001
		Leeds	723
		Glasgow (local government district)	579

THE PEOPLE

Thousands		Total labour force (thousands)	30 630
Population	60 587	Civilian employment (% of total)	
Net increase (annual average 2001-05)	274	Agriculture, forestry and fishing	1.3
Number of inhabitants per km^2	250	Industry and construction	22.0
		Services	76.4

PRODUCTION

Gross domestic product		Gross fixed capital investment	
In £ billion	1 300	In % of GDP	18.1
Per head ($)	39 519	Per head ($)	7 138

THE GOVERNMENT

Public consumption (% of GDP)	22.1	Composition of House of Commons (seats)	
General government (% of GDP)		Labour	351
Current and capital expenditure	44.6	Conservatives	195
Current revenue	41.6	Liberal Democrat	63
Net debt	39.5	Other	37
Last general elections: 5 May 2005		Total	646

FOREIGN TRADE

Exports of goods and services (% of GDP)	28.4	Imports of goods and services (% of GDP)	32.6
Main commodity exports (% of total)		Main commodity imports (% of total)	
Electrical machinery	22.7	Manufactured goods and articles	25.2
Manufactured goods and articles	22.0	Electrical machinery	25.0
Chemicals	15.2	Road vehicles	10.0
Mechanical machinery	11.6	Fuels	9.8

THE CURRENCY

Monetary unit: Pound sterling		August 2007, monthly average of spot rate	
		£ per $	0.497
		£ per €	0.677

Executive summary

The United Kingdom's welcoming approach to globalisation has contributed to a strong growth performance. GDP per capita is now the third highest in the G7, compared with the lowest 10 years earlier. GDP growth has been close to its trend rate of around 2¾ per cent for a number of years, suggesting that the amplitude of the economic cycle is smaller now than in previous decades. This strong performance is not only due to the willingness to embrace the opportunities offered by globalisation, but also to sound institutional arrangements for setting monetary and fiscal policy as well as a period of robust trading partner growth.

Despite offshoring, employment has grown steadily and unemployment is low. But the labour market position of many low-skilled workers needs to be further improved. The participation rate of some groups is low and others suffer from poor incentives to progress in work. To raise the adaptability of the workforce the government has invested in education. It is also spending more on fighting poverty and has been addressing weaknesses in the transport and health systems. The budget deficit remains large, and slower growth in government expenditure will be required over the coming years, as well as more effort to ensure good value for money in public spending. Against this background, further rewards from globalisation can be reaped by addressing the following challenges.

Improving prospects for the least skilled to benefit from globalisation

- Because the benefits of globalisation are potentially greater with a flexible labour force, primary and secondary schools need to make sure all young people acquire core skills before leaving full-time education.

- More needs to be done to improve education outcomes for young people from low socio-economic backgrounds. A faster transition to a more equitable allocation of school funding would help and more should be done to encourage the best teachers to move to the most disadvantaged schools.

- Incentives to join the workforce and to progress in work should be improved for certain groups such as second-income earners, lone parents, and incapacity beneficiaries. This may require reducing marginal effective tax rates and providing greater access to child-care support. A slower rise in the minimum wage may also improve the employment prospects of the low-skilled.

Enhancing business conditions for productivity growth and job creation

- Planning regulations need to give more weight to economic considerations to promote firm entry and local plans should ensure that more land is freed up for development.

- Sufficient levels of investment in the transport infrastructure should be ensured, while the potential for more extensive road-pricing to reduce congestion should be explored.

- Tax competitiveness should be improved by continuing to broaden the corporate tax base while cutting the rate. The corporate tax system should be simplified and there may be room to shift taxation to less mobile sources.

OECD ECONOMIC SURVEYS: UNITED KINGDOM – ISBN 978-92-64-03772-4 – © OECD 2007

ISBN 978-92-64-03772-4
OECD Economic Surveys: United Kingdom
© OECD 2007

Assessment and recommendations

The United Kingdom has embraced globalisation and been rewarded with a strong growth performance

Living up to the challenges posed by globalisation is the over-arching theme of this *Economic Survey*. Compared with its large European neighbours, the United Kingdom has been more proactive in adapting to international economic forces. This is reflected in support for free trade, openness to foreign direct investment, a willingness to open its labour markets to the citizens from the new EU member countries that joined in May 2004, the adoption of regulatory policies that promote efficiency and a macroeconomic policy framework that has enhanced economic resilience. This willingness to embrace the opportunities offered by globalisation is generally backed by widespread support among key groups, including politicians, trade union leaders and employers. This has been rewarded with a stronger economic performance. The level of gross domestic product (GDP) per capita is now the third highest in the G7 (after the United States and Canada). Ten years earlier it was the lowest in this group. The United Kingdom's GDP per capita ranking among all OECD countries has also improved. GDP growth has been close to its trend rate of around 2¾ per cent for a number of years, suggesting that the amplitude of the economic cycle is smaller now than in previous decades.

The near-term outlook is more uncertain, given recent financial market turbulence

Despite buoyant activity in recent years, strong inward migration has contributed to an easing in labour market tightness. Although the unemployment rate has crept up over the past two years, particularly among young unskilled school-leavers, it is still relatively low at around 5½ per cent. Consumer price inflation temporarily spiked to just above 3% earlier this year, partly because of unusually large increases in electricity and gas prices, but has since dropped back to just under 2%. Looking ahead, the interest rate increases over the last year, together with recent financial market volatility, are expected to slow the housing market. Prior to the recent financial market turmoil the OECD projected growth of 2¾ per cent this year and 2½ per cent next year, with inflation remaining close to the 2% target. However, although indicators of economic activity have been robust in 2007 to date, there is now a risk that growth will be weaker going forward, which could imply a need for interest rate reductions. A slowing in growth, together with reduced profitability in the City, could also reduce tax revenues and imply a rise in the budget deficit, which is still relatively high by international comparison.

Earnings growth has remained moderate, despite significant concerns earlier this year that the spike in inflation might push up wage inflation. Strong inward migration helped in this regard by filling skill shortages and preventing labour market bottlenecks. Wage bargainers typically use as their inflation benchmark the retail price index. However, neither this index nor the consumer price index (CPI) are ideally suited for this purpose. An improved index would be based on the CPI but include a better measure of housing costs. The UK authorities should continue to support the development of the CPI index to include housing.

The size of government has grown and the deficit remains large

Government revenues and outlays – but particularly the latter – have trended upwards over the past few years as a share of GDP, albeit from relatively low levels by UK historical standards. Increased spending was a deliberate policy choice, motivated by the desire to improve certain government services, notably health and education. This contrasts with a general tendency towards spending restraint in most other OECD economies. The government deficit has fallen from 3.4% of GDP in 2003 to 2.7% in the year to March 2007, but the cyclically-adjusted budget shortfall is still substantial and significantly larger than in most other OECD countries. There is a need to further reduce the government deficit, which will require much slower growth in government expenditure – as the 2007 Comprehensive Spending Review promises to deliver – and more effort devoted to ensuring that publicly-funded services provide good value for money.

In 2005 the government renegotiated the policy that would have raised the normal public sector pension age from 60 to 65 for existing workers from 2013 in return for a commitment from unions that they would agree other reforms in the pension schemes to recover equivalent costs to those that would be lost by retaining the existing pension age for existing workers. Some of the subsequent negotiations have yet to be finalised and the final savings are not yet known, but the government is optimistic that the measures should deliver significant cost reductions.

The fiscal rules could be refined

The golden rule explicitly permits the government to borrow to pay for capital investment while the sustainable investment rule puts a limit on the extent of borrowing – by limiting public sector net debt to 40% of GDP. The golden rule only requires that the current budget is in surplus or balance over the cycle, and so does not require the accumulation of surpluses. Thus, it does not by itself explicitly address the perceived need to go further in preparing the public finances for the long-term challenges due to the ageing of the population. However, the government publishes annually the Long-Term Public Finance Report, which provides a comprehensive assessment of long-term fiscal sustainability, including the impact of ageing. Moreover, by separating current and capital spending, the fiscal rules have helped to tackle the United Kingdom's historical bias against capital spending and low investment in public infrastructure. The rules have also put the public finances on a more sound and sustainable footing than in previous economic cycles and have played an important role in anchoring expectations and improving the transparency of fiscal policy. But some refinements to the rules could be considered. In particular, the golden rule relies on the notion of a clearly defined economic cycle, which has become harder to identify given that the economy has remained close to full capacity for a prolonged period of time. In addition, revisions to the cycle dates have occurred, which may have undermined the credibility of the golden rule. The golden rule could be made less reliant on cycle dating and output gap estimates, possibly by replacing it with a positive target level for the current budget balance over the medium-term, together with a comprehensive independent auditing of revenue projections. This could be accompanied by mechanisms that put a tighter constraint on overall spending and prevent the spending of revenue windfalls. The fiscal framework should also be transparent about fiscal drag, either through indexing tax brackets to wage growth or through efficiency enhancing tax reform. In addition, greater account should be taken of the large off-balance-sheet liabilities, which are not currently monitored under either rule. This could be done by publishing estimates of other public sector liabilities on a regular basis alongside those of public sector net debt and by setting a ceiling on a broader measure of public sector liabilities.

Productivity has been boosted by foreign direct investment, multinational enterprises and offshoring

There are a number of channels through which globalisation has spurred productivity. Openness to trade has promoted competition and encouraged economic resources to shift towards those sectors in which the United Kingdom has a comparative advantage. As a result, the manufacturing sector has shrunk as a proportion of total output, while knowledge-intensive and other business services have grown. This means that the United Kingdom is little affected by head-to-head competition from the emerging markets. Offshoring has facilitated productivity growth by allowing UK firms to re-locate lower-value-added production and service functions (such as information technology) to lower-cost locations, while increasingly specialising in areas of comparative advantage. There is evidence that foreign direct investment and multinational enterprises – particularly those from the United States – have also contributed to productivity growth, by facilitating the transfer of new technologies. Somewhat fortuitously, living standards have also been boosted by terms-of-trade gains, because the United Kingdom has tended to import those goods which have experienced the largest price falls, while being a leading services exporter, where prices are rising. In addition, the United Kingdom is nearly self sufficient in oil and the terms of trade have therefore not been much affected by higher world oil prices. There are some uncertainties regarding the extent to which these positive benefits can be relied on in the future. Compared with many other OECD countries, the labour share of income has been relatively stable over the past decade, rather than declining. This may be a positive reflection of policies that encourage labour to move to where it is most productive and policies that have ensured a relatively low rate of structural unemployment.

Globalisation reinforces the need to raise skill levels

Technological change over the past two decades has significantly raised the level of cognitive skills required for many jobs, including many that were considered relatively low-skilled in the past. Moreover, the strongest employment growth and the largest wage increases have been in professions that require cognitive skills involving good judgement and complex communication. Recognition of these facts by both the public and policymakers explains why there is now much greater pressure on the education system to equip more pupils with better skills. However, the educational performance of the UK population is below the standard of the best performing OECD countries. The government has responded by spending more on education and by expanding capacity in key areas such as pre-primary and upper secondary education. Some measures of performance, such as secondary school completion rates, have been improving although they have further to go. However, it is difficult to evaluate the extent of improvements in cognitive skills as the lags between spending and outcomes are long and some domestic measures of education performance may have been biased by target-driven output measures. To permit more comprehensive evaluation of progress, the government should ensure continued participation in international tests of cognitive ability, such as the Programme for International Student Assessment (PISA) and the Programme for International Assessment of Adult Competences (PIAAC).

And more needs to be done to break the cycle of perpetuating inequality

As globalisation raises the return to higher education, the impact of education policy on the labour market outcomes of those from disadvantaged backgrounds is increasingly important, particularly in the United Kingdom, where occupational and education mobility is lower than in many other OECD countries. The government has addressed this with a broad range of policies, including funding formulas that aim to direct additional resources to areas with a higher proportion of pupils from deprived backgrounds. Performance in the most disadvantaged schools has improved, but overall the socio-economic gaps remain large. One explanation may be that local authorities and schools are not distributing funds as intended by the central government, resulting in inequitable outcomes. To correct this imbalance the government should promote the transition to a more efficient and equitable allocation of funds by reviewing the funding allocation procedures. More research should be done into determining how resource mixes within schools can help to narrow the socio-economic gaps and the pros and cons should be evaluated of introducing a differentiated voucher system of funding, where pupils from poorer families receive vouchers that are valued more highly than those for the general population. Also, given the importance of teacher quality, more should be done to encourage the best teachers to move to the most disadvantaged schools.

More money for schools is no guarantee of better results

There is no strong empirical link between aggregate education spending and pupil achievement so that additional resources do not automatically translate into better results. Given the need for tight expenditure control, this suggests that the focus in education spending should shift to improving the efficiency of existing spending. The key priority should be to continue to promote a focus on the acquisition of core literacy and numeracy skills for pupils at all age levels. The government is considering raising the number of years of compulsory education or training but care should be taken to ensure that greater quantity of education is not sought at the expense of quality. One way the United Kingdom has tried to ensure spending efficiency is through the use of sophisticated school benchmarking together with the setting of targets. While the benchmarking exercise has provided a lot of information, the focus on targets may have made progress more difficult to evaluate, by inducing "gaming" of the targets. All targets should be designed in a way that limits the potential for gaming, by ensuring an interactive performance management system that captures the complexity of the education process. To improve evaluation, it should be ensured that performance measures are not the same as the targeted outputs, unless other mechanisms are in place to guard against gaming.

The flexible labour market has facilitated structural change and inward migration has eased labour market tightness

Compared with most other OECD countries, the United Kingdom has relatively few distorting labour market regulations. As a result, job-to-job mobility between similar industries is relatively high, suggesting that resources shift quite smoothly. The labour market is also better at getting the unemployed back into work than labour markets in the country's large European neighbours, although some Scandinavian economies have much higher unemployment outflow rates.

Strong economic growth over the past decade helped to reduce the unemployment rate from around 8% in 1996 to a low of around 4½ per cent in 2004. Since this was the same year that the United Kingdom opened its labour markets to workers from the new EU member countries, an influx of migrants helped to fill skill vacancies and cool inflationary pressures in the labour market. Since then the unemployment rate has crept up to around 5½ per cent, but it is unclear whether increased immigration is partly responsible. Relatively little is known about migration flows and the characteristics of the migrants. Statistical monitoring of the stock of migrant labour should be improved.

Policy needs to better equip lower skilled workers for globalisation

As in many other OECD countries, the wages of those at the top of the earnings distribution have increased much faster than those of the rest of the population. These top earners seem to be reaping the biggest gains from globalisation. Among the rest of the population, the earnings distribution has not changed much. In part this is because minimum wage increases and tax-benefit changes have cushioned low-income households. In addition, those with mid-level skills may be as affected by globalisation and skill-biased technical change as those with very low skill levels, since many medium-skill jobs are vulnerable to offshoring, while many low-skill service sector jobs must be done at home. However, at least so far, the real median wage has risen in line with productivity, in contrast with a number of other OECD countries.

The pace of increase in the minimum wage should be slowed

The introduction of the minimum wage has mitigated the increase in wage inequality. To date, the minimum wage does not appear to have had a significant adverse effect on employment. However, there are some signs that this could be occurring in certain low-skilled industries. Consequently it may be prudent to increase the national adult minimum wage and the youth wage by less than median earnings in order to foster employment of the low-skilled.

The tax and benefit system should be modified to improve incentives to up-skill and work

It is widely agreed that the ideal way to improve income prospects for the low-skilled is to facilitate higher labour force participation and encourage up-skilling. With respect to participation, the UK record is mixed: on the one hand, the UK tax-benefit system has been successfully designed to minimise unemployment traps for most people. However, high child-care costs continue to create a high implicit tax rate on second-income earners returning to work, reducing labour force participation among this group. Incentives for low-skill second-income earners to participate in the labour market should be improved by providing greater access to child-care support. At the same time, there are concerns that the same "make work pay" policies may have left certain groups of low-skilled workers in "low-wage traps", with reduced incentives to invest in further education and training. Improving these incentives is not easy, since reducing marginal effective tax rates in one place tends to push them up in others. Nevertheless, modifications to the tax-and-benefit system should be considered in order to reduce the marginal effective tax rate faced by lone parents and one-earner couples when extending their hours or when progressing in work. Extending the availability of child-care support could also enhance incentives for low-skilled parents to engage in further education. To do this, the child-care element of the Working Tax Credit should be extended to low-skilled parents undertaking approved courses of study. Work testing for lone parents should also be made more stringent, along the lines suggested in the government's recent Green Paper. Currently the United Kingdom has one of the most lenient regulations in this respect in the OECD.

Further reform to active labour market policies is needed to help the most disadvantaged groups back to work

Significant efforts have been made to help those on sickness and disability benefits back to work. The Pathways to Work pilots have successfully used work-focused interviews, targeted support, and financial incentives to help people to better manage their health conditions and get back to work. New welfare legislation will further enhance the financial incentives for claimants to return to work while providing enhanced financial security for the most severely sick and disabled. This will take effect in late 2008. The Pathways to Work scheme should be extended on a mandatory basis to the full stock of claimants, if the pilots are successful and cost-efficient. More attention should be given to the health status of job-seekers on unemployment benefits, and those with jobs who are reaching the end of their entitlement to sickness pay and benefits, so as to identify the need for earlier support and minimise the number of transfers onto the incapacity benefit. A new active labour market initiative focused on those without work in the most disadvantaged areas was introduced in 2006, but no evaluations of its effectiveness are yet available.

To boost productivity growth, better planning regulations, transport infrastructure and higher skill levels are needed

Productivity growth has remained strong in international comparison, but has slowed since the turn of the century. Investing in the human capital of the young is probably the most important lever to lift trend productivity growth, but there are also some other policy areas that can be improved:

- One priority should be to facilitate the entry of new businesses by reforming and simplifying planning regulations, especially in retail trade, as suggested by the Barker Review. Similarly, more land should be freed up for development by reconsidering the boundaries of the "green belts" in fast-growing areas. Ways to improve incentives for land development should also be considered.

- Good transport links are important for the efficient movement of goods and to support labour market efficiency and flexibility. After many years of under-investment in transport infrastructure, transport investment has picked up in recent years but still looks insufficient to meet the targets outlined in the government's Ten Year Plan for Transport. Looking ahead, ongoing investment will be required and more efforts should be made to ensure that infrastructure investment does not fall short of that envisaged in the Ten Year Plan. Spending should be targeted on key strategic growth areas, as recommended by the Eddington Review, and the government should continue to examine options for addressing road congestion and environment impacts, including the introduction of a nationwide road congestion pricing system.

- A key policy to boost innovation performance has been the introduction of research and development (R&D) tax credits, although it is uncertain whether these represent a cost-effective use of tax-payer funds.

- More broadly, innovation and productivity can be supported by raising the general skill level of the workforce. Workforce skill levels do not compare well with those of the best performing countries. The UK government has plans to address this including through publicly-funded adult training that focuses on the most disadvantaged groups, which currently receive little training. Greater private investment in training is needed as well, in order to raise skills at all levels. In terms of evaluating progress, the government should focus more on international measures of adult cognitive skills as well as on measuring the outcomes from domestic qualifications in terms of employment and pay progression.

Globalisation increases the importance of raising tax revenues in the most efficient way so as to maintain competitiveness

Globalisation creates a tension between the need to spend on social safety nets and the need to maintain tax competitiveness, which may reduce revenues. This pressure has encouraged governments to make the corporate income tax system more efficient by cutting statutory corporate tax rates and broadening the base. As the two have offset each other, corporate tax revenue as a share of GDP has been maintained. The United Kingdom was ahead in the game of cutting rates, but has lost ground more recently. It will thus be important to continue with the strategy of broadening the tax base, while cutting the rate. However, there are likely to be limits as to how far this can go, because tax competition also plays out on the base. The United Kingdom's system of worldwide taxation creates incentives for headquarters to relocate offshore. Thus the government should consider the case for moving to a dividend exemption system of corporate income taxation, which exempts foreign source dividend income from domestic tax. The government has recently published a paper to consult on this issue. Moreover, the complexity of the tax system has increased, in part reflecting a need to respond to increasingly complex financial and commercial structures. However, there is room for simplification.

The degree to which globalisation might undermine the ability to tax corporate income remains uncertain. The location of production is determined by many factors, among which the corporate tax regime is not necessarily the most important. To the extent that globalisation makes it harder to tax mobile factors of production, there may be room to shift taxation onto immobile ones. Property taxation is already high by international comparison, but there is room to raise value added tax (VAT) revenues. By European standards the standard VAT rate is relatively low and includes many exemptions. Thus, there is scope for broadening the base. More radical reform possibilities should also be considered, even though they all have advantages and drawbacks and few have been implemented in other countries.

OECD ECONOMIC SURVEYS: UNITED KINGDOM – ISBN 978-92-64-03772-4 – © OECD 2007

ISBN 978-92-64-03772-4
OECD Economic Surveys: United Kingdom
© OECD 2007

Chapter 1

Making the most of globalisation

The United Kingdom's good macroeconomic performance over the past decade has been underpinned by a willingness to embrace the opportunities offered by globalisation, together with regulatory policies that promote efficiency and economic resilience. As a result, productivity growth has remained strong, while the workforce has been boosted by immigration in recent years. Nevertheless, the productivity gap with the United States remains large, and a number of reforms should be pursued in order to further improve growth performance. There is also a need to further reduce the government deficit. This will require much slower growth in government spending and more effort devoted to ensuring that publicly-funded services provide good value for money. In recognition of the need to support those who are least able to benefit from globalisation, policy has focused on supporting the poorest members of the population, with a continued emphasis on encouraging participation in work. Nevertheless, employment rates among the least skilled remain too low. A key challenge is to raise education performance without significant further increases in expenditure, while a related key challenge is to ensure strong incentives for the least skilled to participate in the labour market and to progress in work. Finally, it remains important to ensure that the tax structure preserves the United Kingdom's position as an attractive business location.

The UK's open and flexible approach to economic policy is reflected in support for free trade, openness to foreign direct investment (FDI), a willingness to open its labour markets to citizens from new EU countries that joined in May 2004,[1] and the adoption of regulatory policies that promote efficiency and economic resilience.

Macroeconomic performance has also been strong. The level of GDP per capita now ranks third in the G7 (after the United States and Canada) compared with bottom of this group 10 years earlier. The United Kingdom has pulled ahead of the euro area, particularly since 2000.[2] This strong performance is not only due to the willingness to embrace the opportunities offered by globalisation, but also to a period of strong trading partner growth, as well as strong institutional arrangements for setting monetary and fiscal policy. Nevertheless, while some progress was made in closing the gap in living standards with the United States and Canada in the first half of the 1990s, more recently the gap has remained unchanged. This suggests that there are areas where the economy could be doing better. Some of the key reform priorities – as highlighted in *Going for Growth* (OECD, 2007a) – include: improving transport infrastructure; raising the education achievement of young people; improving the work incentives for lone parents and second income earners; ensuring that publicly-funded services provide good value for money; and getting more disability-related benefit recipients back into work. The government has addressed many of these concerns – in part by raising government outlays. But despite improvement in some areas, the overall extent to which additional spending is paying off is not yet clear, and the fiscal deficit remains relatively large. The unemployment rate also crept up after 2004, particularly among young unskilled school-leavers, before stabilising at around 5.5%.

This *Survey* addresses these issues through the lens of the benefits and challenges posed by the forces of globalisation. To set the scene, the chapter begins with a brief review of recent macroeconomic performance and prospects. This provides the context for highlighting the key channels through which globalisation has benefited the economy, together with the ongoing challenges of: raising productivity growth; up-skilling the population; providing good incentives to participate in the labour market and progress in work; and ensuring that the tax structure preserves the United Kingdom's position as an attractive business location. Broadly speaking, these challenges are similar to those identified by the government in its own review of globalisation issues.[3]

Recent macroeconomic performance and outlook

Stable and healthy GDP growth continues but the outlook is now more uncertain

Output grew by 2¾ per cent in 2006, close to its trend rate, continuing the healthy record of economic stability established since the mid-1990s. There has been some rebalancing of growth away from consumer spending (consistent with subdued real income growth) and toward investment. Business investment in particular has picked up, while residential construction recorded a smaller recovery following some resurgence in housing market activity in 2005 and 2006. Estimates of the output gap have remained close to zero for some time (Figure 1.1). Job creation has also been significant, although a surge in

Figure 1.1. **Key indicators in long-term and international perspective**

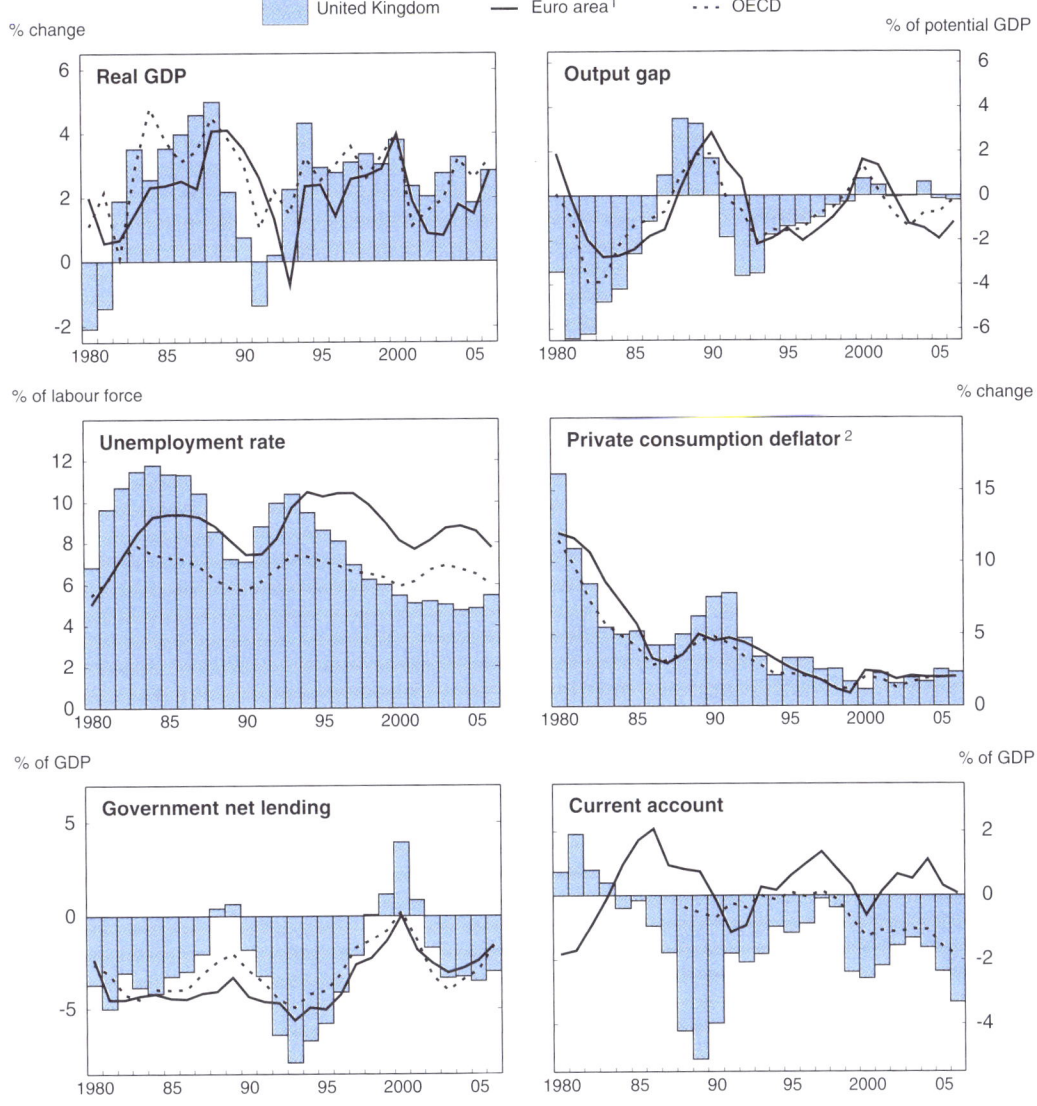

1. Break in series in 1991: western Germany up to then, total Germany thereafter.
2. OECD excludes high inflation countries.

Source: OECD (2007), *OECD Economic Outlook: Statistics and Projections*, No. 81 – online database.

StatLink ⬛⬛ *http://dx.doi.org/10.1787/115588376187*

labour force participation has pushed up unemployment. Labour force growth was in part boosted by older workers delaying their retirement and considerable inward migration from the new EU member countries. Thus, although the unemployment rate had fallen to 4¾ per cent in 2004, it rose again to 5½ per cent by mid-2006 and has been broadly stable since.

Prior to the recent financial market turmoil the OECD projected GDP growth to continue at a pace of around 2½ to 2¾ per cent per annum and inflation close to the 2% target. However, the outlook for both growth and inflation has now become more uncertain and there is a risk that growth will be weaker going forward, which could imply a need for interest rate reductions. A slowing in growth, together with reduced profitability in the City, could also reduce tax revenues and imply a rise in the budget deficit, which is still high by international comparison.

After a long period of low inflation, consumer price inflation picked up from under the 2% target in 2004 to peak at 3.1% in March 2007, before falling back to 1.9% in July. It is a testament to sound monetary management, as well as to the stability of economic conditions, that it took ten years after the Bank was given operational independence from the government before inflation moved more than 1 percentage point away from the inflation target. This outcome triggered the need for an open letter from the Governor of the Bank of England to the Chancellor setting out the reasons why inflation moved away from the 2% target and the policy action that the Monetary Policy Committee took to deal with it (King, 2007). Part of the explanation lies with the fact that the recent period has been characterised by unusually large fluctuations in energy prices; for example, a lack of non-discriminatory access to continental pipelines and gas storage together with insufficient import capacity during 2005 and early 2006 caused the wholesale price in the United Kingdom to rise by significantly more than in continental Europe. More recently, access to new gas pipelines and storage facilities are expected to facilitate the easing in prices throughout the remainder of this year and 2008.

In response to inflationary pressures, the Bank of England raised interest rates five times between mid-2006 and July 2007, bringing the policy rate to 5.75%. The higher interest rates, together with the recent financial market volatility, are expected to have a moderating impact on consumer spending and slow the pace of house price inflation.[4] To date, the growth in average earnings (excluding bonus payments) has been remarkably stable (Figure 1.2). Faced with an inflation spike driven by a supply shock, this is just what one would hope would happen – minimising the chance of the higher inflation rate becoming entrenched in higher inflation expectations. The government has played an important role by keeping the public sector wage settlements at an average of 1.9% for 2007/08 – the lowest in a decade.

Figure 1.2. **Wage inflation more stable than CPI inflation**
Year-on-year percentage change

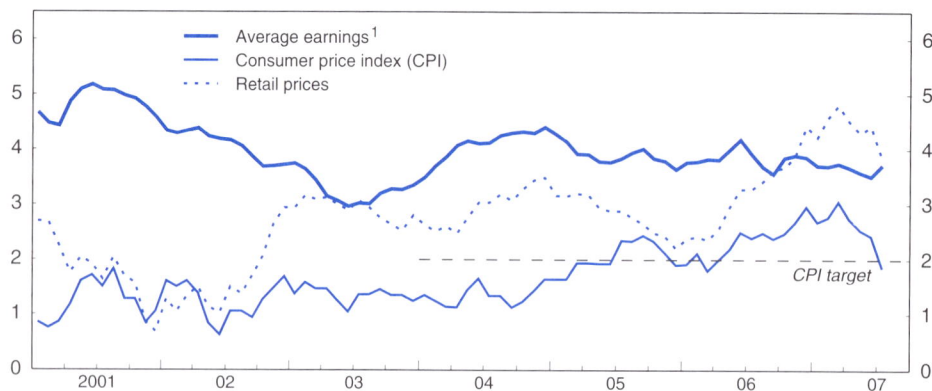

1. Private sector excluding bonus payments; three month average.
Source: National Statistics website, *www.statistics.gov.uk.*

StatLink ⬛ *http://dx.doi.org/10.1787/115600578101*

Inflation measures are not ideal

Although inflation risks have now receded, it remains of some concern that wage bargainers have typically used the retail price index (RPI) (which peaked at 4.8% in March 2007) as their measure of rises in the cost of living, rather than CPI inflation (which pcaked at 3.1%). Approximately 0.5 percentage point of the difference is due to the use of a different index formula in the RPI. Much of the rest reflects a significant increase in housing costs, which in the RPI typically overstates inflation in the true user cost of housing. It would be better to develop an alternative CPI inflation index that includes a comprehensive measure of housing costs, and encourage this to be used as a benchmark for wage negotiations. This would have the advantage of including an expenditure item that is important for most households. Such an index would also make international comparisons of inflation rates more meaningful (see Box 1.1).

Box 1.1. **The case for a new inflation index**

In December 2003 the Consumer Price Index (CPI)[1] replaced the Retail Price Index excluding mortgage interest payments (RPIX) as the basis for the inflation target that the Bank of England's Monetary Policy Committee is required to achieve. Since CPI inflation is typically lower than RPIX inflation,[2] the inflation target was lowered from 2.5% to 2.0% at that time.

Since then, RPIX inflation has taken on a lower profile, but RPI (all items) inflation has continued to play a very important role because it is historically the typical benchmark inflation index for the purposes of wage negotiations and also because the RPI and its derivatives are used to up-rate pensions, benefits and index-linked gilts. The RPI also has the advantage of the familiarity and credibility bestowed by the longer history of the RPI (whereas the RPI has been around since 1947, the CPI was only introduced in 1997).

Unfortunately, however, the importance of the RPI in the wage negotiation process could serve to unduly push up wage inflation, requiring a tighter monetary stance. This is due to two reasons. First, the RPI (unlike the CPI in the United Kingdom or elsewhere) uses the average of relatives (AR) arithmetic mean formula for the aggregation of individual item indexes. Relative to other formulae, this formula increases inflation rates by around 0.5 percentage point (largely because it does not capture the impact of consumers switching to cheaper brands or varieties of products when relative prices change). In contrast, the UK CPI uses the geometric mean (GM) formula which assumes complete substitution. Other countries' CPIs are also calculated using the GM formula, or alternatively using the ratio of averages (RA) formula which also produces results that are comparable with GM.[3] However, if the RPI index were to be re-calculated using a GM formula, this might require redemption of existing (RPI) index-linked gilts.[4]

Second, since 1995 the RPI has included a housing depreciation element, which is based on lagged house prices. However, because house price inflation reflects rises in the price of land, and since land does not depreciate, the price of housing typically overstates housing depreciation costs (Nickell, 2006). The user cost of owner-occupied housing would be better proxied by market rents (e.g. as in the US and Japanese CPIs) or measured directly as the user cost associated with owners' housing capital valued at market prices (as in the US Personal Consumption Deflator).[5]

While the RPI suffers from these two disadvantages, the CPI is not an ideal choice as a reference index for wage negotiations either. This is because the CPI does not include the most important components of owner-occupied housing costs, which constitute an important expenditure item for most wage and salary earners. In recognition of this omission, the Office for National Statistics (ONS) is participating in a Eurostat task force assessing the possibility of including in the harmonised consumer price index (HICP) an index of owner-occupied housing costs. Although Eurostat identified this issue as a priority in 1997, final results of the pilots are not expected before the end of 2009.

Box 1.1. **The case for a new inflation index** (*cont.*)

What might an alternative inflation index look like? Figure 1.3 shows two indicative alternatives: RPI inflation adjusted for the formula bias; and CPI inflation plus the housing component of the RPI. Both of these alternative inflation rates average somewhere in between the CPI and RPI inflation rates, and normally tend to move quite closely together, with the exception of the 2004-05 period when other coverage differences between the two indexes served to push up the inflation rate of the CPI relative to the RPI.[6]

Figure 1.3. **Alternative measures of inflation**
Per cent

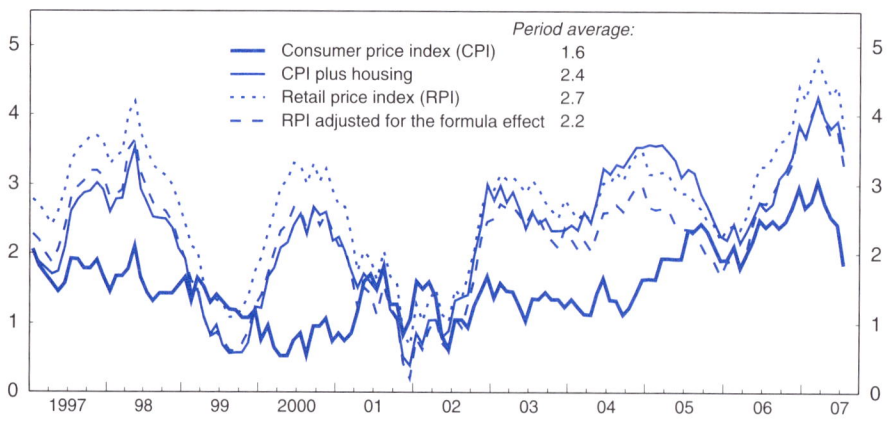

	Period average:
Consumer price index (CPI)	1.6
CPI plus housing	2.4
Retail price index (RPI)	2.7
RPI adjusted for the formula effect	2.2

Source: National Statistics website, *www.statistics.gov.uk* and OECD calculations.

StatLink 🔍📊 *http://dx.doi.org/10.1787/115600683223*

Since such an alternative measure of inflation would be preferable to the RPI as an inflation benchmark for wage negotiations, the government should support the development of the CPI to include housing, either using the index development that the ONS has been undertaking, or by pushing for faster incorporation by Eurostat of housing costs into the HICP. A new index would also significantly assist international comparisons of inflation. At present, the CPI is comparable with HICP inflation rates for other EU countries. For non-EU countries, however, neither the RPI nor the CPI is comparable since the RPI suffers from the AR formula bias and the CPI excludes a measure of owner occupied housing cost, whereas all non-EU OECD countries' CPIs include such a component.[7]

1. The inflation index published as the CPI in the United Kingdom is the same as the Eurostat measure of the Harmonised Index of Consumer Prices (HICP).
2. Since January 1997, CPI inflation has averaged 0.7 percentage points lower than RPIX inflation.
3. See ONS (2007) for further discussion.
4. The prospectus for index-linked gilts states that if any change should be made to the coverage of the basic calculation of the (Retail Prices) Index which, in the opinion of the Bank of England, constitutes a fundamental change in the index which would be materially detrimental to the interests of stockholders, the Treasury is required to offer gilt holders the right to redeem their stock.
5. See Cournède (2005) for further discussion of alternative ways of measuring owner-occupied housing costs.
6. For example, the CPI includes items such as unit trust and stockbroker charges, overseas students' university fees and other accommodation costs in university halls of residence, which are excluded from the RPI.
7. For further details see Christensen *et al.* (2005).

Fiscal policy

The government's fiscal policy objectives are implemented through two fiscal rules, against which the performance of fiscal policy is judged. The *golden rule* states that over the economic cycle, the government will borrow only to invest and not to fund current spending. The *sustainable investment rule* states that public sector net debt as a proportion of GDP will be held at a stable and prudent level (currently defined as being less than 40% of GDP). The fiscal rules have been successful in a number of respects. For example, by separating current and capital spending, the fiscal rules have helped the government to tackle the UK's historical bias against capital spending. Compared with previous economic cycles, the introduction of fiscal rules and clear objectives for fiscal policy have also helped to put the public finances on a more sound and sustainable footing.

In Budget 2007 the Treasury estimated that the cycle that began in 1997 may have ended in early 2007, although this assessment is yet to be confirmed. Over this period it is likely that the golden rule was met, since it is estimated that the cumulative current budget balance over this period was around 0.1% of GDP.[5] The general government fiscal balance is estimated to have averaged –1.3% of GDP over the same period, with a large surplus early on and a large deficit later.

Relative to fiscal outcomes in the previous two decades, this is a positive outcome, and the golden rule deserves credit for helping to constrain fiscal discretion. Nevertheless, given that the golden rule is expected to be met by such a small margin, a binary "success" judgement seems inappropriate, just as a "failure" judgement would be inappropriate if the rule was to be missed by a similar margin. Experience with the golden rule over the past 10 years has highlighted two weaknesses. First, the credibility of the golden rule may have been undermined to some extent by revisions to the start and end dates of the economic cycle, since these revisions occurred at times when it appeared likely that the rule might not be met (see Chote *et al.* [2007] for a detailed discussion). This problem stems largely from the difficulties associated with estimating the output gap and dating the cycle; different techniques produce different results and all are subject to data revisions. It is particularly difficult to date the end of a cycle *ex ante*. Second, the "over the cycle" formulation of the rule means that the goal of permitting automatic stabilisers to operate fully may be compromised if pro-cyclical fiscal tightening is required towards the end of a cycle in order to meet the rule (as illustrated by Honjo [2007]). Related to this, the fact that the cycle may have recently ended with a current deficit means that a tighter fiscal policy will be required over the new cycle, as foreseen in Budget 2007 fiscal projections. An international comparison shows that the UK fiscal balance is in a relatively worse position than most of the other G7 countries; the most recent data shows smaller deficits in France, Germany and the United States, while Canada continues to run a fiscal surplus. However, UK net debt as a percentage of GDP is lower than in all the other G7 countries except Canada.

Scope for improving the golden rule

To address these concerns, a number of suggestions have been made. To address the credibility concern some economists have suggested that estimating the output gap and identifying the cycle could be contracted out to an independent body. Another possibility, that would address both the credibility and pro-cyclicality concerns, is to reduce the reliance of the rule on cycle dating and the output gap altogether. Such an approach is supported by the fact that the amplitude of the economic cycle has become much smaller – at least partly thanks to a reduction in policy-induced shocks – and a clearly defined economic cycle is now harder to identify (as illustrated by the output gap panel in Figure 1.1). Instead of aiming to balance the current budget over a cycle, the Treasury could instead aim for a particular (positive) target level for the current budget balance over an appropriate time horizon. As pointed out by Chote *et al.* (2007), the history of current budget balance forecasts suggests that fiscal policy is already run as though it expects to deliver a current budget surplus of around 0.7% of GDP after five years (Figure 1.4). However, in the event that non-policy shocks are more pronounced in future economic cycles, it may not be optimal to attempt to target such surpluses within a five year horizon.

Figure 1.4. **Successive budget forecasts have had a similar end-point**

Cyclically-adjusted current budget surplus in per cent of GDP

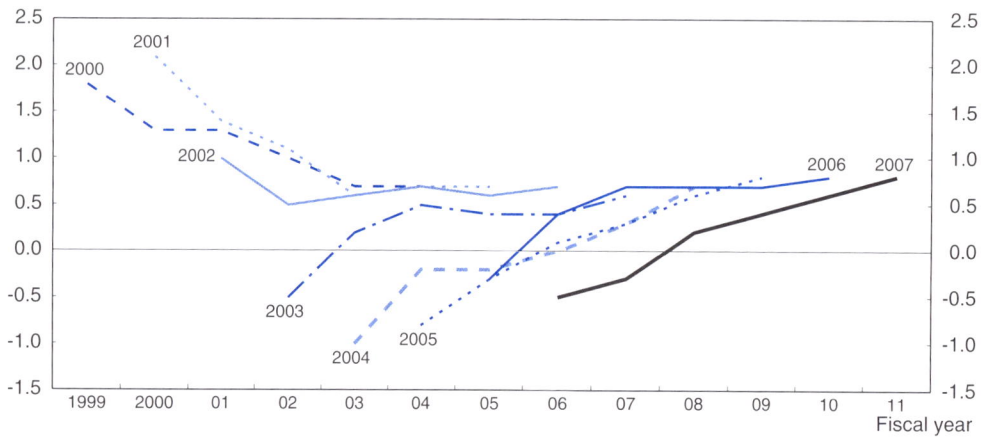

Source: HM Treasury, Budget Reports.

StatLink 🖳 *http://dx.doi.org/10.1787/115607248748*

A more forward-looking fiscal rule would have several advantages. First, it would not be necessary to cyclically adjust the current budget balance since it could be assumed that any output gap would have closed within a five year period. Second, there would be no need to date the cycle. Third, it would permit the automatic stabilisers to operate fully. Fourth, it would redirect attention from the binary judgement of whether or not the golden rule has been met, to the broader picture of fiscal policy. Finally, the desire for fiscal policy credibility, in the absence of a binary "success" judgement, might encourage the Treasury to improve fiscal transparency and more explicitly quantify the uncertainties inherent in their fiscal projections. The Treasury Select Committee's report on the 2007 Budget (House of Commons, 2007a) also recommended that the government review the golden rule with a view to making it more forward-looking and less dependent on the dating of the economic cycle.

Since such an approach would be forward-looking, the Treasury would not be required to make up for past slippage (in the event of larger than expected deficits over the past few years) or be permitted additional fiscal loosening (in the event of unexpectedly good fiscal outturns). It is this forward-looking feature of the rule that would ensure that the automatic stabilisers could work, even towards the end of a cycle. Nevertheless, accountability for past policy and forecasting errors would take on greater importance. In particular, unbiased revenue projections would become more important under a forward-looking rule, suggesting a potentially greater role for auditing of the Treasury's assumptions. While the National Audit Office (NAO) is auditing some specific assumptions, a requirement for broader NAO audit of key fiscal assumptions would significantly enhance fiscal accountability.

What target level might be set for the current balance five years ahead? Although the golden rule targets *balance* in the current budget over the course of the cycle, in practice this goal is interpreted as requiring a balance or surplus. It would also make sense for a rolling forward-looking target to be positive, for three reasons: first, the Treasury's forecasts for the public finances have generally been over-optimistic since 2001, suggesting a need for some buffer if persistent deficits are to be avoided; second, even if Treasury forecasts switch to being consistently pessimistic (and there is evidence that forecast errors tend to be serially correlated) there is a case to be made for targeting a small surplus (say ¾ per cent of GDP) in order to make some compensation for the government's growing off-balance sheet liabilities (see following discussion); third, a positive target would be required to avoid the forward-looking rule imposing a looser constraint on debt than does the golden rule (Honjo, 2007).[6]

Complementing the sustainable investment rule with other liability measures

While the golden rule explicitly permits the government to borrow to pay for capital investment, it only requires that the current budget is in surplus or balance over the cycle, and so doesn't by itself explicitly address the perceived need to go further in preparing the public finances for the long-term challenges due to the ageing of the population. To address these concerns, the sustainable investment rule puts a limit on the extent of borrowing by requiring that the public sector's net debt remains at a "stable and prudent" level. Over the economic cycle that began in 1997 this was defined as a level of less than 40% of GDP. Over the past decade, net public debt was first reduced from 44% of GDP in 1997 to around 30% in early 2002 before it began to gradually trend up again, reaching 37% in April 2007. Looking ahead, net public debt is expected to rise slightly further in the near future. Sustainable debt calculations suggest that, under plausible assumptions, the government could sustain public sector net investment of around 2% of GDP a year without breaching the net public debt ceiling.[7]

An overall assessment of fiscal sustainability should, however, also consider the government's off-balance-sheet liabilities and long-term spending and revenue trends. Table 1.1, based on Chote *et al.* (2007), compares the size of public sector net debt (around 37% of GDP) with official estimates of three other public sector liabilities: i) public sector pension liabilities; ii) the future flow of payments to private finance initiative (PFI) providers under contracts already signed; and iii) Network Rail obligations. Official

Table 1.1. **Estimated value of various future public sector obligations**

	Date	Billion £	% of GDP
Public sector net debt	April 2007	498	37
Public sector pension liabilities (estimate)	March 2005	530	≈ 42
Future PFI liabilities, signed deals (estimate)	December 2006	100	≈ 8
National rail debt	September 2006	18	≈ 1
Total		**≈ 1 100**	**≈ 87**

Source: Public sector net debt from HM Treasury; public sector pension liabilities from the Government Actuary's Department, available at: *www.gad.gov.uk/Pensions/docs/2006_Public_Sector_Pension_Cashflow_projections_methodology.pdf*; future PFI (private finance initiative) payments from Table B24 of HM Treasury (2006), *Pre-Budget Report*; Network Rail debt from Table 9, of Network Rail Ltd, *Interim Financial Statements, six months ended 30 September 2006.*

estimates of these other liabilities are not as up-to-date as those for public sector net debt. A full actuarial valuation of public sector pension liabilities, for example, is normally undertaken only once every four years. However, the government publishes annually the Long-Term Public Finance Report, which provides a comprehensive assessment of long-term fiscal sustainability and which has discussed the different types of liabilities that exist. Since 2004 the Long-Term Public Finance Report has also shown public service pension projections – produced by the Government Actuary's Department – explicitly.

Table 1.1 shows that unfunded public sector pension liabilities are larger than total net public sector debt. Not only that, but the £530 billion estimate is expected to be revised up.[8] The government should also take other actions to reduce the size of these liabilities. For example, further changes could be made to public sector pension schemes to reduce the size of liabilities. In 2005 the government renegotiated a policy to raise the normal public sector pension age from 60 to 65 for existing workers from 2013 in return for a commitment from unions that they would agree to negotiate other reforms to the pension schemes that would recover equivalent costs to those lost by retaining the existing pension age of 60 for existing workers (e.g. by reducing pension generosity and/or by raising employee contributions). Since scheme-specific negotiations are still ongoing, the final savings figure is not yet known. Meanwhile, recent reforms to the basic State Pension include some further increases in the private sector retirement age and should improve private saving incentives (Box 1.2).

Box 1.2. **Recent changes to the State Pension System**

In addition to addressing poverty concerns, one of the key policy goals of reforming the state pension system was to improve incentives for voluntary savings, particularly among low and middle-income earners – by improving coverage, reducing the extent of means-testing, particularly its expected growth in the future, and by simplifying the rules. These challenges were discussed in more detail in the last *Economic Survey* (OECD, 2005a).

The 2007 Pensions Act is expected to address these concerns through a number of channels:

● From 2010 the basic State Pension will become more widely available (by increasing the contributory credits available for caring responsibilities and by lowering the minimum number of contribution years to 30).

● From 2012 (subject to affordability) the basic State Pension will be up-rated on the basis of increases in average earnings instead of prices. As well as making the basic State Pension more generous, this should significantly reduce the number of people who would qualify for means-testing in future.

A second Pensions Bill later this year will introduce private pension reforms from 2012:

● Automatic enrolment, mandatory 3% employer contributions, and a new low cost scheme of personal accounts should encourage higher take up of private pensions and ensure that earners (particularly low-to-middle-income earners) have access to a simple, low cost pension scheme in which to save.

With respect to the fiscal implications, higher take up of private pensions, including in personal accounts, will increase the cost to the government of pension-scheme-related tax relief. In the longer term there will be some offsetting cost savings as the retirement age for women increases from 60 to 65 between 2010 and 2020, before increasing gradually for both men and women after that in line with increases in life expectancy, reaching 68 by 2046. Nevertheless, there remains scope to further simplify the state pension system and to consider ways to further enhance savings incentives for low to middle-income earners.

The other two public sector obligations are smaller, although future PFI liabilities are significant. PFI initiatives are often a cost-effective way of financing public investment. However, compared with conventionally-financed investment projects, PFIs typically add less to public sector net debt (because they do not capture future government liabilities in terms of the commitments to pay private firms a rental price for the use of capital assets). Thus, as long as public finance assessments focus predominantly on net public debt statistics, fiscal transparency is reduced, and the government may have an incentive to finance more projects *via* PFI or public-private partnerships in order to keep a lid on the monitored statistic (net public sector debt). To prevent this, the government should set a ceiling on a broader measure of public sector liabilities. In addition, the 40% ceiling for public sector net debt should be confirmed for the new economic cycle. Box 1.3 summarises the proposed improvements to the fiscal rules.

Box 1.3. **Improving the fiscal rules**

Both the golden rule and the sustainable investment rule have played an important role in anchoring expectations and improving the transparency of fiscal policy. However, the rules have some important limitations. This box summarises the proposed improvements.

Reduce the reliance of the golden rule on cycle dating and output gap estimates

● Reformulate the golden rule to make it less dependent on cycle dating, for example by targeting a positive level for the current budget balance over an appropriate time horizon (*e.g.* five years). This should be accompanied by a requirement for a broader NAO audit of key fiscal assumptions.

● Introduce mechanisms that put a tighter constraint on overall spending by preventing the spending of cyclical revenue windfalls.

Take greater account of off balance sheet liabilities

● Publish estimates of other public sector liabilities on a regular basis alongside those of public sector net debt.

● Confirm the 40% ceiling for public sector net debt and set a ceiling for a broader measure of public sector liabilities.

The 2007 Spending Review will be challenging

In many other OECD countries, expenditure rules are becoming a popular way of ensuring fiscal discipline (Guichard *et al.*, 2007). Expenditure rules have two main merits: they force governments to prioritise spending within a fixed overall envelope; and they avoid the risk inherent in fiscal or current balance targets of running pro-cyclical fiscal policy in good times, forcing counter-cyclicality when the economy turns down.[9] By contrast, the UK's *Spending Review* framework provides a relatively comprehensive means for controlling government spending at the departmental level on the basis of fixed, three-year Departmental Expenditure Limits (DEL) for each government department which account for 60% of public expenditure. However, it does permit the expenditure limits to be revised upward to reflect both discretionary policy decisions (such as education initiatives announced in the last Pre-Budget Report) and non-discretionary items (such as the cost of military operations in Iraq and Afghanistan) where this is consistent with meeting the fiscal rules (for example, if government revenues are stronger than expected or if the limits of the rule are not yet binding). Actual real spending has indeed exceeded that planned in all Spending Reviews since 1998 and in some cases substantially so (IFS, 2007). This reflects, in large part, the government's preference for higher government spending to the extent permitted within the broader framework of fiscal sustainability as implemented through the fiscal rules. As a share of GDP, total government spending has crept up and is now approaching that of Germany. Government spending as a percentage of GDP has already overtaken that of Canada in the last 10 years, and if it overtakes that of Germany this year, the United Kingdom will move into the 3rd highest spending position in the G7 (Figure 1.5, upper panel).[10]

Figure 1.5. **Government expenditure and revenue**
Per cent of GDP

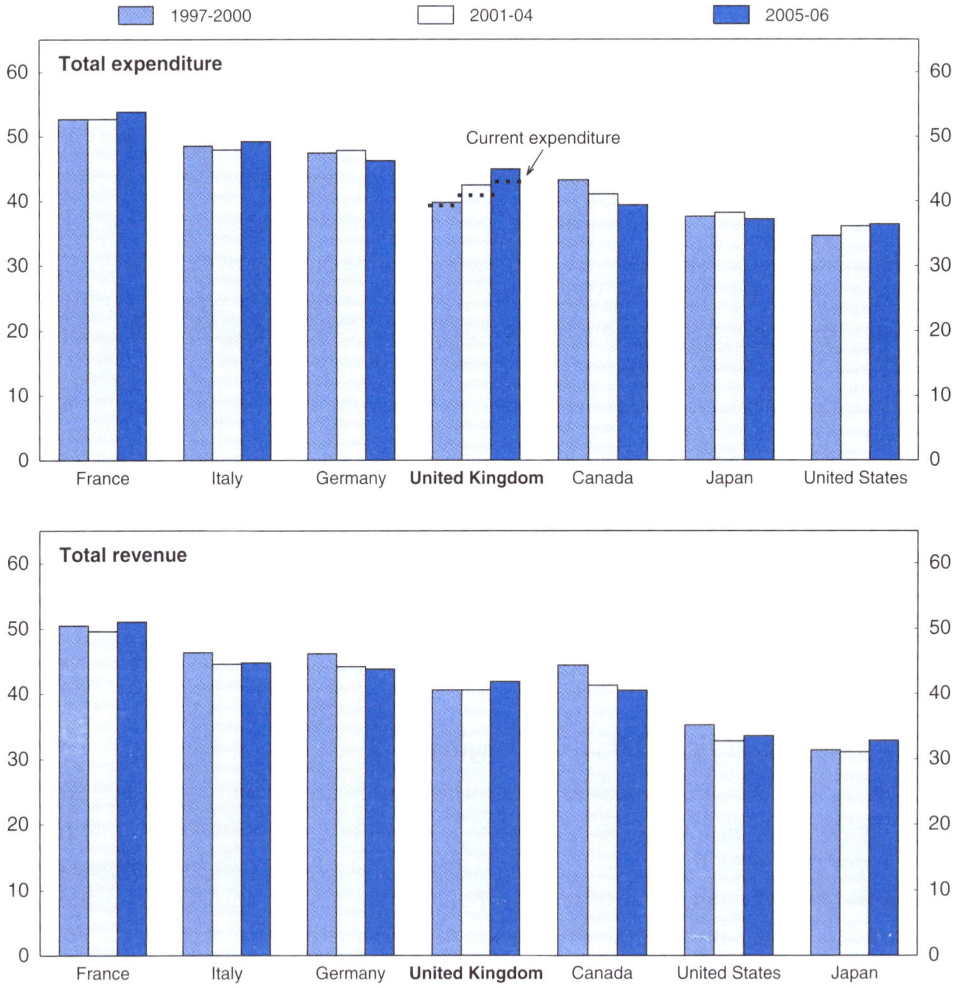

Source: OECD (2007), OECD Economic Outlook: Statistics and Projections, No. 81 – online database.
StatLink ⎙⎘ http://dx.doi.org/10.1787/115610211167

After its peak in 2000, general government net lending as a per cent of GDP deteriorated significantly, before gradually beginning to improve again more recently (see Figure 1.1). The larger than expected deficits over the 2001-04 period were due to a combination of falling public sector current receipts as a percentage of GDP together with a deliberate government decision to significantly raise current expenditures as a percentage of GDP over this same time period. More recently, current receipts have recovered to previous levels and the deficits can be attributed largely to higher rates of expenditure. As a result, the next economic cycle – if it begins this year – will start with a current budget deficit, suggesting that higher revenues or lower spending will be required to meet the golden rule over the next cycle. Raising the tax burden further is not an attractive option. Many economists (e.g. Botman and Honjo, 2006) argue that it would be better to reduce transfers or spending than to raise taxes, due to the adverse effects of higher taxes on labour supply and capital accumulation – and this Survey argues that human capital is an increasingly important component of capital accumulation. While the government has announced that it will not raise VAT and income taxes, it projects that the tax/GDP ratio will rise by 0.8% of GDP between 2006/07 and 2008/09. Much of this increase is due to fiscal drag,[11] which should be seen as an explicit policy choice for raising additional revenues. Indeed, Figure 1.5 (bottom panel) shows that the tax burden has crept up over the last 10 years, compared with small decreases in four of the other G7 countries. The fiscal framework should also be transparent about fiscal drag, either through indexing tax brackets to wage growth or through efficiency enhancing tax reform. Chapter 5 discusses the possible impacts of globalisation on the tax structure.

The government agrees that slower spending growth is required and the 2007 Budget projects that total public spending will grow by around half a percentage point more slowly than GDP in each of the three years from 2008/09 to 2010/11 (after having expanded by around 0.9% faster than GDP on average between 2000/01 and 2005/06). Public spending as a percentage of GDP is now projected to fall by about 0.6 percentage points over the next three-year period. This tight overall envelope sets the scene for a tough Comprehensive Spending Review, with the allocation of this envelope between departments and priorities due to be announced in October 2007. Roughly 30% of the Departmental Expenditure Limits (DEL) had already been announced by Budget 2007, including those for education and science, which will see their expenditure growing in line with GDP. More challenging allocations – involving expenditure settlements of spending declines or no real growth – have been announced for some other ministries, although these cover only around 10% of total DEL. The National Health Service (NHS), which has seen the largest spending increases over the past decade, is likely to see expenditure rising further as a percentage of GDP. Although some hospital trusts are continuing to run deficits, the overall position of the health system's finances improved over 2006/07. Nevertheless, further efficiency gains will be required if the NHS is to achieve its key targets without a return to the large deficits of 2005/06. After strong growth in public sector earnings in previous years the government is so far succeeding in restraining average public sector salary increases in 2007. This is important in order both to limit government expenditure and to ensure that wage increases are consistent with the 2% inflation target. Overall, raising the efficiency of public sector spending remains a key challenge facing the government and more efforts need to be made to ensure that higher expenditure results in significantly higher standards of service delivery. Concerning education, Chapter 2 discusses the need to focus more on encouraging higher educational attainment, without significant further increases in expenditure, while Chapter 4 assesses spending on transport, another priority area.

Globalisation has contributed to strong productivity growth

While the UK's openness to the forces of globalisation is not new, the recent emergence of low-cost countries such as China has led to an intensification of both international trade and foreign direct investment (FDI), both of which have grown much faster than GDP (see OECD, 2007b for a discussion of globalisation trends).

Increasing trade in services has been another important feature of globalisation in recent years – underpinned by advances in communications technology. Yet overall it is still at relatively low levels; total trade in services accounted for only around one-third of that in goods in 2005 (Figure 1.6, upper panel). In terms of export market share, however, the UK economy is performing better in services (middle panel). In most components of services the United Kingdom runs a trade surplus, with the travel and transportation components being important exceptions (bottom panel). Overall, the surplus on trade in services (around 2½ per cent of GDP) plays an important role in mitigating the deficit on trade in goods (around 6% of GDP) although the current account deficit was still 3.6% of GDP in the first quarter of 2007.

For both goods and services the United Kingdom trades most with other OECD countries. Although the share of non-OECD countries in total world trade has risen from around one quarter at the start of the 1990s to around one-third, non-OECD countries accounted for only about 20% of total UK trade in 2004; the UK's largest single trading partner is the United States (approximately 10% of total goods trade and 20% of total services trade), although the euro area as a whole is much more important (50% of goods trade and 40% of services trade). The UK's exports to China are still very small (up from 0.5% of total exports in 1995 to 1.3% in 2005), but imports from China are becoming more important (up from 1% of total imports in 1995 to 3.7% in 2005).

Compared with trade, financial transactions have been an even faster-growing segment of international transactions and FDI statistics reflect the increasing interdependence of the United Kingdom with other economies. In absolute terms the United States has traditionally been both the largest foreign investor and the largest recipient of FDI flows in the OECD. When measured as a share of GDP, however, the relative importance of the United Kingdom as a destination and source of FDI becomes more evident (Figure 1.7, upper panel). However, a large proportion of FDI has been driven by acquisitions and mergers, i.e. a change of ownership, rather than creation of new businesses or capacity enlargements of existing firms.[12]

Trends in the components of FDI flows are consistent with the increasing importance of the services sector. Between 1992 and 2003, the UK's inward and outward investment positions in services rose from around 40% of total FDI to around 60%. While the manufacturing share of total FDI dropped, both inward and outward manufacturing sector FDI still increased as a percentage of GDP (Figure 1.7, lower panel).

The forces of globalisation have shaped the economy

The UK philosophy of openness to international economic forces is reflected in a general absence of protection for failing industries. The manufacturing sector has shrunk as a proportion of economic output (to less than 15% of total gross value added), with resources shifting to areas of comparative advantage, such as business services. Indeed, the share of business services in total economy-wide value added increased from less than 1.5 times that of manufacturing in 1980 to more than 3.5 times by 2003 (Figure 1.8, upper panel). While most other G7 countries have also experienced declining value added shares

Figure 1.6. **Trade indicators**

Average trade to GDP ratios[1]
Per cent

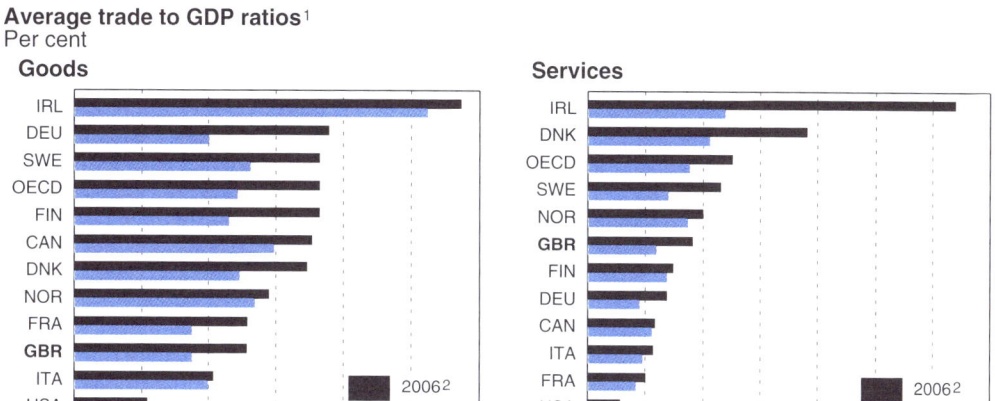

Export market shares[3]
Annual percentage growth, 1995-2005

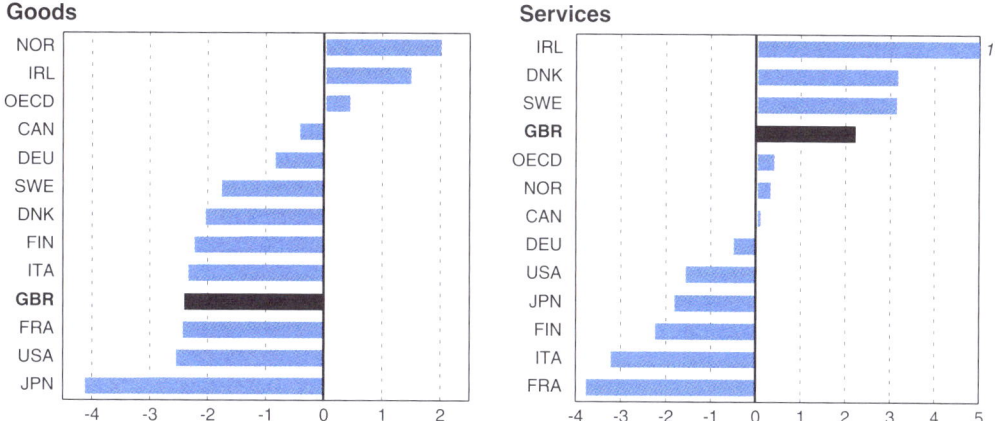

Net exports of services
Per cent of GDP

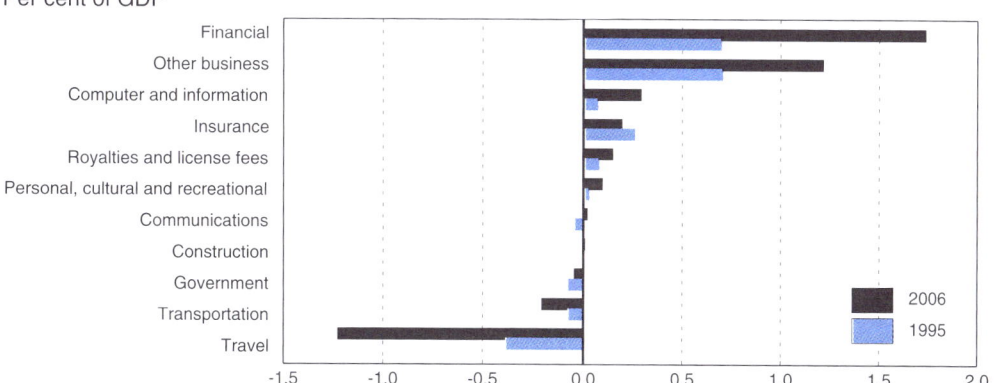

1. Calculated as ([exports + imports]/2)/GDP*100. OECD is an unweighted average excluding Belgium.
2. 2004 for Mexico; 2005 for Canada, Ireland, Japan (estimated), United States and OECD.
3. In current prices. OECD is an unweighted average.

Source: OECD (2007), *National Accounts of OECD Countries* – online database, September; IMF (2007), *Balance of Payments Statistics* – CDROM, August; National Statistics website (2007), *Balance of Payments: Trade in Services*, June, *www.statistics.gov.uk.*

StatLink ⫘ *http://dx.doi.org/10.1787/115622118677*

Figure 1.7. **Foreign direct investment in the G7 – flows and stocks**
Per cent of GDP

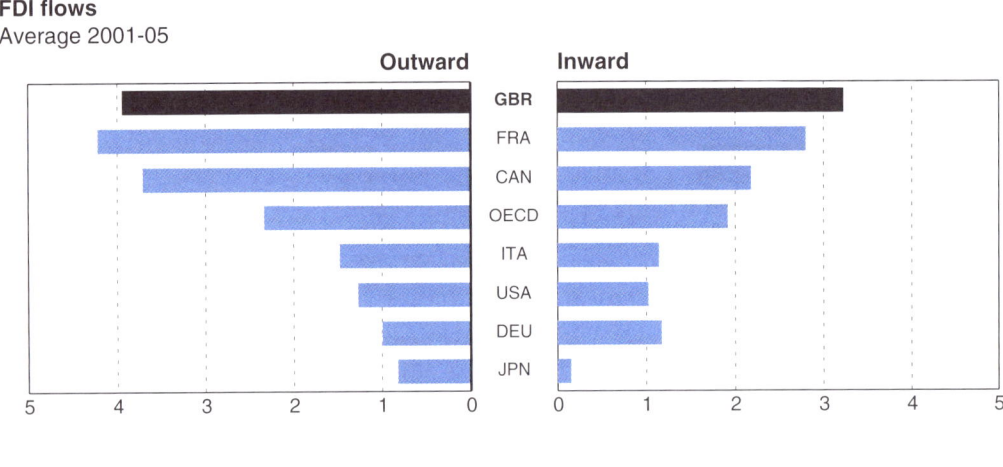

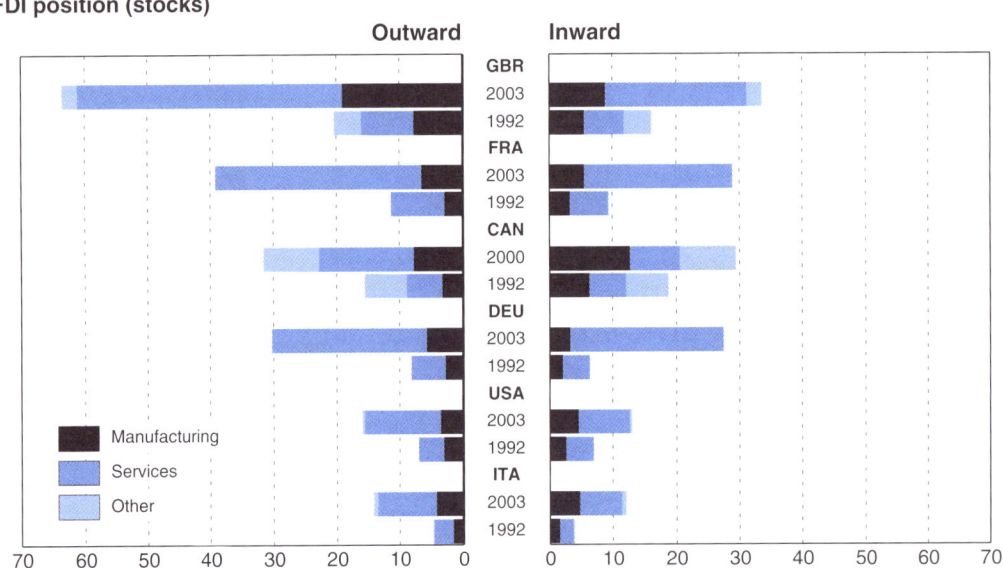

Source: OECD (2007), *International Direct Investment Statistics* and *National Accounts of OECD Countries* – online databases, January.

StatLink ⫶⫶⫷⫸ *http://dx.doi.org/10.1787/115633335218*

in manufacturing[13] and all have experienced rising value added shares in business services, these trends have been the most marked in the United Kingdom.

Similar trends can also be observed in employment. Figure 1.8 (lower panel) shows that by the early 1990s the United Kingdom already had one of the largest shares of employment in business services (relative to the other G7 economies) and one of the lowest in manufacturing. Even so, employment has continued to shift in this direction, particularly into knowledge-intensive services, where the United Kingdom now has the largest employment share among the G7, outstripping the United States.

Even though trade openness is facilitating the process of creative destruction in the United Kingdom, the results of a poll released at the end of 2006 (GMF, 2006) suggest that British workers are more likely to view free trade in a positive light than people in the other

Figure 1.8. **The resource shift from manufacturing to services can be seen in value added shares and in employment**

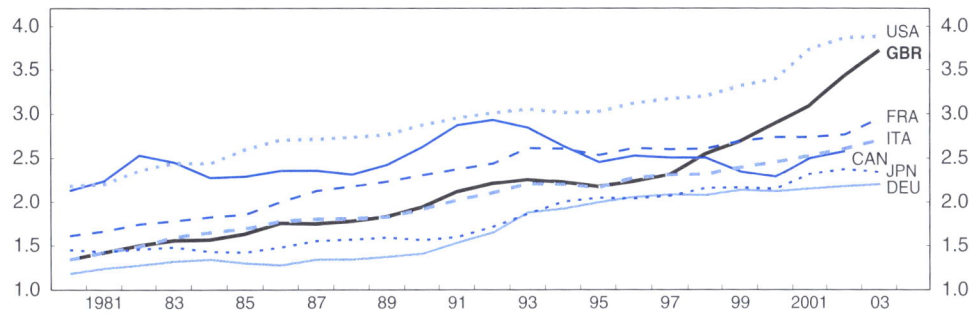

Ratio of value added shares in business services to manufacturing

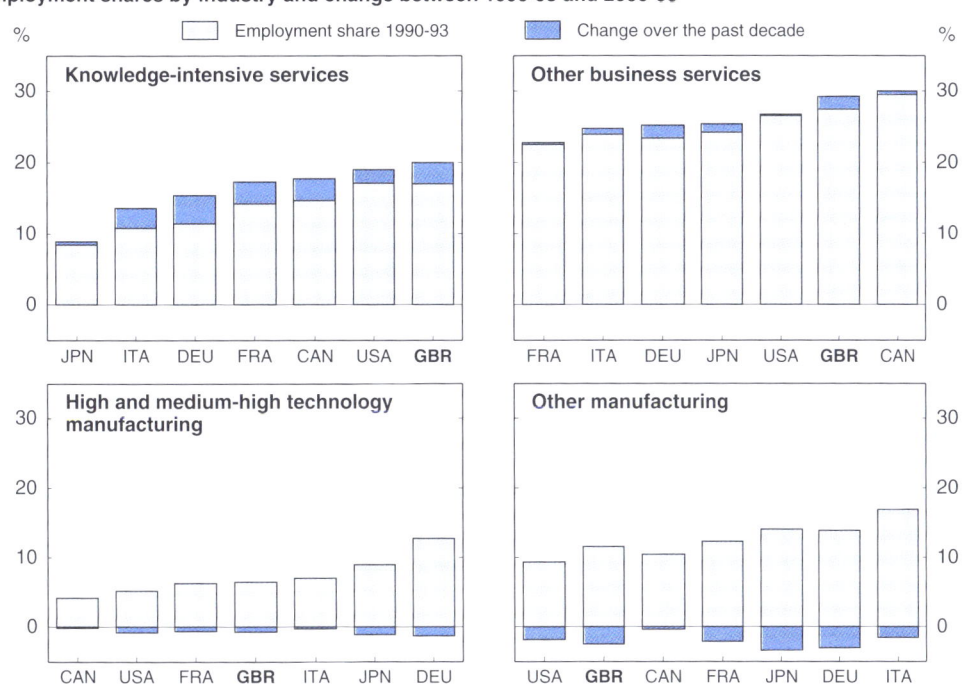

Employment shares by industry and change between 1990-93 and 2000-03[1]

1. For Germany and France, data is up to 2002 only. For Japan the knowledge-intensive services definition excludes post and communications as data is not available since 1999. For the United Kingdom, high-technology manufacturing data is available up to 2002 only. For Italy service sector employment data begins in 1992.

Source: OECD (2006), STAN Indicators database, www.oecd.org/sti/stan/indicators.

StatLink ⋐⋑ http://dx.doi.org/10.1787/115650647310

six countries polled (France, Germany, Italy, Poland, Slovak Republic and United States). Although half of all UK respondents thought that freer trade costs more jobs than it creates, this proportion was lower than in all the other countries except Poland. Perhaps more importantly, 77% of respondents in the United Kingdom thought that they benefited personally from free trade – more than in any other country polled. Relatively positive public opinion in the United Kingdom may reflect the government's more positive attitude to free trade (relative to that of the United States and most other European countries), together with the support of trade union and business leaders.

Finally, the resource shift from manufacturing into services is also evident in measures of export specialisation. Figure 1.9 uses the Revealed Symmetric Comparative

Figure 1.9. **Trade data also illustrate the UK's comparative advantage in services**

Degree of specialisation measured by the Revealed Symmetric Comparative Advantage (RSCA) index in selected sectors (service sectors shown in bold)[1]

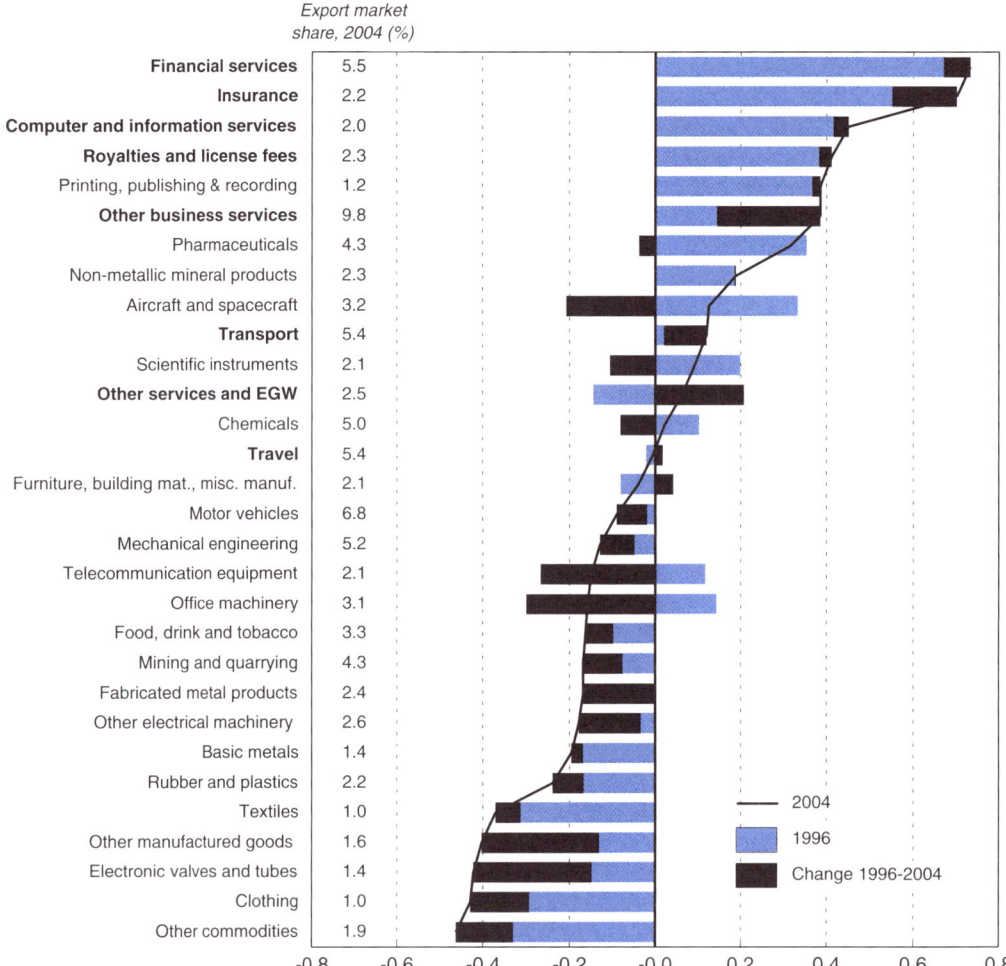

1. RSCAs are shown for all commodities whose UK export share is more than 1%. Others are aggregated into three combined categories as follows: 1) Other services and EGW – construction; electricity, gas and water supply; government services; communications; personal, cultural and recreational services. 2) Other commodities – forestry; wood and products of wood and cork; mineral oil refining, coke and nuclear fuel; leather and footwear; agriculture; pulp, paper and paper products; fishing. 3) Other manufactured goods – building and repairing of ships and boats; radio and television receivers; railroad equipment and transport; insulated wire; other instruments (optical instruments and photographic equipment).

Source: OECD calculations based on the United Nations COMTRADE and UNCTAD databases.

StatLink ᴍᴸ᠍ᴾ *http://dx.doi.org/10.1787/115653375337*

Advantage (RSCA) index to illustrate the UK's degree of specialisation in different export sectors.[14] This analysis shows that it is the service sectors in which the United Kingdom currently enjoys a higher than average export market share, and also that the UK's degree of specialisation in these sectors has increased over the past decade.

While the importance of manufacturing has been sliding relative to that of services, the United Kingdom still boasts a number of world class manufacturing firms. These firms tend to be in those sectors in which the United Kingdom continues to enjoy a higher than average export market share (see Figure 1.9): printing, publishing and recording; pharmaceuticals; non-metallic mineral products; aircraft and spacecraft; scientific instruments; and chemicals. However, in most of these sectors the UK's degree of specialisation has been slipping over the past decade. Moreover, Figure 1.9 shows that in all other manufacturing sectors the United Kingdom now has a negative RSCA index (implying a lower than average export market share), and that the United Kingdom has been further reducing its specialisation in these sectors over the past decade.

Service sectors are less exposed to competition from emerging markets

While these resource shifts are, in part, a *response* to the emergence of economies heavily endowed with unskilled labour, such as China, the UK's pattern of economic specialisation seems to have already been poised to benefit from such globalisation. If economic policy had protected low-skill-intensive industry in the late 1970s and 1980s, the more recent competition from emerging markets might well have proven fatal for these industries, prompting costly adjustments. Instead, by the mid-1990s the United Kingdom had already developed a specialisation in sectors (such as financial services) that are less exposed to competition from emerging low-wage economies such as China. The sectors in which the United Kingdom has specialised are also some of the fastest growing sectors.

Consistent with Coleman's (2006) model, the United Kingdom has thus been able to benefit from globalisation in the form of a rising terms of trade (discussed further below). Not surprisingly, the correlation between the United Kingdom's RSCA index in the different export sectors and that of the dynamic Asian economies is negative, implying that there is little head-to-head competition and globalisation is more an opportunity than a threat (Figure 1.10).

Figure 1.10. **RSCA correlations between selected OECD countries and the dynamic Asian economies**[1]

In 44 aggregated sectors

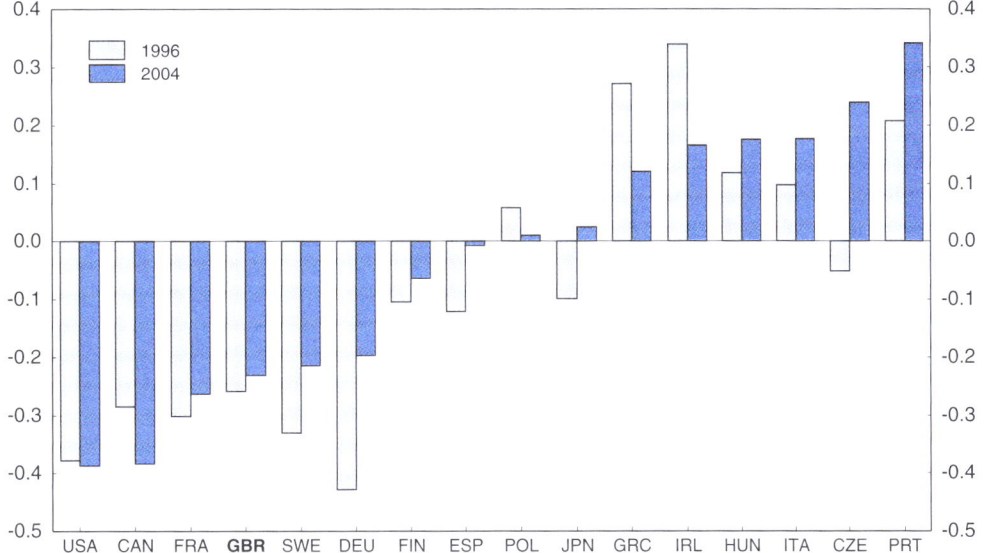

1. The correlation is a rank correlation between the Revealed Symmetric Comparative Advantage (RSCA) of each OECD country with those of the dynamic Asian economies (Chinese Taipei; Hong Kong, China; Indonesia; Malaysia; Phillipines; Singapore and Thailand) plus China and India. These latter RSCAs are calculated using extra-regional trade data except for services where it is not available. In the case of missing data on services exports it was assumed that a country's exports grew at the same rate as world growth in that service.

Source: OECD calculations based on the United Nations COMTRADE and UNCTAD databases.

StatLink ⧉ http://dx.doi.org/10.1787/115654761654

However, during the last 10 years the UK's exposure to and degree of competition with the emerging markets seems to have increased slightly. On the one hand this may suggest diminishing complementarities in export patterns with the emerging markets and increasing competition. On the other hand it could be interpreted as indicating the development of intra-industry trade. In contrast to the United Kingdom, some southern (Italy, Portugal) and eastern European countries already have significant positive correlations between their sectoral specialisation and that of the dynamic Asian economies. The high correlation for Ireland is harder to interpret, given its sensitivity to aggregation effects.[15]

Globalisation has helped to keep productivity growth strong

Although UK productivity growth has lagged that of the United States in recent years (see Chapter 4 for further discussion) there is a growing body of evidence indicating that the impact of globalisation has been positive. In other words, it is likely that productivity growth would have been slower – perhaps more in line with that of the United Kingdom's large European neighbours – in the absence of policies that promote openness and attract foreign investment.

There are at least three channels through which globalisation can spur productivity, and some of these have already been operating for some time. First, openness to trade promotes competition and encourages the weakest firms to exit the market. Second, openness to FDI and the presence of foreign multinational enterprises can facilitate technological transfers and spill-overs of best practice to domestic firms. Third, and more recent, advances in information and communication technologies have eroded the boundaries between tradable and non-tradable goods and reduced the need for different stages of production to take place near each other. This has led to the geographical fragmentation of value-added chains, permitting firms to cut costs in low value-added areas through offshoring and redirecting resources to what they do best (see Baldwin [2006] for an overview). Outsourcing or offshoring[16] of key business inputs (such as the provision of information and communication technology [ICT] services) has become common, and this may also facilitate the diffusion of productivity enhancing technologies.

Given the UK's comparative advantage in producing services, this helps to explain the faster expansion of services relative to manufacturing (although in absolute terms manufacturing has also been growing, reflecting the success of those sectors where the United Kingdom is highly competitive). Indeed, relative to other OECD countries the sectoral composition of output in the United Kingdom is heavily slanted towards (high growth) knowledge-intensive services and away from low growth sectors (Figure 1.11).

Offshoring has enhanced productivity

There is increasing evidence that offshoring – a manifestation of the increasing fragmentation of production processes – facilitates productivity growth by allowing UK firms to specialise in core functions in which they add the greatest value-added, while re-locating lower-value-added production abroad to low cost locations. For example, Criscuolo (2006) found that a 10 percentage point increase in services offshoring intensity by British firms during 2000-03 was associated with a 0.4% increase in total factor productivity after controlling for other dimensions of global engagement, industrial affiliation, regional location, capital intensity and age. Similarly, Girma and Gorg (2004) show that services outsourcing in manufacturing industries between 1980 and 1992 was

Figure 1.11. **The sectoral composition of output**
Per cent of total value added, 2003[1]

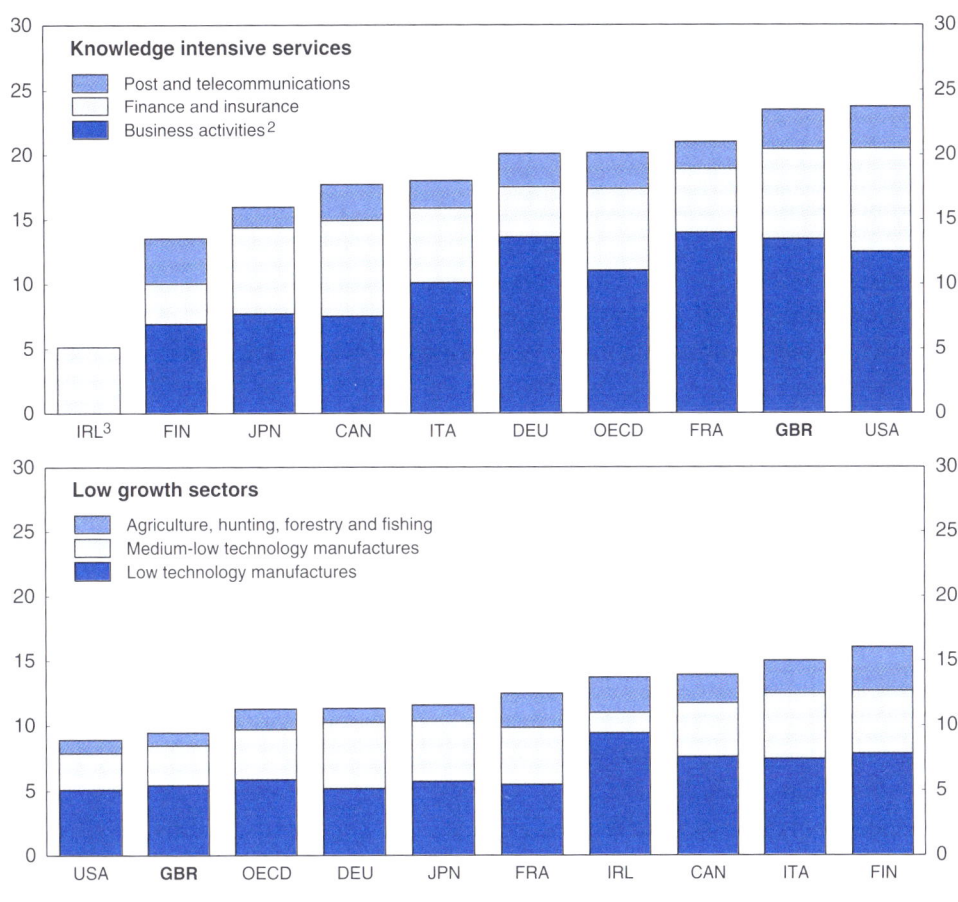

1. 2002 for Canada, Germany and Ireland. The OECD average covers 18 countries only and shows 2001 data for knowledge intensive services and 2002 for low growth sectors.
2. Renting of machinery and equipment, computer related services, research and development, other business services.
3. No breakdown available for post and telecommunications or business activities.

Source: OECD (2006), *STAN Indicators database, www.oecd.org/sti/stan/indicators.*

StatLink ᴍᴤᴸ *http://dx.doi.org/10.1787/115662422741*

positively correlated with productivity and that its effect was stronger in foreign-owned establishments.[17] For the United States, Amiti and Wei (2006) found that offshoring of services in US manufacturing industries between 1992 and 2000 had a significant positive effect on productivity, accounting for about a tenth of productivity growth during this period, while offshoring of goods (material) had a smaller effect accounting for approximately 5% of productivity growth.

While offshoring began as a manufacturing sector phenomenon, it is becoming increasingly prevalent in many service sectors also, particularly among firms that already have international linkages, such as multinational enterprises (MNEs).

MNEs play an important role

Theories of international trade suggest that MNEs possess advantages that allow them to compete with domestic firms in local markets despite higher cost and less knowledge of demand and local networks in a foreign country (Markusen, 1995). As such, MNEs contribute to the host country's growth by spurring competition and facilitating the transfer of new technologies. Empirical evidence also confirms that foreign multinationals are normally more productive than domestic firms in all countries – largely because of a selection bias; only the most productive firms are able to bear the fixed costs associated with becoming multinational (Griffith *et al.*, 2004).

MNEs and FDI play an important role in the UK economy. For instance, the share of foreign-controlled affiliates' turnover in manufacturing is 35% – the second highest among the G7 economies after Canada (OECD, 2005b). Moreover, the share of workers employed by foreign MNEs is close to 20% in manufacturing and just under 10% in services. Within the services sector the involvement of foreign MNEs is particularly high in wholesale and retail trade where around 30% of employees work for foreign MNEs. However, the most frequent means by which foreign firms enter the United Kingdom is through the take-over of existing firms, rather than through green-field investment (Griffith *et al.*, 2004; OECD, 2006). Since firms that set up new plants through green-field investments are more likely to invest in the state-of-the art technology, the prevalence of firm take-overs may suggest less potential for technological spillovers and productivity gains. However, Bloom *et al.* (2007) find that being taken over by a US multinational increases information technology productivity.

Recent OECD work shows that the productivity growth of foreign manufacturing affiliates in the United Kingdom was more than 6 percentage points faster than that of domestic firms between 1995 and 2001 (Figure 1.12, upper panel) and that their contribution to overall manufacturing productivity growth was larger than in the other large OECD economies (Figure 1.12, middle panel). These findings are consistent with other empirical results suggesting that foreign-owned multinationals tend to be more productive than UK multinationals (Griffith *et al.*, 2004). A number of studies show that US multinationals outperform all others (Bloom *et al.*, 2007), while UK multinationals are on a par with other non-US foreign multinationals (Criscuolo and Martin, 2005). As well as having higher productivity growth, recent OECD work suggests that foreign affiliates also have a higher *level* of productivity in manufacturing – consistent with the idea that MNEs use superior technologies.[18] For example, Criscuolo (2005) finds that output per employee of foreign affiliates is almost three times higher than output per employee in the total UK economy. Compared with other countries, this analysis suggests that the productivity advantage of foreign affiliates is particularly high in the United Kingdom, even after the industrial composition of foreign affiliates is adjusted to match that of the domestic economy (Figure 1.12, lower panel).[19]

The importance of the services sector and the key role played by MNEs highlights the growing importance of the financial services sector. As a major hub, or *cluster*, of financial sector firms, the City of London plays a critical role in the economy. Although its regulatory framework for financial services remains a strength, the UK's growing tax complexity and eroding tax advantage as other countries cut tax rates faster (Chapter 5), pose a risk that the position of the City as a key financial sector cluster could become less secure. That said, the United Kingdom has gained market share of global financial business in recent years, and there is little sign such risk is imminent (Box 1.4).

Labour market tightness has been eased by high net inward migration

Contrary to some fears, the available evidence suggests that openness to trade and capital flows is consistent with high aggregate employment levels (OECD, 2007c; European Commission, 2005). Certainly, this is supported by the case of the United Kingdom, where

Figure 1.12. **The labour productivity advantage of foreign affiliates**

Labour productivity growth in the manufacturing sector[1]

Annual average 1995-2001, % points[2]

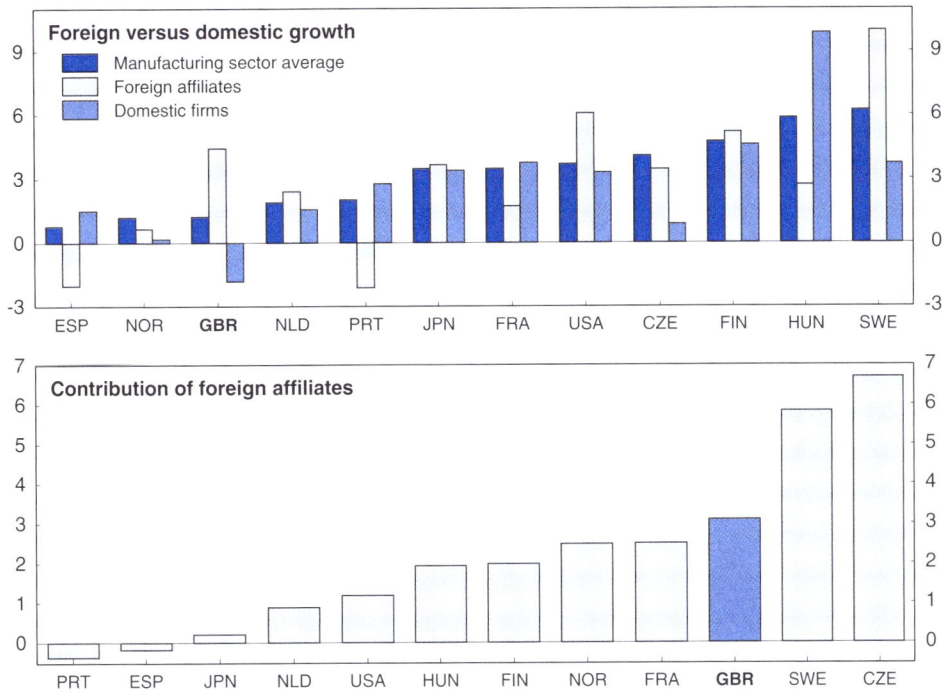

Relative labour productivity in foreign affiliates
2001[3]

Output per employee in manufacturing,
ratio of foreign affiliates to domestic firms[4]

Total economy labour productivity level, US$ of output/hour[5]

1. Labour productivity is measured as value added in constant prices over employment.
2. Or nearest available years: Czech Republic, Hungary and Portugal 1996-2002; Finland 1995-2002; Spain 1999-2001 and United Kingdom 1995-99.
3. Or latest year available for the ratio of foreign affiliates to domestic firms: Czech Republic 2002; Japan 2000; Hungary and the United Kingdom 1999; Portugal 1998.
4. Controls for the fact that foreign affiliates are more likely to be in high technology, high value added industries by keeping the industrial composition of foreign affiliates equal to that of domestic firms.
5. Using 2000 purchasing power parities.

Source: OECD (2006), *Productivity database, www.oecd.org/statistics/productivity* and Criscuolo, C. (2005), "Foreign Affiliates in OECD Economies: Presence, Performance and Contribution to Host Countries' Growth", *OECD Economic Studies*, No. 41, Vol. 2005/2.

StatLink ᵐˢᵖ *http://dx.doi.org/10.1787/115678432266*

Box 1.4. **The City: How safe is the cluster?**

The financial services industry accounts for close to 3½ per cent of employment in the United Kingdom and 8½ per cent of gross value added. As documented earlier in this chapter, this is the sector in which the United Kingdom has the largest comparative advantage, and it is continuing to gain market share: both relative to global exports of financial services and in many specific markets. For example, the UK's share of the global hedge fund industry more than doubled between 2002 and 2006 to 21%, while New York's share fell from 42% to 33%.*

More than a third of financial sector employees work in the City of London (the "Square mile" plus Canary Wharf). In turn, this sector accounts for almost 20% of GDP in London. But other financial centres are also important, most notably Edinburgh. Related professional services (accounting, legal services and management consulting) account for a further 3½ per cent of UK GDP.

History clearly plays an important role in explaining the City's importance in global financial services markets. Other factors, as summarised by Gieve (2007), which help to explain its recent growth include: the flexible labour market; the importance of English as an international language of commerce; the time zone (since the working day overlaps with Asia in the morning and America in the afternoon); the well-established financial infrastructure and telecommunications network; and the confidence that prospective market participants often have that the competitive environment is genuinely open to all. This latter point is often linked to what has been called the Wimbledonisation of the UK financial markets – the fact that the United Kingdom acts to a large extent as host to the sector, which is dominated by foreign players.

Two other factors are important. First, the "principles-based" approach to regulation of the sector is a strength. Although the principles-based approach implies a degree of legal uncertainty, the Financial Services Authority and the English legal system more generally have a reputation for predictability, and the alternative approach of setting more prescriptive rules is unable to keep up with the rapid pace of financial innovation. Second, a key basis for the competitiveness of the City is grounded in the clustering together of a critical mass of international wholesale financial activity. By bringing together a critical mass of financial expertise, individual firms can benefit not only from access to a pool of skilled labour but also from the strong external economies of scale that result from being closely located to other firms.

One potential concern of globalisation is that technological advances might encourage firms to relocate to lower-cost sites, thus undermining the synergies of clustering. However, an HM Treasury (2003a) study to investigate what impact UK euro adoption might have on the financial services sector concluded that most offshoring was of lower-value-added activities (such as back-office functions), and that core wholesale operations still saw the benefits of locating in a cluster. Indeed, they even suggested that technology may have worked in favour of clustering, by making it easier for firms to relocate activity away from their markets and towards the City cluster.

But could the whole cluster move? Not all at once of course. But if firms operating in the financial sector considered that the United Kingdom was no longer a competitive location, they could gradually relocate some or all of their activity to somewhere more competitive. It is even possible that there could be a tipping point, where the departure of one or two large banks could prompt other firms to follow. That said, in recent years, the City has been gaining business, and there is little sign that these risks are imminent. But to make sure things stay that way, policy makers should continue to emphasise sound regulatory policy, macroeconomic stability, openness, and investment in human capital while further efforts will need to be made to improve the business environment. For example, more effort needs to be made to minimise the burden of business regulation, further improve London's transport infrastructure (discussed further in Chapter 4), simplify the tax system and hold ground on tax competitiveness (Chapter 5).

* Most of the empirical estimates in this box are drawn from IFSL (2007).

the unemployment rate has trended down over the past two decades (Figure 1.1) despite increasing openness.

Another aspect of globalisation – rising migration – has also played an increasing role in the UK labour market. Until relatively recently, the United Kingdom had experienced several decades of relatively low population growth, in large part due to much lower rates of net inward migration than countries such as Australia, Canada, Germany, New Zealand, Switzerland and the United States.[20] Since the late 1990s, however, both inflows and outflows of workers have accelerated, but particularly the inflow rate. As a result, annual net inward migration has tripled, increasing from around 0.1% of the population over the 1991-96 period to around 0.3% since 2000. The greatest new influx of migrants has been from the eight new EU member countries that gained access to the UK labour market in 2004, although the net inflow of migrants from other countries has also risen.

The recent inflow of migrants has coincided with an increase in the unemployment rate, but it is not yet clear to what extent these developments are linked. What is clear is that migrants have boosted the pool of available workers, they are more mobile than natives, and there is some evidence that their wages are more flexible (Blanchflower, 2007). This has helped to make the labour market more fluid and wages less sensitive to demand fluctuations. Indeed, the migrant inflow may help to explain why earnings growth has remained relatively moderate, despite reasonably strong growth and the significant pick-up in CPI inflation earlier this year (Figure 1.2). Of course, part of the explanation probably also lies with the more general decline in the bargaining strength of native workers, which has been influenced by other aspects of globalisation, such as the greater mobility of capital. The impact of migration on the labour market is discussed in more detail in Chapter 3.

Heightened competition has changed relative prices

The United Kingdom's openness to globalisation, together with flexible product markets has permitted consumer prices of some manufactured goods to fall by more than those in continental European countries that have more stringent product market regulations (Figure 1.13). This is consistent with a number of studies which find that the greater the

Figure 1.13. **Many traded goods prices have fallen by more in the United Kingdom than in the euro area**

Average inflation rate, per cent, 1997-2007[1]

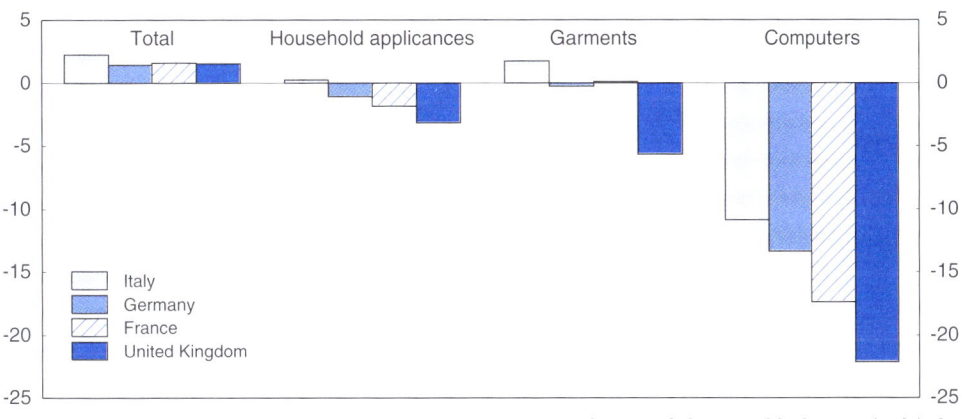

1. Average for January 1997 to July 2007; year-on-year percentage change of the monthly harmonised index of consumer prices.

Source: Eurostat database (2007), Economy and Finance, June.

StatLink ⌗ http://dx.doi.org/10.1787/115680245438

intensity of foreign competition, the greater the indirect effect of lower import prices on domestic producers in import-competing industries (see Pain *et al.* [2006] for a review).

Because the central bank aims at hitting an aggregate inflation target, lower prices of these goods have allowed other prices to rise by more than might otherwise have been the case, leading to a significant gap between services and goods price inflation (Figure 1.14).

Figure 1.14. **Goods prices inflation *versus* services**

Year-on-year percentage change

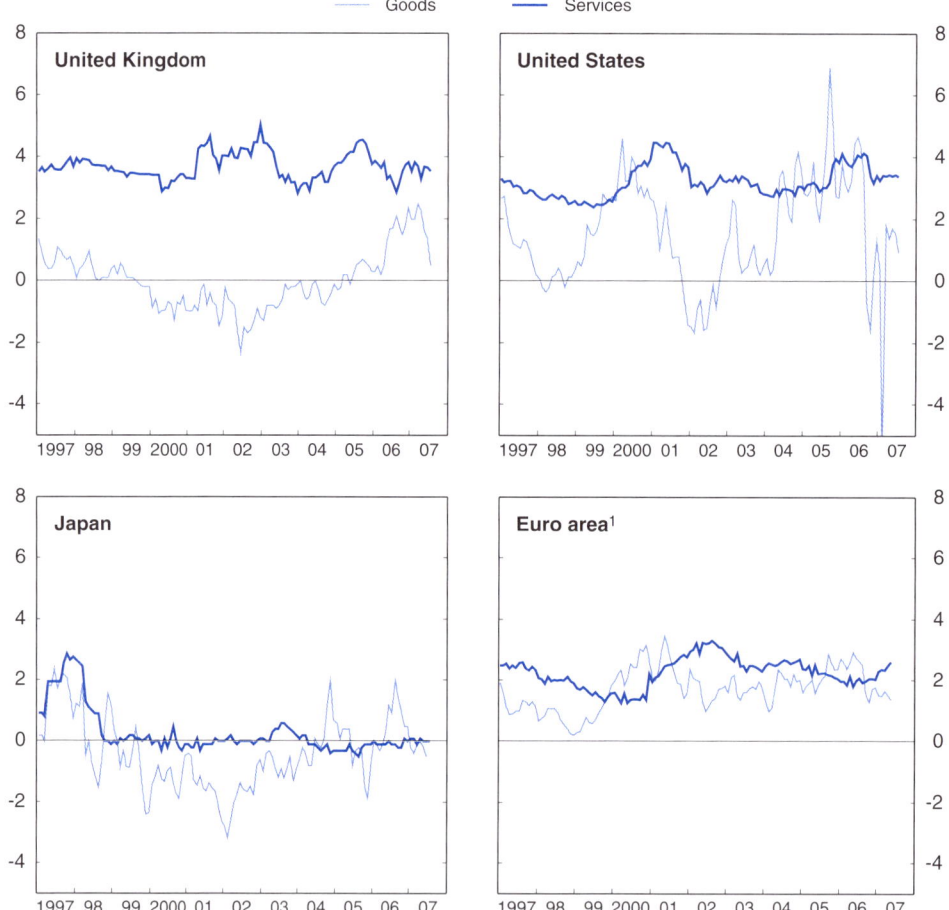

1. Twelve member countries.

Source: UK National Statistics website, *www.statistics.gov.uk*; US Bureau of Labour Statistics, Japanese Statistics Bureau and Eurostat – online databases, September 2007.

StatLink 🔗 *http://dx.doi.org/10.1787/115680483127*

As well as putting downward pressure on some prices, globalisation has also put substantial upward pressure on the prices of oil and other commodities. Although the United Kingdom is roughly self-sufficient in oil (net imports of oil in 2006 were just 0.3% of GDP), the higher oil price still served to redistribute income towards the oil companies and the government and away from non-oil firms and households. So the risk of higher energy prices spilling over into higher wages is still an important concern for the Bank of England. Overall, there is little reason to conclude that globalisation has made the job of the central bank any easier, although it has led to significant changes in relative prices (Box 1.5).

Box 1.5. **Globalisation and monetary policy**

While much has been written about the impact of globalisation on inflation, many of its effects work in opposite directions, making its overall impact uncertain. Moreover, it is difficult to isolate the impact of globalisation from other trends (such as increased central bank credibility).

One thing that is certain, however, is that globalisation represents a shock to relative prices, while the overall price level depends on monetary policy. Thus, for an unchanged inflation rate, globalisation might imply lower prices of the manufactured goods exported by China, and higher prices for all other goods, as seemed to be the case to some extent in the early part of this decade. At the other extreme, it could imply higher prices of imported commodities (such as oil and metals) and lower prices of all other goods. The extent to which the central bank chooses to accommodate such terms of trade shocks (by permitting inflation to slide beneath the target in the first case, or to exceed it in the second) will depend on how firmly anchored medium-term inflation expectations are.

There has been considerable discussion about the extent to which globalisation may have contributed to the flattening of the Phillips curve – or the weakening of the link between inflation and measures of economic slack – that has been observed over the past decade or so. Indeed, there are some channels by which globalisation may have contributed to this flattening. First, the larger global supply of labour and the potential for offshoring have weakened the bargaining power of unions, limiting the extent of upward pressure on wages at times of strong domestic demand. Related to this, there is also some evidence that specialised agencies are used to fill specific vacancies from abroad when the UK labour market is tight (Bean, 2006). Second, increased competition from imports has put downward pressure on profit margins and reduced the procyclicality of mark-ups over marginal cost (Pain *et al.*, 2006). Firms are now more likely to respond to higher costs by putting downward pressure on other input costs and by seeking efficiency gains elsewhere. Third, the increased specialisation of trade has made inflation less responsive to domestic demand conditions (Pain *et al.*, 2006). On the other hand, other globalisation effects would tend to make the Phillips curve steeper (*e.g.* tougher global competition would tend to make wages and prices more flexible). Meanwhile, two important channels completely unrelated to globalisation are likely to have played an important role in the flattening: the improved anchoring of inflation expectations, driven by the increased credibility of central banks; and the related fact that lower trend inflation has reduced the frequency of nominal price adjustments. Empirical research to date has found it difficult to disentangle these effects and identify what impact can be directly attributed to globalisation (see Kohn, 2006), although Helbling *et al.* (2006) estimated that openness contributed to roughly half of the Phillips curve flattening, with improved central bank credibility and the low inflation environment accounting for the remainder.

To the extent that globalisation has contributed to the flatter Phillips curve, its implications for monetary policy are unclear. A flatter Phillips curve implies that the transmission of monetary policy to prices may have weakened; this would normally imply that monetary policy should be more responsive to the output gap. But at the same time globalisation may also be making the output gap even more difficult to measure than is normally the case. This is partly because excess capacity is harder to measure in the service sector, which is growing as a proportion of the economy, and also because the increased availability of migrant workers makes traditional measures of tightness in the labour market less meaningful. To some extent then, monetary policy transmission may be becoming more dependent on the exchange rate and expectations channels, which are more uncertain.

Besides the flattening of the Phillips curve, there is some evidence that the more competitive global market has reduced the pass-through from the exchange rate and from global energy prices into final goods. This has considerably assisted the job of the monetary policy makers, particularly in the face of the recent oil price shock. However, Helbling *et al.* (2006) suggest that the decline in the exchange rate pass-through might only be temporary. At the same time, the fact that globalisation has tended to push the prices of many imported goods down, while pushing energy prices up, has made many policy-makers more wary of ex-energy measures of core inflation.

The bottom line seems to be that while globalisation-related influences have had a big impact on relative prices, they have not obviously made the job of the monetary policy makers any easier, or necessarily more difficult. As before, the challenge of conducting monetary policy under uncertainty remains, and monetary policy makers will need to remain vigilant to ensure that inflation expectations remain well anchored.

A higher terms of trade has boosted incomes

Largely because the United Kingdom has tended to import those goods which have experienced the largest price falls and because the United Kingdom is more or less self sufficient in oil, whose price has been pushed up, the terms-of-trade effect of globalisation appears to be significantly more positive for the United Kingdom than for most other G7 countries (Figure 1.15).

Figure 1.15. **The United Kingdom has benefited from a gain in the terms of trade**

Index, 1995 = 100

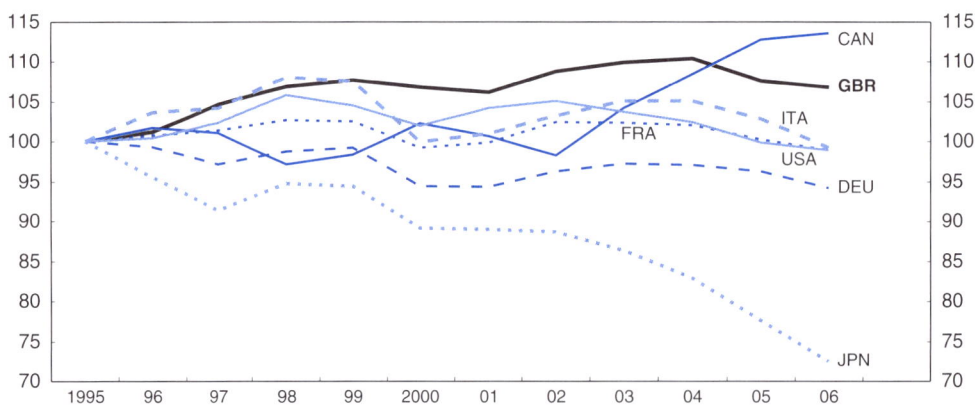

Source: OECD (2007), *OECD Economic Outlook: Statistics and Projections*, No. 81 – online database.

StatLink ᵐˢ᷉ *http://dx.doi.org/10.1787/115706724111*

One way of looking at the overall income growth implications of terms-of-trade gains is to adjust conventional measures of volume-based growth with a terms-of-trade effect to reflect consumption possibilities. This measure of "command GDP" captures the importance of sectors such as knowledge-intensive services, where prices are increasing relative to those of manufacturing goods. This adjusted measure – also discussed in the last *Survey* – suggests that the terms of trade has added about 0.2 percentage points to growth per annum over the last decade in the United Kingdom (Figure 1.16). This is larger than in most OECD countries, except those which are major net exporters of commodities, such as Australia, Canada and Norway.[21]

Figure 1.16. **Command GDP adjustment to annual average GDP growth rate**

1995-2006, per cent per annum

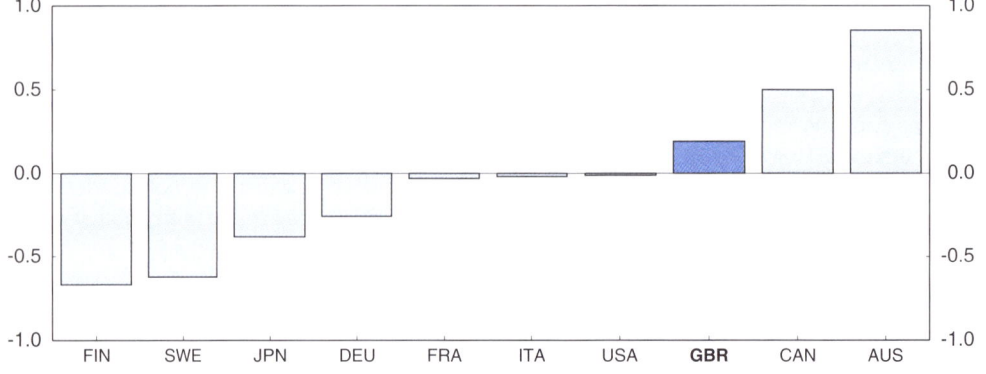

Source: OECD calculations based on OECD (2007), *OECD Economic Outlook: Statistics and Projections*, No. 81 – online database.

StatLink ᵐˢ᷉ *http://dx.doi.org/10.1787/115721787332*

OECD ECONOMIC SURVEYS: UNITED KINGDOM – ISBN 978-92-64-03772-4 – © OECD 2007

The distributional impact of globalisation depends on other policies

Because global integration has expanded the relative supply of labour in the global economy – particularly low-skilled labour – low-skilled workers in developed countries have lost some of their bargaining power. This is reflected in an increased responsiveness of domestic labour demand to the cost of labour abroad *via* trade and outward FDI (initially in manufacturing, and increasingly in services).[22]

At an economy-wide level, it could be expected that erosion in workers' bargaining power would be reflected in a declining labour share of national income. Indeed, such trends are documented by Guscina (2006), Jaumotte and Tytell (2007) and OECD (2007b), with both globalisation and skill-biased technological progress identified as explanatory factors. In the United Kingdom, however, the labour share appears to have a less notable downward trend than in some other countries (Figure 1.17, upper panel).

Figure 1.17. **Labour share of income**
Total labour compensation,[1] in per cent of GDP

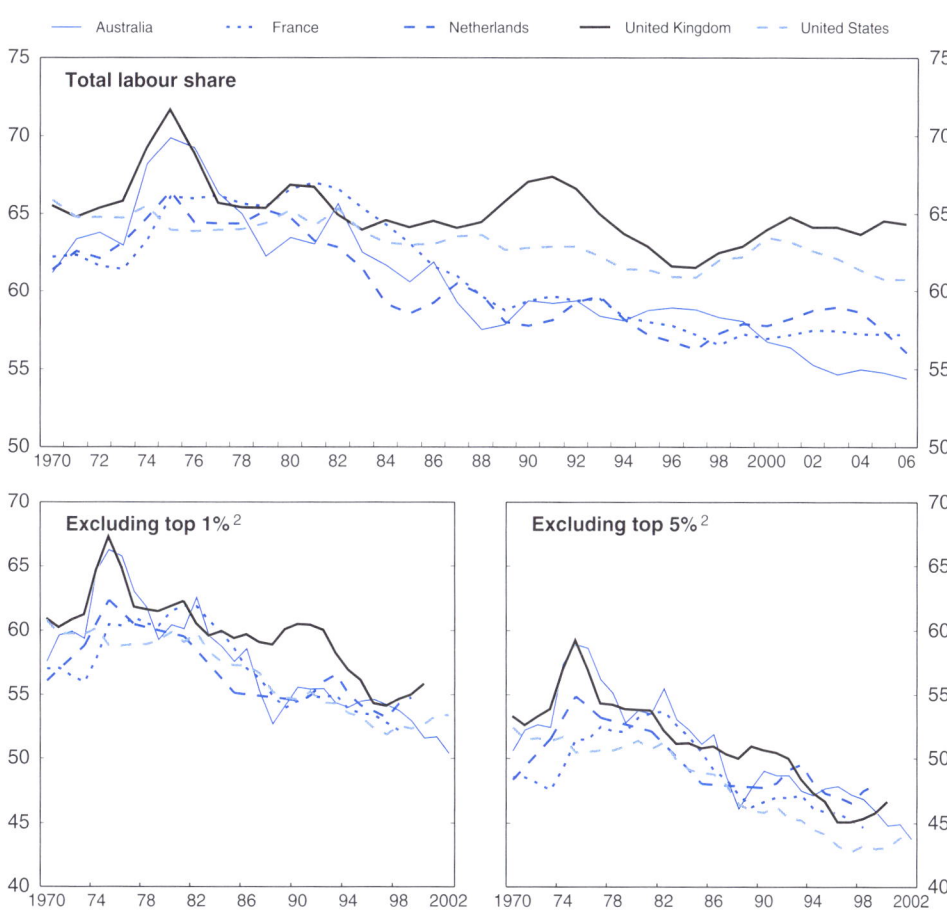

1. Total labour compensation, including employers' social security contributions and imputed labour income for self-employed earners.
2. Data on top income shares are not necessarily consistent between countries and in some cases there may be breaks over time. See Atkinson and Piketty (2007) for details.

Source: OECD (2007), *OECD Economic Outlook: Statistics and Projections*, No. 81 – online database and Atkinson, A.B. and T. Piketty (2007), *Top Incomes over the Twentieth Century*, Oxford University Press.

The factors underpinning trends in the labour share are not fully understood. Nevertheless, Jaumotte and Tytell (2007) identify a number of differences in labour share patterns across countries: *i*) in countries where the labour share is declining, much of the decline can be attributed to the unskilled sectors of the economy, whereas the labour share of the unskilled sectors was quite stable in the United Kingdom; *ii*) although technical change contributed to the reduction of the labour share, its impact was smaller in the United Kingdom and the other English-speaking countries; *iii*) the English-speaking countries have also tended to mitigate falls in the labour share by introducing changes to labour market policies that have benefited the labour share by raising employment, such as policies that have reduced the tax wedge and unemployment benefit replacement. These trends seem broadly consistent with the idea that openness has permitted resources in the United Kingdom to flow into sectors of comparative advantage, where technology is increasingly used as a complement to labour, rather than as a substitute. The stability in the UK labour share is also consistent with the fact that the United Kingdom is relatively less exposed to competition from the emerging market economies than are some other countries. Finally, it is also consistent with trends in earnings growth (documented in Chapter 3), which suggest that the median worker in the United Kingdom has experienced real wage growth broadly in line with labour productivity growth in recent years, unlike the United States where median real wage growth has lagged productivity.

An important trend in income distribution (documented in Chapter 3) is the marked increase in the relative income share of the top earners (Piketty and Saez, 2006). Indeed, when the earnings of the top 1% (or 5%) earners are excluded from the measure of labour income, the adjusted labour share has deteriorated (Figure 1.17, lower panel).[23] In the United Kingdom, most of the decline occurred between the mid-1970s and the mid-1990s. Since then, the adjusted labour share has been relatively stable, despite ongoing increases in the income share of top earners.

Significant challenges remain

While the UK economy has been well positioned to benefit from globalisation, there are still concerns about the extent to which the benefits are being distributed across the population, and an up-skilling of the population will be required to cope with the labour market demands of the future. To date, the government has addressed distributional concerns through higher expenditure in key areas, such as education and poverty reduction. As fiscal constraints have become more binding, however, further expenditure increases are less feasible, emphasising the importance of achieving better value for money in public spending. Globalisation also implies increased competition for the location of businesses and investment and location decisions are affected by the quality of infrastructure, the price of office space, the regulatory environment, and by tax competitiveness. A number of these challenges are discussed in further detail below.

Raising education achievement within a tighter budget constraint

Higher educational standards and attainment is arguably the most important channel by which living standards can be sustained, and raised, in the face of ever sharper competition. Moreover, both efficiency and social justice concerns suggest that it is important to have an education system that can help to break intergenerational cycles of disadvantage. Education spending has increased, and strong efforts have been made to direct higher spending to where it would have the greatest payoffs. Yet it is difficult to evaluate by how much education outcomes have improved. This is partly because some domestic measures of education performance may have been biased by target-driven output distortions. In addition, the lags between expenditure and outcomes are long, suggesting that some further improvements might still come.

An important concern is that the socio-economic gaps in education performance are large. The central government has attempted to address this by directing additional funds to local authorities with a higher proportion of pupils from deprived backgrounds. However, some local authorities have preferred to distribute the funds more equally between schools, undermining the central government's goal. Progress in narrowing the gaps is likely to require faster progress towards a more efficient allocation of funds.

Compared with many other OECD countries, the United Kingdom has relatively low participation by 16 and 17-year-olds in education or training. This is of concern, since globalisation suggests an increasing need for a flexible and skilled labour force that is able to re-train relatively easily in response to changing economic conditions. New financial incentives have helped to raise education participation and the government is now consulting on proposals to introduce more compulsory participation by 16 and 17-year-olds. In addition new vocational diplomas are being developed for young people who do not follow the traditional academic programmes offered at upper secondary school. Chapter 2 discusses these issues and, in the context of the challenges posed by globalisation, highlights the importance of retaining a focus on the acquisition of core literacy and numeracy skills. Given the need for fiscal restraint, the chapter suggests a number of areas where policy improvements can be made without significantly increasing outlays.

Improving work prospects for the least skilled

The key challenge of finding the right balance between transfers designed to reduce poverty and incentives for the low-skilled to participate in the labour market and to progress in work by working longer hours or by up-skilling is discussed in Chapter 3. Large increases in the minimum wage and new in-work tax credits have underpinned an improvement in the disposable income of the poorest workers, relative to the median. But the worsening labour market position of the least skilled is reflected in high inactivity rates, particularly among prime age males, together with higher unemployment rates among school leavers (Figure 1.18).

Up-skilling may be the best path for many workers to improve their labour market prospects, but the marginal effective tax rates for some groups of people are currently too high to make up-skilling worthwhile. Chapter 3 discusses the evidence that labour market outcomes for certain groups have deteriorated, together with policy options for improving labour market outcomes for the least skilled.

Addressing the productivity gap

While relatively strong productivity growth over recent years is gradually closing the productivity gap between the United Kingdom and the large European economies, lower labour productivity still explains most of the GDP per capita gap with respect to the United States (Figure 1.19). Moreover, after having narrowed substantially in the first half of the 1990s, the productivity gap with the United States has remained unchanged. This raises questions about whether current policy settings are sufficient to raise productivity growth and to promote the diffusion of new technologies.

Figure 1.18. **Recent unemployment trends**

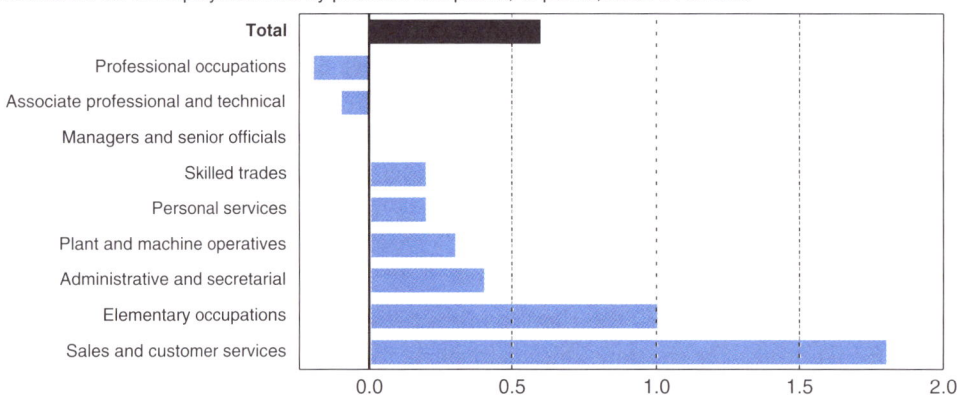

The unemployment rate is higher
Per cent

Especially among the young
Per cent of total unemployed

Age 25-49

Age 16-24

Age 50+

And those in lower-skilled professions
Increase in the unemployment rate by previous occupation, % points, 2002-04 to 2006[1]

Total
Professional occupations
Associate professional and technical
Managers and senior officials
Skilled trades
Personal services
Plant and machine operatives
Administrative and secretarial
Elementary occupations
Sales and customer services

1. Average of quarterly data.

Source: National Statistics website, *www.statistics.gov.uk – Labour Force Survey, Historical Quarterly Supplement* and *Economic & Labour Market Review.*

StatLink *http://dx.doi.org/10.1787/115745816732*

Recent productivity trends are discussed in more detail in Chapter 4, with a number of key weaknesses being identified as explanatory factors. An important area of weakness is the UK planning system and restrictions in business' access to land, which constitute an important barrier to lifting the UK's productivity performance. To address this situation the government commissioned the Barker Review which made a number of suggestions on how the system could be improved by ensuring that more weight is given to economic issues in the planning process. The Barker Review recommendations are being taken forward *via* the Planning White Paper and proposed Planning Bill. However, indications to date are that the government will not follow through on all of the Barker Review recommendations.

Another area of weakness is transport infrastructure, which suffered a long period of underinvestment (both in roads and the railways) over many decades. Railway ownership underwent dramatic reforms over the 1990s and, following the release of the Ten Year Plan for Transport in 2000 and a couple of fatal railway accidents, spending on railway infrastructure has increased. In contrast, investment in road transport remains low by historical standards, although there are currently plans underway to trial road-user pricing

Figure 1.19. **There is still a substantial productivity gap with the United States**

2005

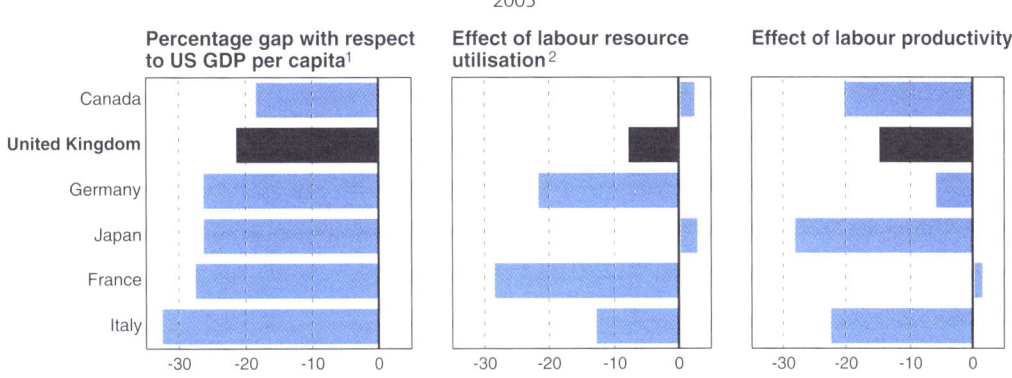

1. Based on 2005 purchasing power parities.
2. Total hours worked per capita.
3. GDP per hour worked.

Source: OECD (2007), *Productivity database*, March, *www.oecd.org/statistics/productivity.*

StatLink *http://dx.doi.org/10.1787/115760302587*

schemes which, if extended nationwide, should provide major congestion benefits. However, this is probably at least a decade away. Further efforts to improve infrastructure are needed.

The Davidson Review 2006 was commissioned to look at the extent to which red-tape and business regulation was impeding business activity and the subsequent 2006 Legislative and Regulatory Reform Act gave the government the power to amend primary legislation by "Legislative Reform Order" (LRO). These new order-making powers are focussed on better regulation outcomes, but more needs to be done, and progress on this front needs to be monitored. Chapter 4 provides more background on how these areas of weakness may impede productivity growth and discusses the policy options for reform. Other key challenges, such as the low general level of skills of the adult population, are also discussed.

Holding ground on tax competitiveness

Concerns have been voiced that greater openness will erode tax revenues, while globalisation raises demands for government programmes that cushion the impact of economic changes. However, internationally mobile activity represents a relatively small proportion of revenues, with corporate tax revenues making up only 8% of the total tax take (Figure 1.20).

Figure 1.20. **Tax revenue by source**

Per cent of total tax revenue, 2004

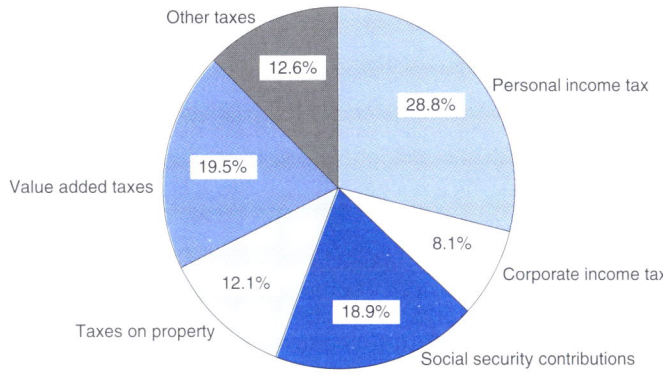

Source: OECD (2006), *Revenue Statistics.*

StatLink *http://dx.doi.org/10.1787/115768355348*

Corporate tax revenues as a share of GDP have not declined, at least to date, despite lower statutory tax rates. Moreover, to the extent that embracing globalisation enhances economic growth, it also implies a larger potential tax base which could strengthen the provision of social welfare, rather than diminish it (Hines, 2006).

Statutory corporate tax rates have declined substantially in the United Kingdom and elsewhere, while tax bases have been broadened. This has rendered corporate tax systems more efficient. While declining tax rates are consistent with tax competition, they do not prove that it has been taking place. But there is a considerable amount of evidence that countries compete on the location of business investment, the location of business headquarters and where company profits get taxed.

The United Kingdom was early in cutting the corporate tax rate and had strong tax competitiveness until the mid-1990s. In the meantime, other countries have caught up and many smaller European countries have considerably lower tax rates, even after the recent announcement to cut the corporate tax rate from 30% to 28% in 2008. However, the UK tax rate is the lowest among the G7 countries, although pressures to cut rates will continue. Chapter 5 looks at the various options to preserve tax competitiveness; these include further tax cuts and base broadening, reducing the complexity of the corporate tax system, and shifting taxation to less mobile factors. More radical options to overhaul the corporate tax system are also discussed; all have some advantages, if also significant drawbacks.

Notes

1. Citizens from two of the accession countries already enjoyed relatively free access to the UK labour market prior to EU expansion. Ireland and Sweden also permitted free movement and the right to work from 1 May 2004, and Finland, Greece, Italy, Portugal and Spain followed suit in 2006. In contrast, public opinion on immigration has become more negative in recent years, leading the United Kingdom to impose restrictions on workers from Bulgaria and Romania when they joined the European Union in January this year.

2. These international comparisons are based on a comparison of GDP per capita converted to US dollars using 2000 purchasing power parities (OECD *National Accounts* database).

3. HM Treasury (2005) summarised the six key policy challenges for the United Kingdom in responding to globalisation as: i) entrenching macroeconomic stability in a more integrated global economy; ii) building an enterprising and flexible business sector where firms can succeed and seize the opportunities presented by a more open and competitive global economy; iii) promoting innovation to drive forward scientific research and knowledge-driven industries; iv) opening the acquisition of skills to secure the right skills profile for the global economy; v) ensuring fairness to provide security for those who need it while providing incentives to work and save; and vi) increasing the energy and resource efficiency of the economy.

4. The links between consumption and housing were discussed in Chapter 2 of the previous *Survey*.

5. For example, see HM Treasury, Budget 2007.

6. Honjo (2007) shows that a rolling forward-looking version of the golden rule (*i.e.* a forward looking rule aiming for "balance" over the cycle), would avoid the risk of pro-cyclicality but in doing so impose a looser constraint on debt over any given cycle.

7. For example, this would be the case as long as the current budget balance averages zero and nominal GDP grows by 5% per annum.

8. For example, it was announced that the unfunded pension liabilities of the NHS rose to £165 billion at 31 March 2006 from £131 billion at 31 March 2005 and from £103 billion at 31 March 2004. Eighteen billion pounds of the most recent re-valuation stemmed from the 1 April 2005 change in the Government Actuary's Department discount rate from 3.5% to 2.8% (House of Commons, 2007b). The liabilities of other public sector pension funds are likely to be similarly revised.

9. For example, cyclical revenue windfalls are often directed into government programmes that tend to be permanent.

10. OECD projections published in the *Economic Outlook* No. 81 (June 2007) suggest that total government disbursements as a percentage of GDP in the United Kingdom will surpass those of Germany in 2007.

11. Fiscal drag refers to the additional tax revenues that are raised by allowing tax allowances and thresholds to increase in line with retail prices rather than earnings. The Treasury estimates that fiscal drag increases current revenues by 0.2% of GDP per annum (HM Treasury, 2003b).

12. See the OECD *Economic Globalisation Handbook*. For example, in 2005 and 2006 the United Kingdom received the highest level of inflows in the OECD ($165 billion, three times higher than FDI inflows in 2004). This figure was boosted by several large cross-border take-overs, such as the early 2006 take-over of Peninsular & Oriental Steam Navigation Company by Dubai Ports World (OECD, 2006).

13. Canada's value added share of manufacturing has remained broadly stable since 1980.

14. For further discussion about the RSCA analysis see Rae and Sollie (2007).

15. While Ireland also appears to be exposed to competition with the emerging markets, this largely reflects Ireland's specialisation in information technology related manufactures. A correlation based on more disaggregated data (1 033 categories) reveals less exposure for Ireland. However, for the United Kingdom the more disaggregate analysis seems to be less appropriate because of the much greater importance it attaches to the manufacturing sectors relative to the service sectors.

16. The terms outsourcing and offshoring are often used interchangeably. Both can be used to describe the process of purchasing intermediate goods and services from foreign suppliers, although outsourcing can also be done domestically, while offshoring always refers to inputs being sourced from abroad and also incorporate international insourcing (importing goods or services from foreign affiliates of domestic parent companies).

17. The study covered the chemical, mechanical and instrument engineering and electronics industries.

18. In services and in low-tech manufacturing sectors the largest contribution of foreign affiliates was due to an increase in employment shares of foreign affiliates, while in medium and high-technology sectors the contribution was mainly driven by stronger productivity growth of existing foreign affiliates.

19. In general it was found (in both the OECD and in the United Kingdom) that the productivity advantage of foreign affiliates was smaller in high-technology sectors (such as chemicals and pharmaceuticals, and machinery and equipment) than in low-technology manufacturing. One explanation for this might be that these high-technology sectors have already been more exposed to global competition through trade.

20. Between 1991 and 1996 the UK population increased by around 0.25% per annum, compared with over 1% per annum in Australia, Canada, New Zealand and United States. More recently, UK population growth picked up to around 0.6% in 2004 and 2005.

21. Norway is an extreme case, with a command GDP adjustment of more than 2½ percentage points. Australia (shown in Figure 1.16) is the second largest. At the other end of the scale, Korea has a particularly large negative adjustment (–2.2 percentage points).

22. OECD estimates suggest that the wage elasticity of labour demand increased from about 0.2 to 0.5 in absolute value between 1980 and 2002, with the evidence for this increase being strongest for manufacturing, one of the most exposed industries. Globalisation, and in particular offshoring, may have played a significant role in causing this change by allowing firms to more flexibly respond to shocks *via* changes in the mix of production at home and abroad (OECD, 2007b).

23. The adjusted labour share is calculated by re-classifying the earnings of the top 1% income earners as a return to (human) capital rather than labour. This share averaged around 6-7% during the 1970s, before gradually increasing to close to 10% by 1990 and 13% by 2000 (Atkinson, 2007). Similarly, the earnings of the top 5% rose from 17-18% in the 1970s to 27% by 2000.

References

Amiti, M. and S.-J. Wei (2006), "Service Offshoring and Productivity: Evidence from the United States", *NBER Working Paper*, No. 11926, National Bureau of Economic Research, Cambridge MA.

Atkinson, A.B. (2007), "The Distribution of Top Incomes in the United Kingdom, 1908-2000", in A.B. Atkinson and T. Piketty (eds.), *Top Incomes over the Twentieth Century*, Oxford University Press.

Baldwin, R. (2006), "Globalisation: the Great Unbundling(s)", contribution to the project *Globalisation Challenges for Europe and Finland,* Prime Minister's Office and Economic Council of Finland, Helsinki, September.

Bean, C. (2006), "Globalisation and Inflation", speech to the LSE Economics Society, 24 October, available at: *www.bankofengland.co.uk*.

Blanchflower, D. (2007), "Recent Developments in the UK Labour Market", speech at the University of Sterling, 26 February, available at: *www.bankofengland.co.uk*.

Bloom, N., R. Sadun and J. van Reenen (2007), "Americans Do I.T. Better: US Multinationals and the Productivity Miracle", *NBER Working Paper*, No. 13085, National Bureau of Economic Research, Cambridge MA.

Botman, D. and K. Honjo (2006), "Options for Fiscal Consolidation for the UK", *IMF Working Paper*, No. 06/89, International Monetary Fund, Washington DC.

Chote, R. *et al.* (2007), "The Fiscal Rules and Policy Framework", *The IFS Green Budget: January 2007*, IFS Commentaries, No. C102, Institute for Fiscal Studies, London.

Christensen, A., J. Dupont and P. Schreyer (2005), "Inflation Measures: Too high – Too low – Internationally Comparable?", paper prepared for an OECD seminar, Paris, 21-22 June, available at: *www.oecd.org/dataoecd/14/18/34987270.pdf*.

Coleman, W.J. (2006), "Accommodating Emerging Giants", *2006 Meeting Papers*, No. 50, Society for Economic Dynamics, New York.

Cournède, B. (2005), "House Prices and Inflation in the Euro Area", *OECD Economics Department Working Papers*, No. 450, OECD, Paris.

Criscuolo, C. (2005), "Foreign Affiliates in OECD Countries: Presence, Performance and Contribution to Host Countries' Growth", *OECD Economic Studies*, No. 41, Vol. 2005/2, OECD, Paris.

Criscuolo, C. and R. Martin (2005), "Multinationals and US Productivity Leadership Evidence from Great Britain", *CEP Discussion Paper,* No. 672, Centre for Economic Performance, London School of Economics.

Criscuolo C. (2006), "Does Offshoring Matter for Productivity?", Centre for Economic Performance, London School of Economics.

European Commission (2005), "Rising International Economic Integration: Opportunities and Challenges", *The EU Economy 2005 Review*, European Economy, No. 6, Office for Official Publications of the European Communities, Luxembourg.

Gieve, J. (2007), "The City's Growth: the Crest of a Wave or Swimming with the Stream?", speech to the London Society of Chartered Accountants, 26 March, *Quarterly Bulletin*, Vol. 47, No. 2, Bank of England, London.

Girma, S. and H. Gorg (2004), "Outsourcing, Foreign Ownership and Productivity: Evidence from UK Establishment Level Data", *Review of International Economics*, Vol. 12, No. 5, Blackwell Publishing.

GMF (German Marshall Fund of the United States) (2006), *Perspectives on Trade and Poverty Reduction: A Survey of Public Opinion*, German Marshall Fund of the United States, Washington DC.

Griffith, R., S. Redding, and H. Simpson (2004), "Foreign Ownership and Productivity: New Evidence from the Services Sector and the R&D Lab", *CEP Discussion Paper*, No. 649, Centre for Economic Performance, London.

Guichard, S. *et al.* (2007), "What Promotes Fiscal Consolidation: OECD Country Experiences", *OECD Economics Department Working Papers*, No. 553, OECD, Paris.

Guscina, A. (2006), "Effects of Globalisation on Labor's Share in National Income", *IMF Working Paper*, No. 06/294, International Monetary Fund, Washington DC.

Helbling, T., F. Jaumotte and M. Sommer (2006), "How Has Globalization Affected Inflation?", *IMF World Economic Outlook*, International Monetary Fund, Washington DC.

Hines, J.R. (2006), "Will Social Welfare Expenditures Survive Tax Competition?", *Oxford Review of Economic Policy*, Vol. 22, No. 3, Oxford University Press.

HM Treasury (2003a), "The Location of Financial Activity and the Euro", EMU Study, HM Treasury, available at: *www.hm-treasury.gov.uk*.

HM Treasury (2003b), *End of Year Fiscal Report*, The Stationary Office, London, December.

HM Treasury (2005), *Globalisation and the UK: Strength and Opportunity to Meet the Global Challenge*, The Stationary Office, London.

Honjo, K. (2007), "The Golden Rule and the Economic Cycle", United Kingdom: Selected Issues, *IMF Country Report*, No. 07/90, International Monetary Fund, Washington DC.

House of Commons (2007a), *The 2007 Budget: Fifth Report of Session 2006-07*, House of Commons Treasury Committee, The Stationary Office, London, April.

House of Commons (2007b), *NHS Pension Scheme and NHS Compensation for Premature Retirement Scheme: Resource Accounts 2005-06*, The Stationary Office, February.

IFS (Institute for Fiscal Studies) (2007), *The IFS Green Budget 2007*, IFS Commentaries, No. C102, Institute for Fiscal Studies, London.

IFSL (International Financial Services) (2007), "International Financial Markets in the UK", International Financial Services, London, available at: *www.ifsl.org.uk*.

Jaumotte, F. and I. Tytell (2007), "The Globalization of Labor", *IMF World Economic Outlook*, International Monetary Fund, Washington DC.

King, M. (2007), Letter from the Governor to the Chancellor, available at: *www.bankofengland.co.uk/ monetarypolicy/remit.htm*.

Kohn, D. (2006), "The Effects of Globalization on Inflation and their Implications for Monetary Policy", Remarks at the Federal Reserve Bank of Boston's 51st Economic Conference, Chatham, Massachusetts, 16 June.

Markusen, J. (1995), "The Boundaries of Multinational Enterprises and the Theory of International Trade", *Journal of Economic Perspectives*, Vol. 9, No. 2, American Economic Association, Nashville TN.

Nickell, S. (2006), "Monetary Policy, Demand and Inflation", speech to the Bank of England's South East and East Anglia Agency on 31 January, available at: *www.bankofengland.co.uk*.

OECD (2005a), *OECD Economic Surveys: United Kingdom*, OECD, Paris.

OECD (2005b), *OECD Handbook on Economic Globalisation Indicators*, Measuring Globalisation, OECD, Paris.

OECD (2006), "Trends and Recent Developments in Foreign Direct Investment", *International Investment Perspectives*, OECD, Paris.

OECD (2007a), *Going for Growth*, Economic Policy Reforms, OECD, Paris.

OECD (2007b), "Making the most of Globalisation", *OECD Economic Outlook*, No. 81, OECD, Paris.

OECD (2007c), "OECD Workers in the Global Economy: Increasingly Vulnerable?", *OECD Employment Outlook*, OECD, Paris.

ONS (Office for National Statistics) (2007), *Consumer Price Indices: Technical Manual 2007 Edition*, Office for National Statistics, London, May.

Pain, N., I. Koske and M. Sollie (2006), "Globalisation and Inflation in the OECD Economies", *OECD Economics Department Working Papers*, No. 524, OECD, Paris.

Piketty, T. and E. Saez (2006), "The Evolution of Top Incomes: A Historical and International Perspective", *American Economic Review*, Vol. 96, No. 2, American Economic Association, Nashville TN.

Rae, D. and M. Sollie (2007), "Globalisation and the European Union: Which Countries are Best Placed to Cope?", *OECD Economics Department Working Papers*, forthcoming.

ANNEX 1.A1

Progress in structural reform

This annex reviews action taken on recommendations from previous *Surveys*. Recommendations that are new in this *Survey* are listed in the relevant chapter.

Recommendations	Action taken since the previous *Survey*
Housing market	
Monitor closely the speed and efficiency of the planning system and progress towards the government's regional housing targets.	Progress is being made towards the government's target of 200 000 homes a year by 2016; net additions rose in 2006 to 185 000 (from around 160 000 in 2005). Planning performance has also improved with over 70% of local authorities now meeting targets for speed, up from around 20% in 2002.
Reform the planning system to increase its responsiveness to housing demand as well as providing greater incentives for local authorities to meet housing growth targets, *e.g.* by disregarding for a period council tax receipts generated by new housing from the calculation of the local authorities grant allocation from central government.	The government has consulted on a proposal to introduce a new Housing Delivery Grant to further improve incentives for housing delivery.
Reform the council tax to make it more proportional to property values and based on more frequent and up-to-date valuations.	Sir Michael Lyons' Independent Review of local government finance in England concluded in March 2007 that revaluation is an important task for a future government.
Public sector management	
Further improve incentives faced by providers of health and education, for example by introducing incentive pay for hospital doctors, and further involving private sector providers to ensure contestability.	The private sector has continued to be involved in providing capacity to the National Health Service (NHS). Take-up of the wave 1 contracts has continued to rise, exceeding 90% of the contracted volumes in recent months, promoting contestability throughout the NHS. The role of private sector providers is increasing in a number of other areas, including the construction of schools (through private finance initiatives) and provision of training providers available to employers. The government is continually reviewing contracts for NHS doctors, and considering the role of incentives. Incentive pay is being brought into the teacher pay system.
Free up additional government resources by applying an interest rate close to government borrowing costs to student loans, rather than a zero real interest rate.	The government plans to appoint an independent panel to review all aspects of the policy, including interest rates, in 2009.
Transport infrastructure	
Maintain investment in transport infrastructure at least at the levels envisaged in long-term spending plans and examine any persistent undershoot with a view to taking remedial action. Consider the case for further raising expenditure on strategic roads.	The Eddington Review has improved the evidence base as regards the case for additional expenditure on transport. This evidence will feed in to the Comprehensive Spending Review, which will address overall investment in transport.
Monitor incentives for local authorities to pursue local congestion charging schemes, *e.g.* by making funds from the Transport Innovation Fund available sooner or by making planned increases in funding for local transport contingent on local plans to tackle congestion.	Funding has been made available to ten local authorities for trial congestion schemes. Incentive funding linked to Local Transport Plans was contingent in part on local congestion strategies. The Congestion Performance Fund has been announced, offering increases in funding to those areas with the greatest congestion problems to go beyond existing local targets, with the first allocations under this scheme being announced.

Recommendations	Action taken since the previous *Survey*
Consider directing more subsidies to railway lines which have the greatest potential for relieving road congestion.	New franchise agreements require train operators to increase capacity where possible. The government will soon set out the capacity increases (including new rolling stock and infrastructure) which it expects the rail industry to provide over the period 2009-14, and for which the government will contribute to funding.
Find further measures for more closely integrating investment decisions between railway infrastructure and train operations.	A process is underway to specify the capacity, punctuality and other improvements the government wants the industry to deliver. The industry will identify the specific measures it proposes to secure these improvements. This process concentrates on high level outputs rather than specific projects, enabling the industry to identify complementary operational and infrastructure measures capable of delivering passenger benefits.

Pensions

Recommendations	Action taken since the previous *Survey*
Simplify the pension system by reducing excessive reliance on means-testing. For example, by raising the basic state pension and indexing it to future earnings rather than prices, with the fiscal costs to be partially covered by raising the state pension age in line with increasing life expectancy and by introducing a cap on tax subsidies to pension savings.	The government has proposed to: link the basic State Pension to earnings from 2012 (subject to affordability); introduce measures to improve coverage for women and carers; simplify the State Second Pension; restrict the spread of means-testing; and raise the state pension age to 68 by 2050 in line with increases in average life expectancy. These proposals are currently before parliament.
Facilitate reforms to promote other sources of income during retirement, such as through mortgage equity release products.	The UK government introduced legislation to bring home reversion plans within the scope of Financial Services Authority (FSA) regulation, establishing a level regulatory playing field in the equity release market. The FSA regime took effect in April 2007.
Consider imposition of some form of mandatory savings in the medium term.	The government has announced proposals to introduce a new system of simple, low cost personal accounts from 2012, along with auto-enrolment and mandatory employer contributions, to encourage low to moderate earners to save for retirement.

Child care

Recommendations	Action taken since the previous *Survey*
Give support for child-care and nursery education priority over extending paid maternity leave. Evaluate the effects of 9 months paid leave before committing to the extension of paid leave to a full year.	Paid maternity leave was extended from 26 to 39 weeks from April 2007. It is therefore too early to evaluate the effects of this specific change, ahead of the government fulfilling its goal of 52 weeks paid maternity leave by the end of this parliament.
Consider ways of developing the quality and flexibility of the supply of child-care services.	The government introduced a £250 million Transformation Fund to improve the quality of the child-care workforce, and aims to have a graduate leader in every full day-care setting by 2015. All local authorities have a statutory duty to ensure sufficient child care, as far as is reasonably practicable, for all parents who need it in order to work or access training. This will involve ensuring the availability of flexible child-care services where the demand exists.

Labour market

Recommendations	Action taken since the previous *Survey*
Continue to roll out the Pathways to Work programme nationally. Extend it to a wider range of existing claimants when there is sufficient capacity.	Pathways to Work currently covers around 40% of the country. By 2008 Pathways will be rolled out to the remaining 60% of the country where it is to be delivered by the private sector and other non-profit organisations. In most areas Pathways is only mandatory for new claimants but existing claimants can volunteer on to the programme. To date about 1 in 15 Pathways' participants have been existing claimants. Localised trials are being conducted on making Pathways mandatory for existing claimants. The findings of these pilots will inform future national decisions on policy for existing claimants.
Make the transfer to the incapacity benefit less automatic by involving specialised occupational health teams earlier in the process of eligibility assessment.	The Welfare Reform Act 2007 will replace the current system of incapacity benefits with a new integrated and simplified Employment and Support Allowance (ESA). ESA will have a clearer balance of rights and responsibilities than the current system. In parallel with the introduction of ESA the Personal Capability Assessment (PCA) – the eligibility test conducted at the start of an incapacity benefit claim – will be changed so screening of applicants is more stringent.

Recommendations	Action taken since the previous *Survey*
Consider shifting health care resources towards mental health.	The government continues to allocate growing volumes of resources to mental health. Between 2001/02 and 2005/06 (latest spending figures available) spending increased by 25% or £983 million.

Innovation policy

Recommendations	Action taken since the previous *Survey*
Evaluate the effectiveness of research and development (R&D) tax incentives before extending their generosity.	In 2006 the United Kingdom commissioned an independent consultancy to conduct a feasibility study into whether an econometric evaluation of the scheme would be possible. The study concluded that it is still too early. The United Kingdom plans to do a full evaluation of the scheme as the data becomes available.
Reconsider the balance of direct funding for R&D between SMEs and larger companies who receive most current support.	The government's main source of direct funding for R&D in both small and medium-sized enterprises (SMEs) and large companies is the Department of Trade and Industry (DTI) Technology Strategy (£178 million a year), which will be administered by an independent agency from July 2007, with an enhanced remit to support innovation across all sectors of the economy. The Sainsbury Review is developing recommendations on how support for innovative SMEs can be further improved.
	Budget 2007 announced a more generous R&D tax credit system for SMEs, subject to state aid clearance.
	The small business research initiative (SBRI) aims to encourage more high-technology small businesses to grow and develop new research capacities. Government departments should purchase at least 2.5% of their R&D from SMEs. The Sainsbury Review of Science and Innovation is reviewing the scheme, and will report this summer. SBRI operates within the EU legal framework, which means that it is not legally permissible to advertise SBRI contracts as being solely for SMEs or for UK-based companies.
Further promote university-business collaboration, *e.g.* by streamlining university governance procedures and providing clearer guidelines concerning intellectual property rights.	The government is providing £110 million a year support for business-university collaboration in England through the Higher Education Innovation Fund, and has published a set of model intellectual property agreements that businesses and universities can use as templates. The Gowers Review reported in December 2006 with a set of recommendations for modernising the UK's intellectual property regime, which the government is taking forward. The Sainsbury Review is developing recommendations on how knowledge transfers between businesses and universities can be further improved.

Skills

Recommendations	Action taken since the previous *Survey*
Do more to improve basic literacy and numeracy so as to provide a stronger foundation for continued learning.	The government recently met its interim target for tackling basic skills challenges in the adult population – over 1.6 million adults have improved their basic skills since 2001.
	The government has carried out a small-scale trial of new functional skills qualifications in mathematics, English and information and communication technology (ICT), and is developing full qualifications for piloting from September 2007. Full roll out is planned from 2010, with functional skills featuring both as a discrete qualification for young people and adults and as part of GCSE, the new diplomas and apprenticeships.
Unify the current array of vocational programmes and diplomas into a limited number. Work with the universities to ensure that the new diplomas give sufficient pathways to continued education including with foundation degrees.	New qualifications are being developed to replace and rationalise the current complex range of provision and qualifications. The reform will create a coherent system of units and qualifications that are easier for learners and employers to navigate, and are focused on skills for life and work, subject and vocational based learning, and personal and social development. Higher education institutions are integrally involved in the development of diplomas, so as to ensure that the qualifications are designed with the possibility of progression into higher education.

ISBN 978-92-64-03772-4
OECD Economic Surveys: United Kingdom
© OECD 2007

Chapter 2

Raising education achievement within a tighter budget constraint

Globalisation, together with skill-biased technical change, is changing the composition of jobs in advanced economies and raising the level of skills required to do them. This has increased the importance of educating a large proportion of the population to much higher standards than in the past. The government has responded to this challenge by raising education spending and expanding the capacity of the education system in key areas such as pre-primary education and increased participation in education beyond the age of 16. The United Kingdom has also pioneered the use of school benchmarking techniques and the use of targets to raise school quality. However, targets may also have biased some measures of education performance. Socio-economic background plays an important role in explaining education performance, and the government has addressed this by the use of funding formulas which direct additional resources to areas with a higher proportion of pupils from deprived backgrounds. There has been some improvement in the most disadvantaged schools but pupils in the middle and lower half of the distribution continue to perform particularly poorly relative to students in countries with the best performing education systems. Overall, the socio-economic gaps remain large. One explanation may be that local authorities and schools are not distributing deprivation funds as intended by the central government, resulting in outcomes which can be seen as inequitable. Stronger measures may be required to correct this imbalance. This chapter proposes a number of avenues for encouraging higher educational attainment, without significant further increases in expenditure.

Globalisation is raising the level of skills demanded in advanced economies

In the United Kingdom, as in other advanced economies, there is some evidence to suggest that many moderately skilled jobs are being "hollowed out" by offshoring and computerisation (Figure 2.1).

Figure 2.1. **Employment share by job quality decile**[1]

Percentage change, 1979-99

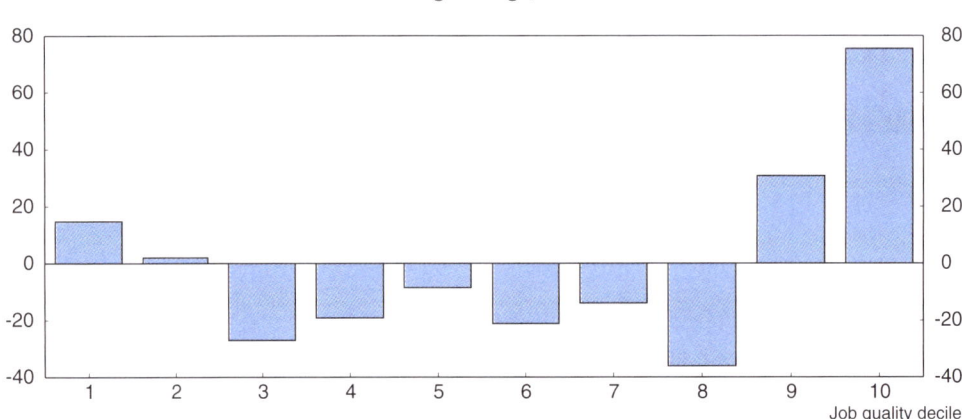

1. Employment data are taken from the Labour Force Survey and the quality deciles are based on median wages in 1979 from the New Earnings Survey. Both use three-digit SOC90 codes.

Source: Goos, M. and A. Manning (2007), "Lousy and Lovely Jobs: The Rising Polarization of Work in Britain", *The Review of Economics and Statistics*, Vol. 89, No. 1, The MIT Press.

Most of the job types that are being hollowed out can be described as routine, involving tasks that rely on very little tacit knowledge and which can be relatively easily specified in rules (*e.g.* call centre work, assembly line work, or the processing of basic tax returns). Some more highly skilled jobs – those that involve a heavy component of rules and standardised procedures – have also moved offshore (*e.g.* technical jobs in programming, engineering, financial analysis, etc.).[1] But there has been strong employment growth in the most skilled and highly paid professions – those that require more abstract cognitive skills involving complex communication with other humans (*e.g.* lawyers, managers) or solving problems and exercising good judgement in the face of uncertainty (*e.g.* scientists, doctors). In contrast, manual low-skilled jobs, most often in service occupations, are unlikely to disappear, even if their numbers are not increasing rapidly.

Importantly, the increasing demand for higher-level skills comes not only from changes in the employment share between occupations, but also because of changing skill demands from within occupations. For example, a bank teller today spends more time selling financial services than performing routine tasks of processing deposits and withdrawals. Similarly a mechanic can no longer function without the ability to read and to work with computerised testing equipment.

Recognition of these trends by both the public and policymakers explains why there is now much greater pressure on the education system to equip more pupils with more advanced skills. For example, the Leitch Review of Skills (Leitch, 2006) concluded that the skills base of the UK economy is too weak, although the focus of that report was predominantly on qualifications. While it is beyond the scope of this *Survey* to discuss how such skills can be taught, common sense would suggest that they would require a strong foundation of basic reading, writing and mathematics. In this context the government's announcement in December 2005 of a renewed emphasis on "basic skills" is very welcome.[2]

Given this context, this chapter focuses on how the compulsory education system is addressing two key problems: first, the fact that the skill level of the workforce (including the younger cohorts) is relatively low and may be impeding faster productivity growth; and second, the fact that the education system still seems to perpetuate rather than break the cycle of inequality. In light of the increasingly binding fiscal constraints of the government, the focus is on ways in which higher primary and secondary education performance can be achieved without significant further increases in spending. Although globalisation may also imply significant benefits from up-skilling the adult population, continuing education, vocational training, and tertiary education are not covered in this chapter, although some of these issues are touched on in Chapter 4.

Education participation rates are low but picking up

The educational performance of the UK population is below the standard of the best performing OECD countries (Figure 2.2). This is reflected in results that are only average on internationally comparable assessments of cognitive skills (see discussion below) and in the UK's relatively low secondary school completion rates. In recognition of this latter point, the government has made significant efforts to raise education participation among 16 and 17-year-olds. One successful intervention has been the Education Maintenance Allowance (EMA) which uses the payment of a small allowance to encourage 16-19-year-olds from poor families to continue in education. Although further participation in education and training is expected, the government is also considering raising the compulsory participation age from 15 to 17 (Box 2.1). In part, this proposal reflects a desire to rank among the best performing countries in the OECD in terms of education participation.[3] This proposal is also supported by evidence that higher levels of education can improve health and lower the probability of being imprisoned or becoming a future welfare recipient.[4]

While raising education participation is an important goal, it is not clear that compulsion is necessarily the best way to achieve it. In the United States there is substantial evidence that higher student achievement leads students to stay in school longer voluntarily (see Hanushek and Woessmann [2007] for a review). For those students who have already performed poorly, and who are unmotivated, it is not clear what the returns to further education and training at ages 16 and 17 would be, particularly since the return on many existing vocational qualifications is low and the new diplomas are yet to be tested.[5] It should also be kept in mind that education participation is a relatively poor proxy for skills, and that a focus on qualifications can hide problems of poor usage and over-qualification. Educational quality – measured by cognitive skills – is a much better measure of human capital than years of schooling (Hanushek and Woessman, 2007), and care should be taken to ensure that greater quantity is not sought at the expense of quality.

Figure 2.2. **Educational attainment by age group and PISA performance**

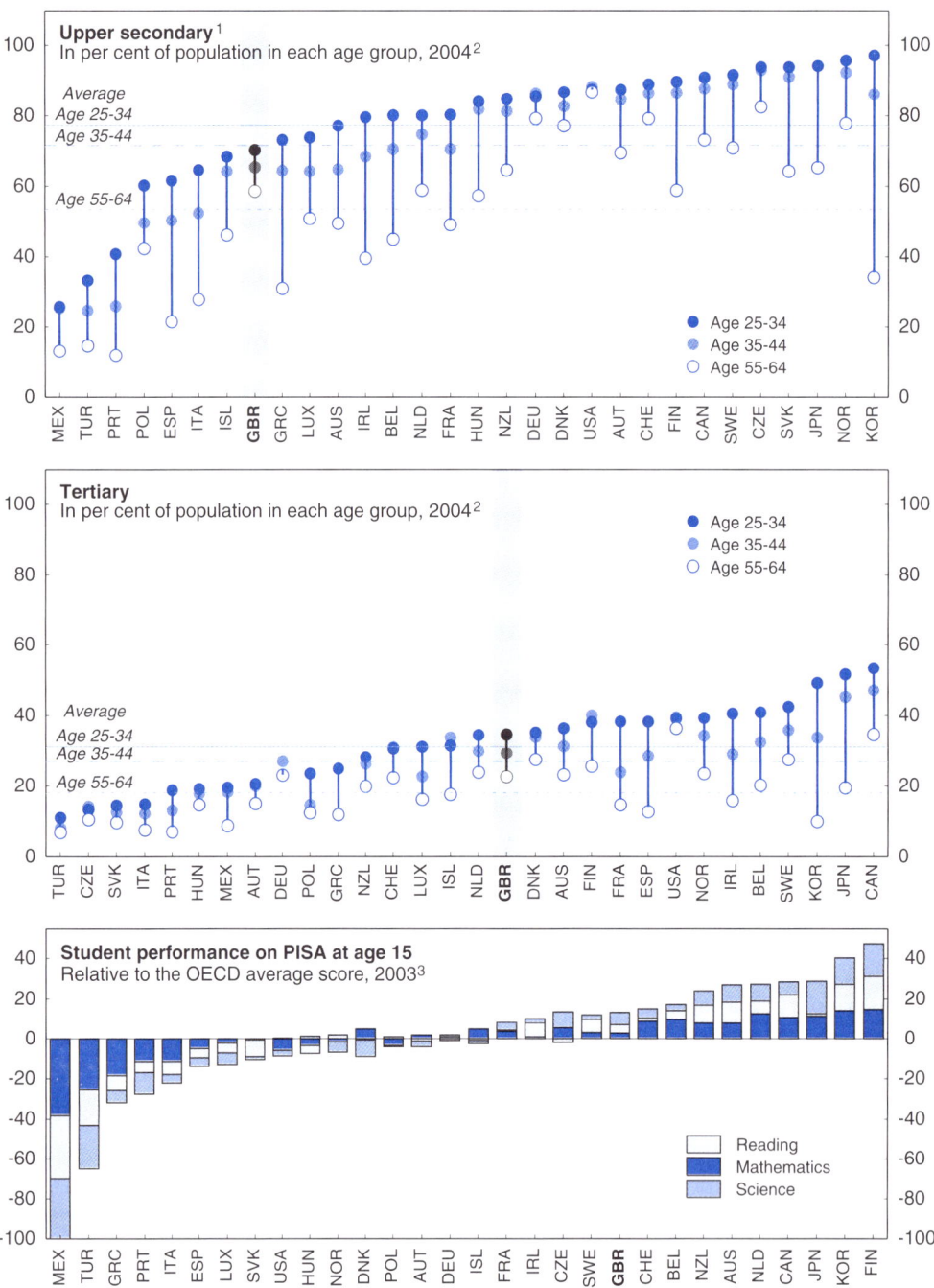

1. Excluding ISCED 3C short programmes except for the United Kingdom where some are included.
2. 2003 for Japan.
3. The bars indicate the average PISA score for each country relative to the OECD average. The contribution of relative performance in mathematics, reading and science is also indicated (these three skills are weighted equally in the total score). Note also that the UK's response rate is too low to ensure comparability with the other countries.

Source: OECD (2006), *Education at a Glance* and OECD (2004), *Learning for Tomorrow's World: First Results from PISA 2003*.

StatLink ᡱᢅᡱ *http://dx.doi.org/10.1787/115804551171*

Box 2.1. **Raising education participation: Coercion or compulsion?**

After fluctuating in the 64-66% range over 1994-2003, the percentage of 16 and 17-year-olds in full-time education increased to 67% in 2004 and to 70% in 2005. Based on evidence from the pilots, some of this increase has been attributed to the education maintenance allowance (EMA), introduced in September 2004, which pays up to £30 per week to 16-19-year-olds from families with an income of less than £30 810 per annum who stay on at school or undertake unpaid training. Payments are stopped for absenteeism and there are bonus payments to reward achievement of agreed learning goals. Including work-based learning and other forms of training, 16 and 17-year-old participation rates have regained previous levels of around 85% after falling back in the late 1990s and early 2000s (OECD calculations based on DfES, 2006a). Moreover, the evidence suggests that the policy is to a large extent displacing individuals from unproductive activities (Dearden *et al.*, 2006).

For 17-year-olds, the participation rate (in education and work-based learning) was 76% in 2005/06 and the government aspires to raise this to 90% by 2015. A naturally increasing trend is expected to be boosted when the new diplomas are implemented. The government is currently overhauling vocational education by replacing the current system of 3 500 separate qualifications with diplomas in 14 broad areas (DfES, 2005). Some of the new diplomas will be available from 2008 in selected areas, and all will be available in all areas from 2013. Although it is too early to judge what the economic returns of these diplomas will be, their goal is to offer a mix of practical and theoretical study for those young people who prefer a more applied approach than offered by the existing qualifications.

Although the government expects to meet its aspiration of 90% participation (in education or work-based training) by 17-year-olds by 2015, it has also proposed to introduce more compulsion by making participation in some form of education or training mandatory until age 18 (DfES, 2007). It is proposed that the policy would be introduced in phases, initially raising the participation age to 17 in 2013, and then to 18 in 2015. Since the majority of young people would be choosing to participate in education or training voluntarily by 2015, compulsion would be binding for a relatively small group. Sanctions, through either a civil or a criminal process, would be introduced for hard core cases who refuse to participate, although the government is trying to develop a process that avoids criminalisation. Young people would have the option of studying either for a general qualification (GCSEs, A-levels, International Baccalaureates), as part of an apprenticeship, or for one of the new diplomas. The government has recently consulted on whether working towards an accredited occupational qualification would be sufficient, or whether young people should also be expected to develop core literacy and numeracy skills. It has argued that compulsion would mean that the education system would need to focus more on the needs of young people who are least likely at present to choose to participate; provide better for them pre-16; and make sure that there are high quality options post-16 which can engage and interest them. However, these benefits could also be achieved by only introducing compulsion for those students who have not already achieved a minimum level of core skills by age 16.

If the proposal to introduce education or training compulsion until age 18 goes ahead, the government proposes to build upon the EMA to ensure that those from low income backgrounds would continue to receive financial support, and that the link between financial support and progression would be strengthened.

In this context the government may wish to consider compulsion only for those pupils who have not already achieved a certain minimum standard of core skills (English and mathematics) by age 16. This would ensure continued focus (by schools and young people) on the acquisition of core skills, both prior to and after age 16, and ensure that the education system prior to age 16 focuses attention on the needs of the lowest performers. Alternatively, compulsion could be delayed until it has been shown that there are significant positive returns to the new diplomas.

The UK's relatively poor level of cognitive skills is reflected in the results of internationally comparable assessments. For example, the International Adult Literacy Survey (IALS), which assessed the proficiency of adult literacy in 20 countries between 1994 and 1998, found that the United Kingdom ranked in the bottom half of the 20 participating countries, and that roughly half the working age population had literacy and numeracy skills at one of the two lowest levels, compared with just a quarter of the population in Sweden, the top performer (OECD, 2000). The IALS judged that the low level of literacy proficiency of these people would make it difficult for them to face new demands, such as learning new job skills, even if they have developed coping skills to manage everyday literacy demands.[6] The United Kingdom did not participate in the update of this survey (known as the Adult Literacy and Life Skills Survey). However, the government has been participating actively in development work for the next adult skills survey (the Programme for International Assessment of Adult Competences – PIAAC). The likely testing window for PIAAC is 2011, which should allow a sufficient time lapse to document any recent improvement in adult cognitive skills resulting from programmes such as the *Skills for Life* initiative.

There is also a need for higher education performance in the compulsory school system if the United Kingdom is to reach the standards of the highest performing countries. Because the UK response rate in the 2003 PISA (Programme for International Student Assessment) study fell below the required level, the results are not fully comparable with those of other countries.[7] With this caveat, the data indicated that the academic results of 15-year-olds in the United Kingdom ranked significantly below the top performers (Figure 2.2, lower panel). A satisfactory response rate was achieved in the 2006 PISA study, although results will not be available until December 2007.

For recent cohorts, the situation may have improved somewhat, at least in terms of primary school level reading skills. In terms of mean reading literacy achievement of children aged about 10, the PIRLS International 2001 survey of student achievement in reading ranked England 3rd, and Scotland 14th out of a total sample of 34 countries, and the 2003 TIMSS study of mathematics skills among 9-10-year-olds placed England 10th and Scotland 18th out of a total sample of 25 countries.[8]

Education is an important tool for spreading the gains from globalisation

As globalisation raises the return to higher education, and worsens the labour market outcomes of some of the lesser skilled, it is important to ensure that the whole population is able to share in the gains. With policy increasingly emphasising the goals of "making work pay" and of facilitating people's integration into the labour market (Chapter 4), the impact of education policy on the labour market outcomes of the disadvantaged is increasingly important, and the use of education as a tool to remedy social disadvantages is justifiable for both efficiency[9] and social justice reasons. However, while education can break intergenerational cycles of disadvantage, it can also act to reinforce them: for example, if education policy is not designed with egalitarian notions in mind (Machin, 2006).

In all countries there is a strong correlation between educational achievement and socio-economic background. In the United Kingdom, however, research suggests that intergenerational social mobility is lower than in many other OECD countries. This shows up in relatively low occupational and education mobility (d'Addio, 2007) as well as low intergenerational income mobility. A common measure of intergenerational income mobility is the fraction of relative income differences between fathers that are transmitted to their sons: the higher this elasticity, the lower is intergenerational income mobility. While this elasticity measure suggests relatively high social mobility in the Nordic countries, Australia and Canada, it suggests the least mobility for the United Kingdom (Figure 2.3).

Figure 2.3. **Intergenerational earnings elasticity – estimates from various studies**[1]

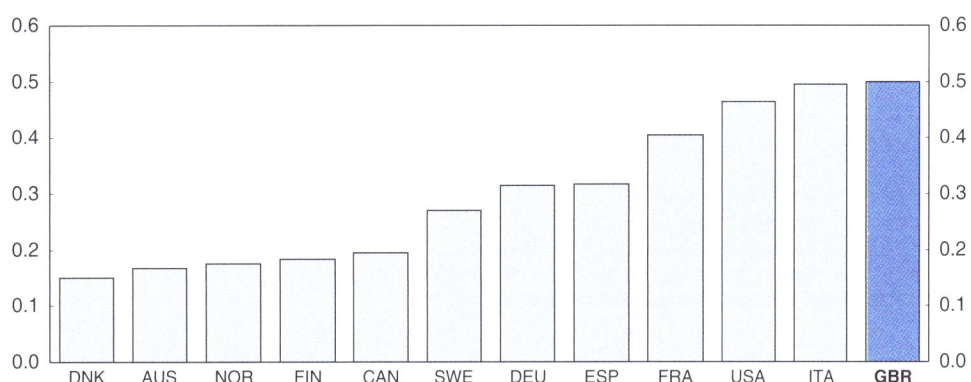

1. The higher the parameter, the higher is the persistence of earnings across generations and thus the lower is mobility.

Source: D'Addio, A.C. (2007), "Intergenerational Transmission of Disadvantage", *OECD Social, Employment and Migration Working Papers, No. 52.*

StatLink ⟳ *http://dx.doi.org/10.1787/115824831540*

Other studies confirm that intergenerational income mobility in the United Kingdom is both low and declining.[10] One explanation is that the expansion of opportunities for university study in the 1980s and 1990s favoured those from better-off backgrounds, thus reinforcing income persistence across generations and depressing the prospects for social mobility.[11] Even today, students from low socio-economic backgrounds are much less likely to have the grades (including English and mathematics) required to enter the academic A-level track at high school which is the main conduit to university study (Figure 2.5). Ensuring that the gains from globalisation are spread more evenly will almost certainly require policies to ensure that more children from lower socio-economic backgrounds receive an education that adequately prepares them for higher education.

Fortunately, cross country analysis suggests that there is no trade-off between high average achievement and equality of educational opportunity. For example, Figure 2.4 shows that the top PISA performers are also countries that achieve a relatively high degree of homogeneity across the distribution of student outcomes.[12]

Figure 2.4. **The best performing countries have the most homogenous outcomes**

2003

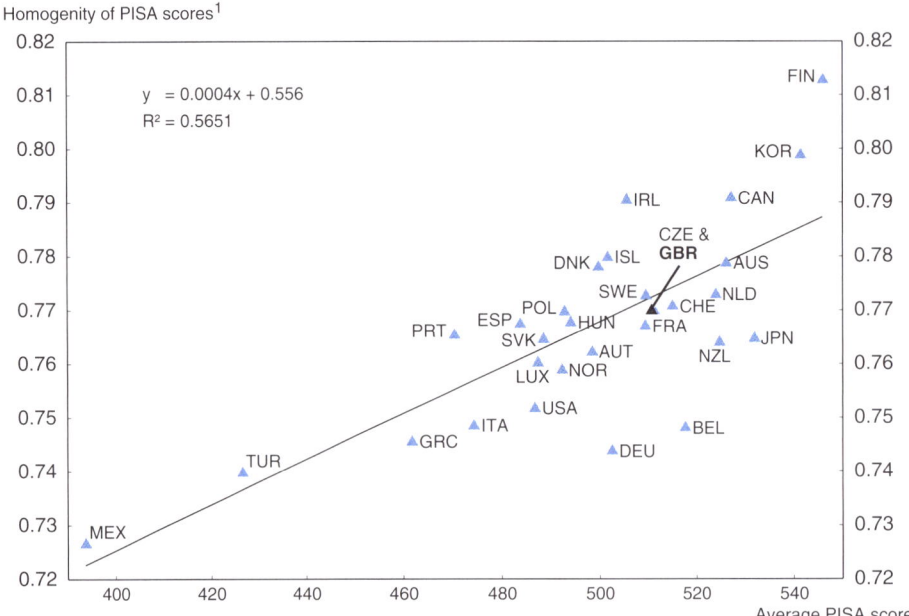

1. Measured by the ratio of the average score of the 25th percentile to that of the 75th percentile (the higher the ratio, the greater the homogeneity in student performance).

Source: OECD (2004), *Learning for Tomorrow's World: First Results from PISA 2003*; OECD (2005), *Education at a Glance*; Sutherland, D. *et al.* (2007), "Performance Indicators for Public Spending Efficiency in Primary and Secondary Education", *OECD Economics Department Working Papers*, No. 546.

StatLink ⬛⬛ *http://dx.doi.org/10.1787/115853336748*

In this context, it is useful to compare the distribution of the United Kingdom's PISA scores with those in the top 7 countries. Keeping in mind the caveats associated with the UK's low response rate in PISA 2003, such a comparison (Table 2.1) suggests that UK pupils at the very top of the performance distribution do relatively well (a gap relative to the top 7 countries of 15-16 points at the 90th and 95th percentiles), whereas the gap is wider further down the distribution (peaking at 23 points at the 25th percentile). The fact that the peak is not at the lowest point on the distribution suggests that UK education policy has ensured that pupils at the very bottom do not fall too far behind. But policies have been less successful at raising the performance of pupils in the middle to bottom half of the education performance distribution. Higher average performance overall would therefore seem to require a levelling up of student outcomes in the middle and bottom half of the distribution.

Table 2.1. **Average PISA scores by percentile ranking: Top seven performers *versus* the United Kingdom[1]**

	5th	10th	25th	Median	75th	90th	95th
Average PISA score top 7 countries	371	407	469	533	598	649	679
United Kingdom	349	385	446	512	579	633	664
Gap: Top 7 – United Kingdom	21	22	23	21	20	16	15

1. The top seven PISA performers are Finland, Korea, Japan, Canada, Australia, New Zealand and the Netherlands. As discussed earlier, it should be noted that the UK's response rate was too low to ensure comparability with the other countries.

Source: OECD (2004), *Learning for Tomorrow's World: First Results from PISA 2003*.

National data on education performance is consistent with this. A comprehensive evaluation of achievement gaps between pupils and schools with differing levels of deprivation up to the year 2005 (DfES, 2006b) found that while average performance has improved across the board, the extent of narrowing of achievement gaps depended on the measures used and whether the comparison was across schools or across pupils. The cross-school comparison showed a clear narrowing in the achievement gap between the *least* and *most* deprived schools when using the benchmark measure of the percentage of pupils achieving five or more A*-C GCSEs or equivalents.[13] However, schools a step above the bottom showed much less improvement, consistent with the results indicated in Table 2.1. In addition, when the alternative measure of five or more A*-C GCSEs *including English and mathematics* was used, there was much less evidence of narrowing (Figure 2.5). Finally, it is not clear whether the gaps have narrowed at all when they are measured across deprived and non-deprived pupils, rather than across schools. For example, Table 2.2 shows that the gap between the percentage of FSM (free school meals) and non-FSM students attaining the five or more A*-C GCSE benchmark narrowed by just over 3 percentage points between 2002 and 2006. However, the gap has not closed at all when measured using the benchmark including English and mathematics.

Table 2.2. **Proportion of pupils attaining GCSE benchmarks**

Percentage of pupils attaining five or more GCSEs or equivalent

	Grades A* to C			Grades A* to C including English and mathematics		
	2002	2006[1]	Difference	2002	2006[1]	Difference
Free school meals	24.1	34.2	10.1	15.3	20.3	5.0
Non-free school meals	54.5	61.5	7.0	43.1	48.1	5.0
Gap	30.4	27.3	−3.1	27.8	27.8	0.0

1.   Revised 2006 figures.
Source: DfES (2006), "Trends in Attainment Gaps in Schools: 2005", *Statistical Bulletin*, Department for Education and Skills and Office for National Statistics, June. Updated to 2006 by DfES.

Government policy initiatives have focused on sharpening incentives and higher overall spending

To raise student achievement, the government has introduced a number of policies which emphasise performance incentives for local authorities, schools and teachers. In addition, education spending has been raised as a percentage of GDP, and efforts have been made to direct the additional spending to areas with the highest pay-off. However in both areas there is room for improvement.

Many institutional settings are exemplary and benchmarking is sophisticated

The UK education system has a number of commendable institutional features, such as significant school autonomy (Gonand, 2007). The United Kingdom has also pioneered the widespread use of benchmarking of schools. New value added measures of performance are now published for all schools alongside Office for Standards in Education (OFSTED) reports and raw measures of performance. These permit school performance evaluation to take into account the relative advantage or disadvantage posed by their pupil intake (Box 2.2).

Box 2.2. **Sophisticated benchmarking to assess school performance**

Each year, Achievement and Attainment Tables are published for each primary and secondary school, indicating the achievement of pupils at different levels. Over time, the indicators published have changed, mostly in positive ways. For example, in December 2005, the "gold standard" indicator for 15-year-old pupils was modified to include a requirement that the core subjects of English and mathematics were included in the qualifying GCSEs. This indicator is now: *the percentage of pupils at the end of year 11 (normally aged 15 or 16) achieving five or more A*-C GCSEs (and equivalent) including English and mathematics GCSEs.*

Since a longer time series is available for the previous indicator (which was the same, but without specifying the English and mathematics requirement), this will continue to be published until 2008. Part of the reason for the importance of this benchmark is that it represents the standard that is required for 15 and 16-year-olds to enter the most academic and most prestigious (A-level) track in upper secondary school. Other indicators, reflecting the achievements of pupils who achieve a lower standard are also published.

The "high performing schools" identified by the above indicators are typically those with the best-prepared students going into them, but not necessarily those where the *value-added* of the school is high, and *vice versa* for bad schools. To address this concern the government has developed more sophisticated techniques for assessing pupils and schools. For example, value added measures have been published in School Achievement and Attainment Tables since 2002. They measure the achievement of pupils in comparison to pupils with similar prior achievement; this is fairer than using raw outcomes since schools can have very different levels of achievement on entry.

More recently, an enhanced indicator, known as Contextual Value Added (CVA) has been developed and published for the first time in the 2006 tables. This aims to take into account other factors that are related to the progress that pupils make in a school, but which are outside a school's control. Factors that have been taken into account in the CVA models include: pupil prior achievement; gender; special educational needs; first language; ethnicity; measures of deprivation; measures of pupil mobility; age; an "in care" indicator; and the average and range of prior achievement within the school. CVA measures have thus replaced the value added measures which were based on prior attainment only. No CVA measures are published for private schools since these schools do not provide the required detailed information about individual pupils.

Since CVA measures are new, it is not yet clear what role they will play in the assessment of school performance. However, they would seem to offer significant potential for more closely evaluating the performance of under-performing schools that currently achieve above the bottom threshold "floor target", and for distinguishing high quality from low quality teachers.

Source: Largely based on DfES (2006), "Publication of 2006 Test and Examination Results in the School and College Achievement and Attainment Tables", Department for Education and Skills, June, *www.dfes.gov.uk/ performancetables.*

But the use of performance incentives is not easy

The educational authorities have also aimed to improve student achievement by emphasising performance incentives for local authorities, schools and teachers. These policies include:

- Merit pay for teachers.

- Expanded choice of schools for pupils.

- The setting of targets and the widespread use of benchmarking to evaluate state-funded schools and identify the best and worst performers.

The introduction of merit pay for teachers has been found to have a positive impact on student achievement in some subjects in England (Atkinson *et al.*, 2004). This avenue for encouraging higher teacher performance is promising, given the importance of teaching quality. For example, Hanushek (2003) cites studies which suggest that having five years of good teachers in a row (*i.e.* teachers at the 85th quality percentile) would overcome the average achievement deficit between pupils from disadvantaged backgrounds and those from higher income families.[14]

Experience to date with "school choice" and on the use of targets is more mixed. While expanded school choice by students and parents can be a powerful tool, by providing pupils with the opportunity to move to a better performing school and by creating competition between schools,[15] choice tends only to work for a well informed and confident clientele and when the supply side is secure enough to be able to adapt properly. In the United Kingdom, it is not clear that pupils and parents in the lowest socio-economic classes are able to take advantage of school choice. A study of pupil mobility by Machin *et al.* (2006) found that pupils that change schools tend (on average) to move to better schools. However, they also found that children from lower socio-economic backgrounds are much less likely to make the move to a better school than are children from wealthier backgrounds. In part, this may reflect the complication of the admissions system and the government has helped to address this by introducing a network of advisers who will provide additional assistance to families that are most likely to struggle with the admissions process. But it also reflects the higher cost of housing in neighbourhoods with the best schools. While the new School Admissions Code (introduced in 2007 for admissions in 2008) encourages schools to reflect the diversity of the communities they serve without excluding or disadvantaging particular social groups, it is likely that most local authorities will continue to give preference to children from the immediate neighbourhood. In this context it will be interesting to follow developments in local authorities (such as in Brighton and Hove) that use random allocation/ballot as a means of allocating some of their school places.

Given the limits to which school choice is likely to work for the lowest socio-economic classes, directing resources towards these pupils may be more important, although there is often some resistance to this at the local authority level (see below). Moreover, since individuals in less advantaged positions often act in ways that serve to perpetuate the *status quo* (Erikson and Goldthorpe, 2002), improved social mobility may require complementary policy interventions beyond simply ensuring equal study opportunities.

Compared with encouraging disadvantaged pupils to move to good schools, it may be much easier to encourage good teachers to move to bad schools. Given that good teachers are often attracted to schools with a high proportion of pupils from advantaged backgrounds, efforts to narrow the gaps between pupils from different backgrounds should consider ways to identify the best teachers (perhaps using CVA measures)[16] and put in place systems and financial incentives to encourage them to move to, and remain at, the most disadvantaged schools (Nickell, 2004). Some small initiatives have explored options in this area. For example, *Teach First* is a recruitment initiative that has aimed at placing high quality graduates into disadvantaged schools. But much more should be done. For example, central government funds could be used to provide bonuses to teachers at disadvantaged schools who consistently obtain higher than expected gains in student performance. Clearly this would require a very different set of teacher management policies from those currently in place.[17] The government has, in its 2007-08 Remit Letter to the Training and Development Agency for Schools, asked it to look creatively at how it can use the resources and levers at its disposal to ensure that schools serving areas of high disadvantage have good-quality teachers and support staff in post. This might include consideration of how financial incentives could be used.

The focus on targets may have made progress more difficult to evaluate

The introduction of education targets for the United Kingdom has been accompanied by a significant improvement in educational attainment (particularly at the primary level in England) as measured by the targets themselves. However, an important concern is that the presence of targets may be producing perverse effects and biasing the measures of performance. Such perverse effects – often referred to as "gaming" – have been well documented in the performance management literature[18] and may include: ratchet effects, threshold effects and unmonitored output distortions.[19]

Some evidence of gaming in education became apparent when the benchmark target was changed from the percentage of students achieving any five A*-C GCSE grades to the percentage achieving five such grades *including English and mathematics*. Performance on both benchmarks has improved (Figure 2.5), but the improvement is less when measured using the more challenging indicator. With the benchmark change some schools slipped very considerably down the league tables and some principals admitted that they had pushed children towards taking easier vocational exams to push their schools up the league tables.[20] Since five A*-C GCSE grades including English and mathematics is the normal benchmark for entry into the academic A-level track at upper secondary school, one of the adverse effects of this target may have been to limit the number of students qualifying for university entrance.

Consequently, an important question is how to shape performance measurement so as to make it meaningful for schools and teachers as well as for those evaluating performance. De Bruijn (2007) argues that targets encourage perverse behaviour because they take only limited account of the complexity of the profession. Thus, he suggests that performance management should meet the following three criteria if it is to fulfil its function properly: interaction, variety and dynamics. In the case of schools, this would mean that the system of performance management should be developed in *interaction* between evaluators and schools/teachers so as to ensure trust in the system. At the same time, the complexity of teaching children should be reflected in a *variety* of performance indicators, and greater emphasis should be placed on school *processes*, rather than outputs, so that performance management can be *dynamic* – permitting adaptation to changing conditions. While these features are undoubtedly already present to some extent in England's performance management system, most media and political focus is on the much narrower range of benchmark indicators which may weaken the effectiveness of the system overall.

Another problem is that the incentive effects of targets usually rely on some reward and sanction mechanisms. But these are difficult to implement. In England it is the Permanent Secretary for the Department for Education and Skills who is responsible for meeting most of the government's education targets, rather than the schools themselves.

Figure 2.5. **Attainment gaps across schools by deprivation level**[1]

Percentage of pupils attaining five or more GCSEs or equivalents

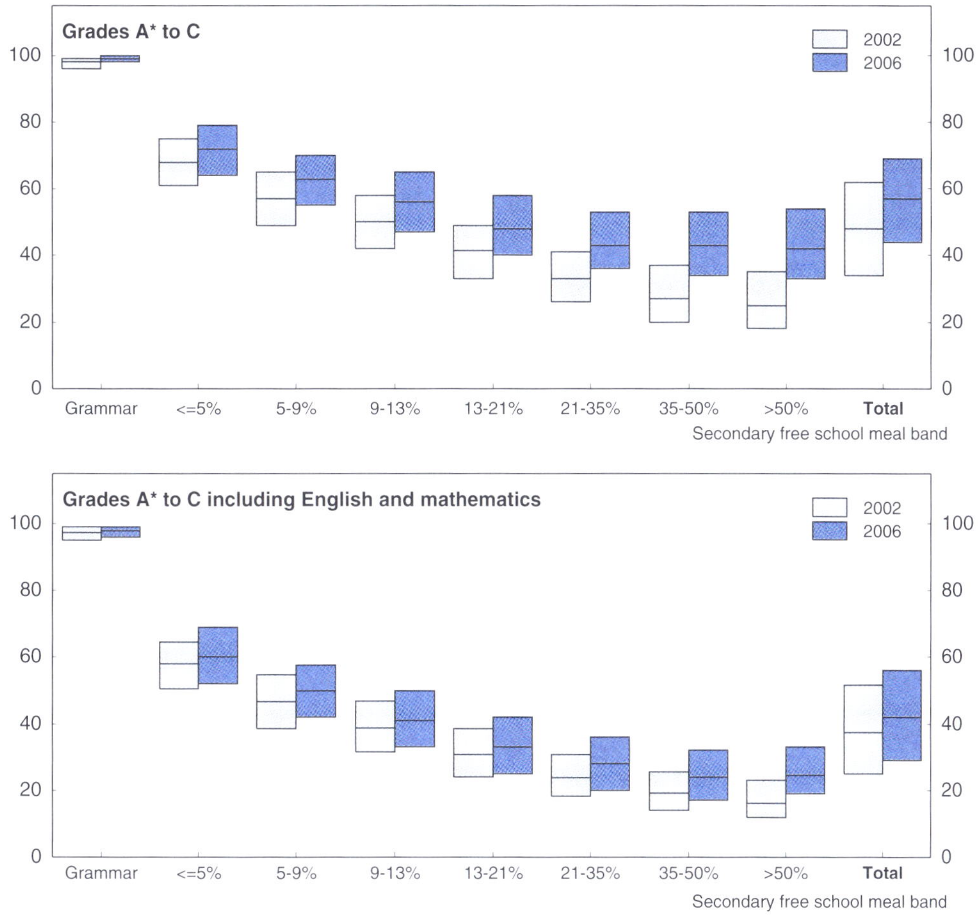

1. The rectangular boxes represent the difference between the upper and lower quartile containing 50% of the schools in each free school meal band. The solid line across the rectangle represents the median school.

Source: DfES (2006), "Trends in Attainment Gaps in Schools: 2005", *Statistical Bulletin*, Department for Education and Skills and Office for National Statistics, June. Updated to 2006 by DfES.

StatLink ᕮᕮᕮ *http://dx.doi.org/10.1787/115863714253*

Furthermore, it is not clear how poorly the Department would have to perform relative to the targets in order for the Secretary to be sanctioned. There may be a case for increasing the accountability of school principals.

Nevertheless, schools do have incentives to perform well, even if these are not directly linked to the targets. For example, the best performing schools are rewarded with increased autonomy and a light-touch inspection regime.[21] They also benefit from the popularity associated with high rankings on "league tables" published by the press (although the league tables only reflect raw performance, rather than value added). At the other end of the spectrum, the worst performing schools (especially those that fail to meet the key floor target of at least 25% of 15-16-year-olds achieving five or more GCSE subject passes at grades A*-C) come under closer scrutiny from the local authority. For such schools, inspection reports from the OFSTED are more frequent and carry a high weight in decisions on whether to place the school under "special measures" (which often involve the principal being replaced). For schools that are performing a little above the critical floor target for OFSTED action, however, the incentives for improvement may be relatively weak. More recently, the government has begun piloting a different approach to improving performance, which involves a greater focus on pupil progress and testing achievement at appropriate points. The pilots include individual tuition out of school hours in English and mathematics for pupils entering Key Stages below national expectations (of whom a significant proportion will be from disadvantaged backgrounds) and the use of financial premia to reward schools who are successful in raising the educational performance of this group of pupils.

Higher spending on education does not automatically improve outcomes

The econometric literature on the relationship between education spending and pupil achievement suggests a need to be very careful about how additional resources are spent. While different methodologies often produce different findings, most reviews of the literature tend to reach the same conclusion: that some measurable school inputs do sometimes matter, but that the magnitude of the effects found are quite small, and that it is therefore hard to provide unequivocal support for the idea that more resources are required to achieve higher educational outcomes.[22] For example, consider the debate on the effectiveness of reducing class sizes; some researchers (Hanushek, 2003) conclude that smaller class sizes have no distinguishable effect on test scores, while others (Krueger, 2003) interpret the same literature differently and argue that class size reduction does improve student achievement. Even taking the most favourable estimates, however, Carneiro and Heckman (2003) argue that the return on reducing pupil-teacher ratios is sufficiently low as to render a focus on reducing class size unwise.[23] The OECD PISA database also suggests that higher spending does not automatically translate into higher performance; a cross country correlation between education inputs and PISA performance finds no clear positive correlation (Figure 2.6).

Of course, these findings do not imply that the level of resources is irrelevant.[24] There is significant evidence that high quality interventions in the early years can effectively promote learning and improve parenting skills in poor families.[25] There is also evidence suggesting that higher quality teachers can raise the test scores of students, as discussed earlier. These findings suggest that governments may maximise the return on education spending by directing a high proportion of public spending towards ensuring the development of both cognitive and non-cognitive skills (e.g. social skills and motivation) in the early years. If it can be ensured that young people have developed the key cognitive and non-cognitive skills that are needed in the workforce by age 16, then a higher compulsory school age may not be required (see earlier discussion). Finding ways to give principals more discretion in rewarding and sanctioning teachers would also help.

The government has made an effort to increase spending where the return is greatest

Education spending in the United Kingdom is not particularly high by international standards (Figure 2.7), but it has risen from 4.7% of GDP in 1996/97 to 5.5% in 2005/06. Looking ahead, Budget 2007 announced that education spending would remain constant as a share of GDP over the next few years. The view of the government is that "additional expenditure has a positive, if relatively modest, impact on attainment" (DfES and HM Treasury, 2005). However, the government has also made a commendable effort to

Figure 2.6. **Higher spending does not automatically translate into higher attainment**

Spending on education and education attainment

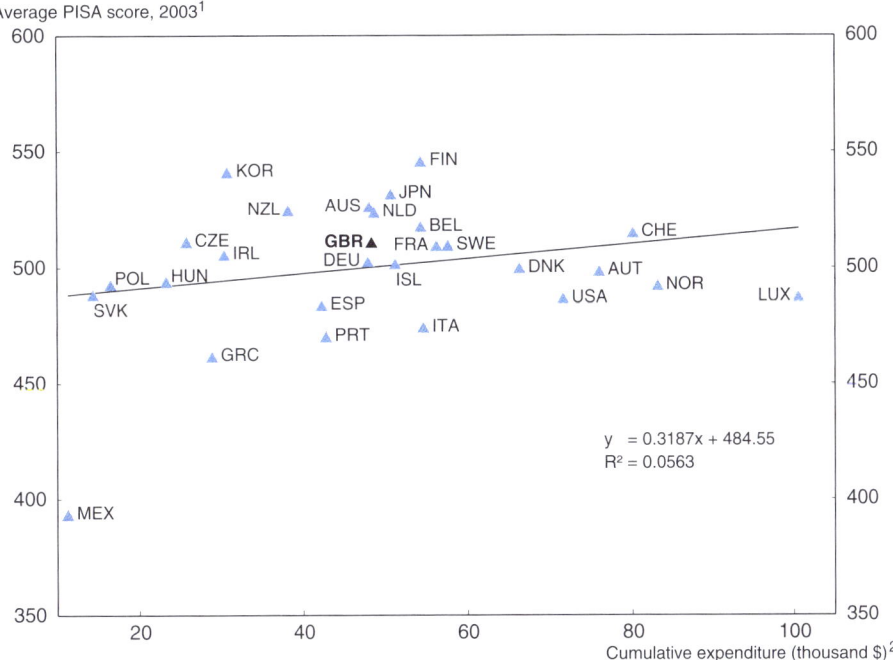

Number of teachers per student and education attainment

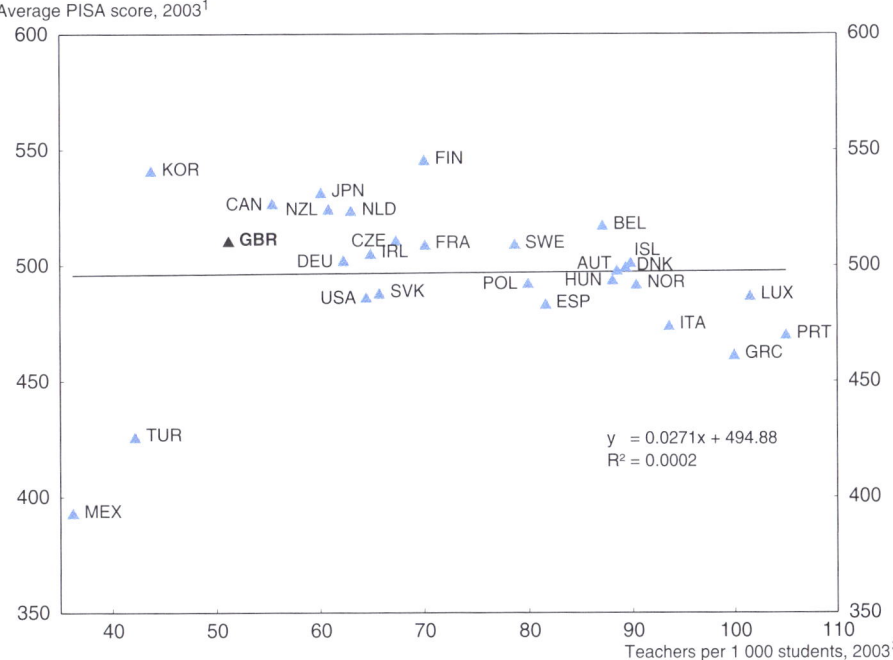

1. Student performance on the combined reading, scientific, mathematical and problem solving scales. Note also that the UK's response rate was too low to ensure comparability with the other countries.
2. Estimated cumulative total spending between 1993 and 2002 on a student aged 15 in 2002, converted to 2002 US dollars using purchasing power parities for private consumption. Public institutions only for Hungary, Italy, Luxembourg, Poland, Portugal and Switzerland.
3. In primary and secondary education based on full-time equivalents. Ireland includes post-secondary non-tertiary staff. 2001 data for Canada and Denmark; 2002 for Portugal.
Source: OECD (2004), *Learning for Tomorrow's World: First Results from PISA 2003*; OECD (2005, 2006), *Education at a Glance*; Sutherland, D. *et al.* (2007), "Performance Indicators for Public Spending Efficiency in Primary and Secondary Education", *OECD Economics Department Working Papers*, No. 546.

StatLink ⧉ http://dx.doi.org/10.1787/115867523325

Figure 2.7. **Education resources in the United Kingdom are not high but they are rising**

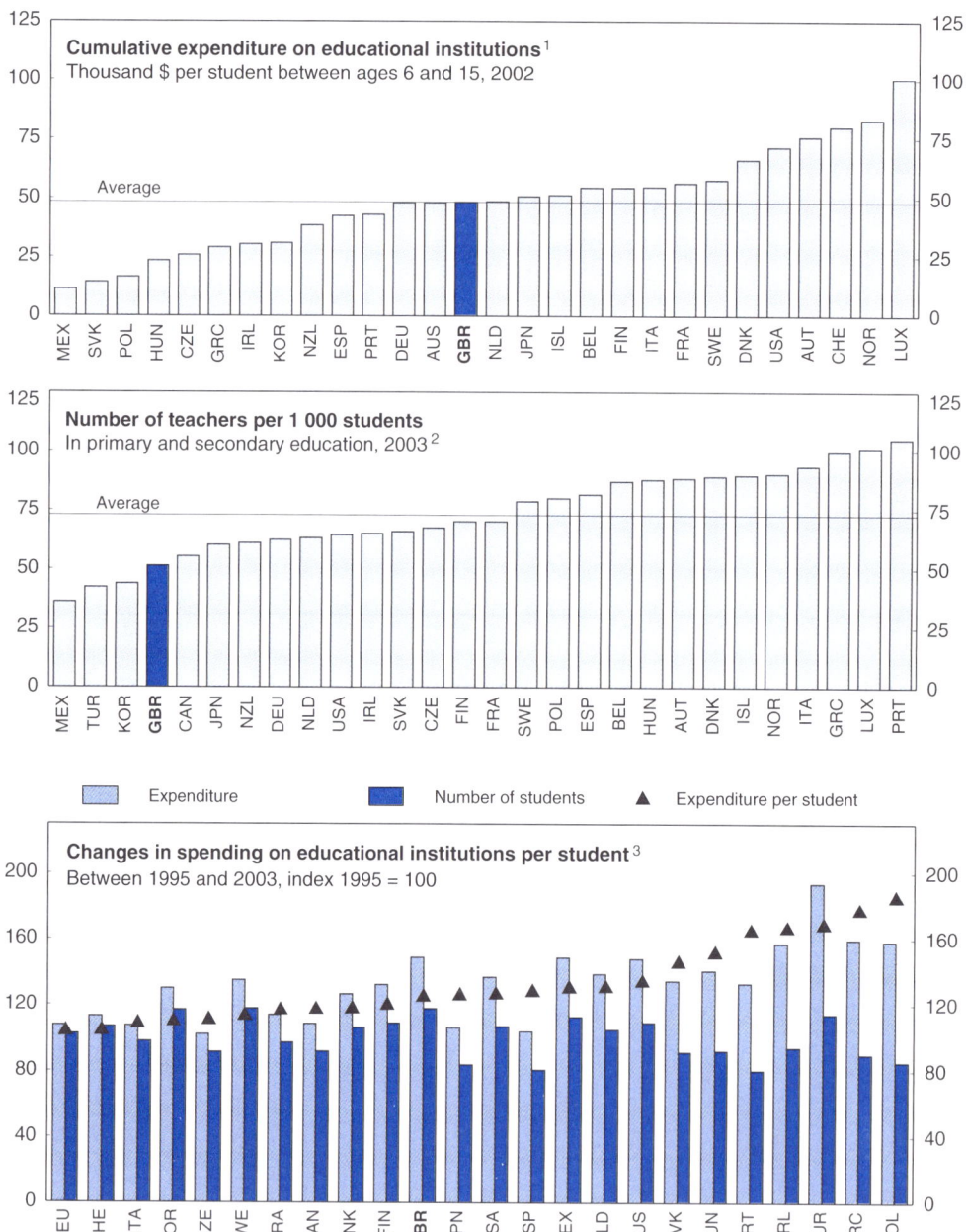

1. Estimated cumulative total spending between 1993 and 2002 on a student aged 15 in 2002, converted to 2002 US dollars using purchasing power parities for private consumption. Public institutions only for Hungary, Italy, Luxembourg, Poland, Portugal and Switzerland.
2. Based on full-time equivalents. Ireland includes post-secondary non-tertiary staff. 2001 data for Canada and Denmark; 2002 for Portugal.
3. Primary, secondary and post-secondary non-tertiary education in 2003 constant prices. Public expenditure and public institutions only for Italy, Poland, Portugal, Switzerland and Turkey; public expenditure only for Greece and New Zealand; public institutions only for Hungary. 1995 to 2002 data for France. Post-secondary non-tertiary is included in both upper and secondary education for Denmark and Japan.

Source: OECD (2005, 2006), *Education at a Glance*; Sutherland, D. *et al.* (2007), "Performance Indicators for Public Spending Efficiency in Primary and Secondary Education", *OECD Economics Department Working Papers*, No. 546.

StatLink ▒▒▒ *http://dx.doi.org/10.1787/115877674700*

identify where the impact of increased spending is greatest. All sectors of the education system have benefited from higher spending. Until 2005/06 pre-school education had benefitted the most. However, spending at the pre-primary level fell in 2006/07 and the total increase is now greatest in tertiary education (Figure 2.8).

Figure 2.8. **Real expenditure growth has increased across all levels of education**[1]

Index, 1998/99 = 100

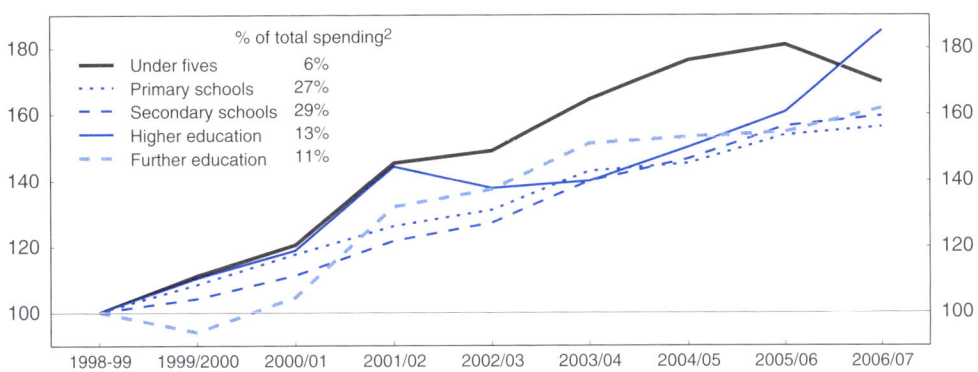

1. Education and training expenditure in current prices converted to constant prices using the GDP deflator.
2. Per cent of total education and training expenditure, average 1998/99-2005/07.
Source: HM Treasury, *Public Expenditure Statistical Analyses* (PESA), HM Treasury and Office for National Statistics.

StatLink ᴬ⁵ᴸᵃ *http://dx.doi.org/10.1787/116052052632*

Within the primary and secondary school budget, the government has concluded that the impact of additional spending "... is greatest when expenditure is targeted on the most deprived schools and towards pupils who are eligible for free schools meals". More specifically, the government claims that the impact of a marginal increase in expenditure on students aged 14 is three times as great for mathematics and four times as great for science when targeted on pupils eligible for free school meals (DfES and HM Treasury, 2005). The unusually low level of intergenerational social mobility in the United Kingdom (discussed earlier) also suggests a need to direct resources at programmes to improve the outcomes of those from deprived backgrounds. Blanden *et al.* (2007) suggests that this could be done either by universal interventions that are more effective for poor children (such as high quality pre-school) or by directing additional resources at poorer schools or communities.

Another, more radical approach, might be to introduce a differentiated voucher system where pupils from poorer families receive vouchers that are valued more highly than those for the general population. Legislation to modify the Chilean voucher system in such a way is currently under discussion in Chile, with the new differentiated vouchers expected to be introduced in 2008 (OECD, 2005a). The advantage of this approach – if combined with levers to ensure that the additional money is used for the disadvantaged child – is that it would create incentives for schools to focus attention on attracting pupils from disadvantaged backgrounds by more directly addressing their educational needs.

Local authorities have flattened the distribution of education spending

The government's efforts to ensure that increases in education spending are spent where the return is highest, have nevertheless not always been implemented as intended. This is because the control over the allocation of funds to individual schools belongs not to the central government but to the local authorities. Since different local authorities use different funding formulas, schools in deprived areas receive greatly varying levels of funding depending on their local authority's approach (Box 2.3). As a result, the government has concluded that "the impact of funding in boosting the attainment of children from deprived backgrounds is not being maximised".

There are a number of reasons why local authorities have not allocated a higher proportion of funding to the most deprived schools. A government survey of local authorities found that some authorities were simply unaware that they received funding specifically to meet the costs of deprivation. Others were aware, but did not think deprivation-based funding was very important. Many local authorities preferred to treat schools equally. Some local authorities even reported that their advisory bodies (the schools forums) had criticised the targeting of funds, preferring a "flatter" distribution than was warranted by the incidence of deprivation (DfES and HM Treasury, 2005).

In response to these problems the government announced that local authorities must discuss with their advisory bodies (the schools forums) how they can better target deprived pupils. The central government has also begun to publish exam results for free school meal (FSM) and non-FSM pupils by local authority area so as to highlight which local authorities are making the most progress in closing the gaps. Nevertheless, many local authorities are likely to resist, particularly in cases where re-allocating deprivation funding towards the most deprived schools according to the assumptions used in the national funding formula would result in reduced funding for the least deprived schools. Even in less extreme cases, many local authorities do not support the central government focus on deprivation. For example one local authority responded: "… generalised exhortations to widen (funding) differentials are not likely to be successful. The majority … will tend to want smaller scale differentials than the Department may envisage. Greater prescription may be needed if these aspirations … are to be achieved" (DfES and HM Treasury, 2005).

If sufficient progress is not made voluntarily then the central government has said that it would consider imposing more conditions on funding allocations. But this is clearly seen as a last resort. There is little political willingness to be associated with funding re-allocations that may result in reduced funding for some schools in the medium term, even if the current situation is recognised as inequitable. In addition, there remain advantages to local autonomy. Not only does it permit flexibility in response to local needs, but it can also encourage innovative responses to problems.

In this context, it seems that more should be done to encourage a fast transition to a more equitable distribution of funding, while safeguarding local authority autonomy. In particular:

- To make it clearer how funding should be allocated in the future, the central government should consider promoting a "first best" national benchmark formula, with local deviations encouraged in cases where local authorities can identify relevant local factors that are not taken into account in the benchmark formula.[26] Such an approach would safeguard flexibility for local authorities to respond to local needs when required, while also providing local authorities with more guidance than at present. Such an approach could also facilitate the funding allocation process for those local authorities that face resistance within their communities and from their schools forums.

- To promote transition away from history-dominated formulas, the government should consider offering local authorities greater flexibility to depart from the minimum funding guarantee (MFG) methodology, so that local authorities that wish to promote a transition to more equitable formulas do not necessarily have to apply to the Secretary

Box 2.3. **Funding formulas *versus* flexibility: The allocation of education spending in England**[1]

In England, there is no national funding formula through which the central government funds schools directly. Rather, each of the 150 local authorities (LAs) receives bulk education funding from the central government and is responsible – in consultation with the schools forum[2] – for distributing it between the pre-school, primary and secondary schools in that area.

Since 1990, when local management of schools first began, at least some proportion of the school funding that local authorities have received has been intended to address social deprivation. During most of the 1990s the formulas used by LAs to fund schools were subject to approval by the central government, and there was some expectation (but no requirement) that formulas would include provision for funding for pupils with special educational needs (SEN). During this period some LAs first began to use eligibility for free school meals (FSMs) as a proxy indicator for "low-level" SEN.[3] Since the current government came to power, however, increasing emphasis has been placed on the role of deprivation funding. For example, authorities were urged to review their formula provision for deprivation in 1998; subsequently a requirement (albeit very modest) was introduced into the regulations (see below).

The education resources directed from the central government to the local authorities are largely based on a basic entitlement for all pupils attending schools in that LA, together with top-ups to address the costs of additional educational needs (AEN), population sparsity, and area costs (*e.g.* to address the variability of costs – principally labour costs – between different parts of the country). The portion of funding intended to address deprivation costs is currently within the allocation for AENs. In 2005/06 it amounted to around £1 630 per year per pupil with AEN.[4] This funding is expected to meet the costs directly associated with social deprivation and the costs of supporting children for whom English is not the native language. Separate funding is delivered to meet the costs of supporting children with "severe" SEN. As a baseline, local authorities are funded on the assumption that at least 12% of pupils have AEN. The AEN top-up is thus provided to those authorities where more than 12% of pupils have AEN. The percentage of pupils with AEN is estimated using national socio-economic indicators.[5]

After deducting central expenditure from a local authority's Schools Budget, the authority has considerable flexibility over how to allocate funding among the schools in that region, including over how much funding is actually allocated at the local level to meet the costs of AEN. Essentially, LAs have been free to use whatever school funding formula they wish, with the only requirement related to AEN being that LAs must have at least one factor in their formula based on the incidence of social deprivation. However, in reality this requirement does not impose any significant obligation on LAs, since it does not imply a minimum of spending on deprivation.[6]

In addition to allocation flexibility, LAs have also had the possibility of using council tax revenues to provide additional funding for schools (the majority of cases) or of allocating less than the full schools budget to schools, with the remainder being used to meet other LA outlays (the case of around one-third of LAs). This freedom to provide less than the full schools budget to schools has now been curtailed with the introduction in the 2006/07 year of a new schools funding system, known as the Dedicated Schools Grant (DSG). Under this system, LA Schools Budgets are fully funded by the central government, and LAs are obliged to allocate the full amount to schools. LAs can add to this funding if they choose, but with the advent of the ring-fenced DSG, most do not. For the initial two years of the DSG, the amount that each authority receives is partly based on up-rating previous allocations to schools. This means that for the next three years at least, schools that had previously part-funded school spending with council tax revenues are receiving higher per-pupil allocations from the central government than those that were previously under-spending their schools allocation. It has not yet been decided whether to return to a formula-only funding approach from 2011 or whether the higher education allocations received by the first group will be locked in for longer.

Box 2.3. **Funding formulas *versus* flexibility: The allocation of education spending in England**[1] *(cont.)*

Under the DSG system, LAs retain the flexibility to allocate funding between schools as they choose. However, in light of evidence that LAs have not accurately or consistently directed the deprivation element of the AEN funding towards schools in deprived areas, the central government is now exerting increased pressure on LAs to progress towards a funding formula which targets deprived pupils adequately from the 2008-11 funding period. The implicit threat has been made of greater conditionality of allocations in the case that LAs do not make sufficient voluntary progress. However, this is clearly seen as being a last resort. One possible disadvantage of the DSG system is that it is now more complicated to derive a straightforward AEN figure for each authority. However, the government has stated that it will ensure that it is clear how much of an authority's total DSG allocation is intended to address AEN, and how much to address deprivation.

One of the main challenges in rectifying the current situation is that of transition. Because of the relatively small amounts currently being allocated for deprivation in some local authority areas, many of the most deprived schools should be given a considerable increase in funding. However, in most cases this would require reduced funding for the least deprived schools, which is politically difficult, even if it would represent a significant improvement in the efficiency of education spending. The transition to more efficient funding formulas may also be undermined by the Minimum Funding Guarantee (MFG) which, introduced in 2004/05, guarantees all schools a minimum percentage increase in their funding per pupil from one year to the next. While the goal of this guarantee is very worthwhile – to provide schools with stability of funding – it may also serve to unduly constrain the transition to more efficient and equitable funding formulas. The specific guidelines for the MFG do permit local authorities to put in place their own phasing arrangements. However, it is stressed that this is a facility that should be used only in exceptional circumstances (with the approval of their schools forums)[7] and if a proposal affects more than 20% of an authority's schools (50% of pupils from 2008/09), the authority must also seek approval from the Secretary of State.[8] For local authorities that are already reluctant to increase the degree of funding differentials between schools, the default of history-based funding underpinned by the MFG could easily undermine the government's other goals.

The central government should encourage local authorities to make a relatively fast transition to more efficient funding. In conjunction with other incentives, this would be facilitated by taking deprivation-targeted funding out of the formula used to determine the MFG so that local authorities can proceed in this direction without having formally to apply for permission.

1. This box draws heavily on DfES and HM Treasury (2005), and on discussions with Department for Education and Skills staff. While this box focuses on England, it should be noted that Welsh local authorities have even greater freedom to determine funding for schools than do English LAs; they are responsible not only for allocating funding between schools but also for determining within the overall available budget how much they allocate to education.

2. Each local authority is required by law to set up a schools forum, a body representative of local schools, made up of at least 15 people. The schools forum must be consulted on all plans for school spending and for changes to the funding formula.

3. Low-level SEN refers to less severe special educational needs. Funding for more severe SEN is delivered separately and is not covered in this box.

4. This figure stems from a baseline cost of meeting AEN of £1 780, as estimated by PricewaterhouseCoopers (2002), reduced to £1 460 to account for the proportion of relevant costs which are funded through grants. For example, the Leadership Incentive Grant has provided grants of up to £135 000 directly to the most deprived secondary schools (scheme being modified in scope from 2006).

5. Indicators currently used include: the number of children in each LA of parents on income support; the number in receipt of a working family tax credit; the number of 5-10-year-olds with English as an additional language; and the number of children from low-performing ethnic groups.

6. At least one authority implemented this rule by giving all its schools £1 each through the social deprivation factor. At the other end of the spectrum, an estimated 12 authorities provided more deprivation funding to schools than would have been implied by the central government formula.

7. "Schools Forum Guidance Note 3 – the minimum funding guarantee", accessed 12 September 2007 as document number 4 – The Minimum Funding Guarantee at: *www.teachernet.gov.uk/docbank/index.cfm?id=9369*.

8. Details can be found at: *www.teachernet.gov.uk/docbank/index.cfm?id=11544*.

of State for permission to deviate from the MFG methodology (see Box 2.3 for further discussion). While a rapid transition would be ideal from the perspective of spending efficiency, this would need to be weighed against the possible costs caused by turbulence in funding levels for some schools. In such cases, longer transition periods should be acceptable – but the medium-term goal should be made clearer than it is at present.

Other analysis also suggests room to improve education spending efficiency

Another way of assessing the efficiency of education spending is to look at measures of productivity in the education sector. Following the Atkinson review (Atkinson, 2005), the national account measures of government output and productivity are being gradually improved and several measures of education productivity are now available. The main (national accounts) measure of productivity is now based on a volume measure of input which makes adjustments for estimates of teachers' pay and uses a new measure of capital services. The national accounts output measure also includes a quality adjustment to proxy for the improvements that are indicated by various domestic measures of pupil performance. An alternative measure of productivity adjusts the volume of output for changes in quality using the upward trend in GSCE exam results (ONS, 2007).[27] This alternative measure suggests that education productivity in the United Kingdom increased by 2.1 percentage points per year from 1996 to 1999, before falling by about 0.7% per year more recently (Figure 2.9). While quality adjustment using GCSE exam results is in line with the Atkinson Review recommendations, one potential problem with it is that the GCSE measure of progress is also a school output target, suggesting a risk of target-driven output distortions. In the case of all productivity measures, it is worth noting that academic attainment is not the only outcome of the education system. The government's aim is for education to enhance the wellbeing of children and young people more generally, but wellbeing is much harder to measure than attainment.

Figure 2.9. **Measures of education productivity**
Index, 1996 = 100

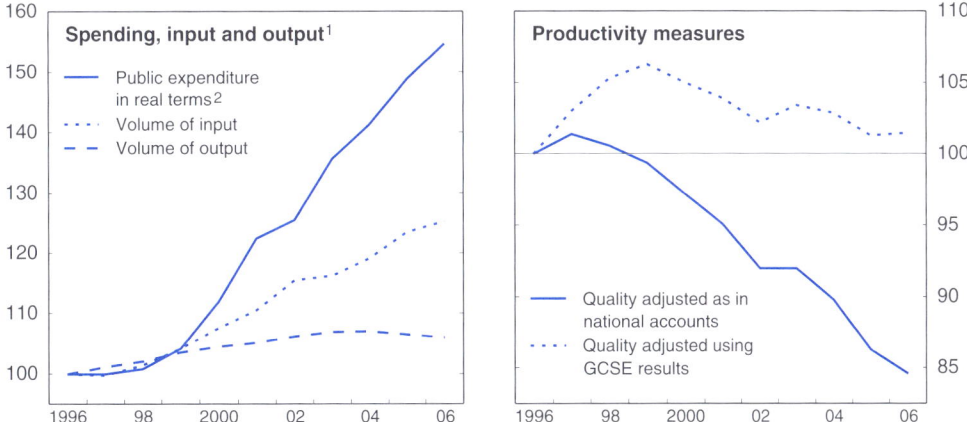

1. Input and output volumes consistent with current national accounts.
2. Nominal central government and local authority spending deflated using the GDP deflator which can be interpreted as the volume of alternative consumption foregone.

Source: ONS (2007), "Public Service Productivity: Education", September, available at: *www.statistics.gov.uk/articles/nojournal/Education_productivity_2007_main.pdf*; HM Treasury (2007), *Public Expenditure Statistical Analyses* (PESA), HM Treasury and Office for National Statistics.

StatLink ⟶ *http://dx.doi.org/10.1787/116063055146*

Finally, results from an OECD project aimed at drawing cross-country comparisons of efficiency in public spending on primary and secondary education also suggest that the United Kingdom – along with other OECD countries – could improve the efficiency of education spending (Sutherland *et al.*, 2007). These results, together with the academic literature investigating the link between spending and performance, suggest that more efforts should be made to carefully monitor and evaluate education policy interventions so as to get a better understanding of what works, particularly with respect to enhancing the educational performance of those from disadvantaged families. While the UK government has devoted considerable effort to identifying the most cost effective uses of education spending, significant progress is yet to be made in determining the effects of different resource mixes in schools. Indeed, a significant focus (at least in terms of communication with the public) is still placed on raising input levels. For example, the government's promise to close the funding gap between state and private schools[28] does not seem to be justified. While it is true that pupil performance is higher at private schools than at state-funded schools, it is not clear to what extent this is due to different student characteristics, the peer group effect, to better funding, or to better teaching quality. With respect to the impact of higher expenditure and other policy initiatives to date, evaluation is complicated by the fact that some of the measures of performance may have been biased by target-driven output distortions. In addition, the lags between expenditures and outcomes are long, so some improvements may be yet to come through.

Box 2.4. **Summary of recommendations on education**

Focus on teaching core functional skills and evaluate progress on these skills

- Continue to promote a focus on the acquisition of core literacy and numeracy skills for pupils at all age levels and ensure that this focus is not compromised by the goal of expanding the average number of years of schooling.

- Ensure continued participation in international tests of cognitive ability, such as PISA and PIAAC.

- Design all targets in a way that limits the potential for gaming, by ensuring an interactive performance management system that captures the complexity of the education process. Ensure that key performance measures are not based on targeted outputs.

Facilitate a narrowing of the socio-economic gaps

- Consider ways of encouraging the highest quality teachers to move to the most disadvantaged schools – such as giving bonuses for high quality teaching performance at such schools.

- Promote a national benchmark formula for local authorities to use in allocating funding between schools, while still permitting flexibility (*i.e.* deviation from the benchmark formula) to meet local needs.

- Promote the transition to a more efficient allocation of funds by providing standard procedures for taking deprivation-targeted funding out of the formula used to determine the Minimum Funding Guarantee. Permit smoothed transitions to the improved formulas in cases where significant school funding volatility for some schools would result. However, make clear the medium-term goal of equitable funding allocation.

- Evaluate the pros and cons of introducing a differentiated voucher system of funding (as in Chile) where pupils from poorer families receive vouchers that are valued more highly than those for the general population.

- Encourage research into determining which resource mixes within schools are most successful at narrowing socio-economic gaps.

Notes

1. Autor *et al.* (2003); Levy and Murnane (2006).

2. DfES (2005). The previous benchmark indicator for school performance was the percentage of pupils at the end of year 11 (normally aged 16) achieving 5 or more A*-C GCSEs (and equivalent). This indicator has now been modified to include a requirement that the core subjects of English and mathematics are included in the qualifying GCSEs (see Box 2.2 for further discussion). In addition, a general (GCSE) diploma will be introduced to recognise those who achieve this standard.

3. The government's consultation Green Paper states: "We already have a challenging aspiration to get to 90% participation in education or training among 17-year-olds by 2015, and we are confident of reaching this. However, even 90% participation will not put us among the best performing countries in the OECD" (DfES, 2007).

4. Lochner and Moretti (2004); Feinstein (2002) and Coelli *et al.* (2007).

5. See Box 8.1 in OECD (2005b) for a literature review.

6. The IALS survey was taken by a sample of the population aged 16–65 (in the United Kingdom the sampling took place in 1996). In the United Kingdom, 23% of people were found to be performing at the lowest level of literacy (level 1), compared with just 7% in Sweden, the top performer. These people have very poor skills (*e.g.* they may be unable to determine the correct amount of medicine to give a child from information printed on the package). Some 28% of the population in the United Kingdom (19% in Sweden) were classified at the second lowest level of literacy (level 2). At this level respondents can only deal with material that is simple, clearly laid out, and in which the tasks involved are not too complex. Level 3 (31% in the United Kingdom; 39% in Sweden) is considered a suitable minimum for coping with the demands of everyday life and work in a complex advanced society. Levels 4 and 5 (18% in the United Kingdom; 35% in Sweden) describe respondents who demonstrate command of higher-order processing skills.

7. In order to ensure that PISA yields reliable and internationally comparable results, the OECD requires that the initial response rates should be at least 85% at the school level (95% after "replacement") and 80% at the student level. However, because of a low response rate in England, the United Kingdom fell significantly short of these standards, and even after "replacement" achieved a final response rate of only 77% at the school level and 78% at the student level. As a result, it is not possible to say with confidence that the UK's sample results reliably reflect those for the national population, with the level of accuracy required for PISA (OECD, 2004, pp. 326-327). Subsequent research (Micklewright and Schnepf, 2006) has found that responding pupils had statistically significantly higher average scores and less dispersed scores than pupils who did not respond, and that the variance of scores was higher in non-responding schools. This was estimated to have caused a bias in both the mean and variance of the scores, with the authors estimating that the bias would shift England's position by about one place in a ranking of countries.

8. IEA (2003). Note that both the Progress in International Reading Literacy Study (PIRLS) and the Trends in International Mathematics and Science Study (TIMSS) country samples included non-OECD as well as other more advanced countries.

9. Countries such as the United Kingdom where the relationship between socio-economic background and student performance is strong do not fully capitalise on the skill potential of students from disadvantaged backgrounds, suggesting inefficiency because of wasted talent.

10. Blanden *et al.* (2004) showed that intergenerational earnings mobility had fallen over time in Britain when comparing individuals born in 1958 and 1970. Earlier studies also found that intergenerational mobility was low (*e.g.* Solon, 2002).

11. Between 1981 and the late 1990s, young people from the poorest 20% of families increased their university graduation rate by just 3 percentage points, compared with a rise in graduation rates of 26 percentage points for those born to the richest 20% of parents (Blanden and Machin, 2004).

12. Very similar results are obtained using alternative measures of homogeneity, such as the 10th/90th or 5th/95th percentile ratios.

13. The GCSE is the General Certificate of Secondary Education. Two measures of the change in the gap were used: i) the absolute change in the gap in achievement and ii) the *odds ratio*, which is defined as the probability of one group of schools attaining the benchmark, divided by the probability of the other group. Both measures showed a clear narrowing of the gap between the percentage of pupils achieving five or more A*-C GCSEs and equivalents in the least deprived *versus* most deprived schools. The least deprived schools were those with ≤ 5% of pupils eligible for free school meals (FSMs) while the most deprived schools were those with > 50% of pupils eligible for FSMs. See DfES (2006b) for further details.

14. Unfortunately, the characteristics of good teachers are not well defined, making it difficult to select good teachers through legislation or regulation. For example, a number of studies, including Hanushek (2003), have found little correlation between teacher qualifications and teacher quality, or between teachers' salaries and teacher quality. The use of merit pay may thus be more likely to reward the best teachers.

15. Bradley and Taylor (2002), Levačić (2004) and Gibbons *et al.* (2006) find small positive associations between competition and school performance in the United Kingdom.

16. Currently, however, CVA is only available for the whole school and it is not possible to link pupil progression to individual teachers using national data.

17. At present, most teachers move through the main salary scale by one point for each year of satisfactory service. Schools have the discretion to advance excellent performers by two points in any year, although in practice only around 1% of teachers have been awarded such double increments. More experienced teachers (those on an upper pay scale) also have the possibility of performance-based salary increments. However, there are currently no incentives to encourage the best teachers to move to under-performing schools. Like most countries, the United Kingdom has teacher contractual arrangements that make significant changes difficult.

18. See de Bruijn (2007) for a detailed discussion. For a review of gaming effects in the English health sector, see Bevan and Hood (2006).

19. The three main forms of gaming that have been identified are: i) *ratchet effects,* whereby "next year's" targets are based on this year's performance, meaning that managers have a perverse incentive not to exceed targets this year even if they could easily do so; ii) *threshold effects*, which may disproportionately reward those with mediocre performance crowded near the target range while providing no incentive for improvement (or even a perverse incentive) for those doing better than the target; and iii) *output distortions*, whereby efforts to achieve the target come at the cost of performance deteriorations in other unmeasured areas of performance.

20. For example, as reported in *The Times*, "Most pupils fail to reach gold standard in GCSE core studies", 11 January 2007.

21. The highest performing schools (approximately 30% of schools in 2006) are subject to a "light touch" inspection regime. These schools are identified primarily on the basis of performance statistics and their previous inspection report.

22. For example, Vignoles *et al.* (2000), Hanushek (2003) and Carneiro and Heckman (2003).

23. Consistent with the US literature, a review of the UK literature (Vignoles *et al.*, 2000) concluded that there is almost no UK evidence that smaller class size leads to better outcomes. Dustman *et al.* (2003) found some positive impact of smaller class size in the United Kingdom on the decision to stay on in full time schooling at 16. However, the estimated impact is very small.

24. As Hanushek (2003) interprets the literature: "There clearly are situations where small classes or added resources have an impact. It is just that no good description of when and where these situations occur is available, so that broad resource policies … may hit some good uses but also hit bad uses that generally lead to offsetting outcomes."

25. See Carneiro and Heckman (2003) for a review of the literature. Using data from the British Cohort Study of children born in 1970, Blanden (2006) found that higher early test scores were an important factor in helping children from poor families achieve economic success as adults. Note, however, that some argue that these payoffs decay rapidly unless bolstered with interventions that can continually offset social disadvantages through the whole education sequence (*e.g.* as discussed by Machin, 2006).

26. DfES and HM Treasury (2005) found *no examples* of local authorities linking the allocation of deprivation funding to the assumptions in the national formula about the typical costs of additional educational needs (*i.e.* the PricewaterhouseCooper's figure quoted in Box 2.3).

27. The National Accounts output series is based on the number of full-time-equivalent pupils in the state sector adjusted by a constant +0.25% per year. The alternative measure attempts to adjust more carefully for performance increases using measures of progress on national tests.

28. In 2005/06, independent (private sector) day schools spent in the region of £8 000 per pupil compared with roughly £5 000 in the public (maintained) sector. The 2006 Budget set out the government's aim to increase real public school spending per pupil to 2005/06 private sector day school levels, although the timetable for achieving this goal was not specified. Goodman and Sibieta (2006) show that approximately £600 additional spending per pupil (in real terms) was already implied under existing spending plans by 2010/11, leaving further increases of £2 400 per pupil (in real terms) before the £8 000 target will be met. If school spending per pupil were to be

increased in line with real GDP growth (approximately 2½ per cent a year) then it would take 14 years to meet the target. By then private sector spending, which has been growing broadly in line with "service sector" inflation rates, would undoubtedly be much higher.

References

d'Addio, A.C. (2007), "Intergenerational Transmission of Disadvantage", *OECD Social, Employment and Migration Working Papers*, No. 52, OECD, Paris.

Atkinson, A. *et al.* (2004), "Evaluating the Impact of Performance-related Pay for Teachers in England", *CMPO Working Paper*, No. 04/113, University of Bristol, December.

Atkinson, A. (2005), *Atkinson Review: Final report*, Palgrave MacMillan, available at: *www.statistics.gov.uk/about/data/methodology/specific/PublicSector/Atkinson*.

Autor, D.H., F. Levy and R.J. Murnane (2003), "The Skill Content of Recent Technological Change: an Empirical Exploration", *Quarterly Journal of Economics*, Vol. 118, No. 4, The MIT Press, Cambridge MA.

Bevan, G. and C. Hood (2006), "What's Measured is what Matters: Targets and Gaming in the English Public Health Care System", *Public Administration*, Vol. 84, No. 3, Blackwell Publishing.

Blanden, J. *et al.* (2004), "Changes in Intergenerational Mobility in Britain", in M. Corak (ed.), *Generational Income Mobility in North America and Europe*, Cambridge University Press.

Blanden, J. and S. Machin (2004), "Educational Inequality and the Expansion of UK Higher Education", *Scottish Journal of Political Economy,* Vol. 51, No. 2, Blackwell Publishing.

Blanden, J. (2006), "'Bucking the Trend': What Enables those who are Disadvantaged in Childhood to Succeed later in Life", *Working Paper, No.* 31, Department for Work and Pensions.

Blanden, J., P. Gregg and L. MacMillan (2007), "Accounting for Intergenerational Income Persistence: Noncognitive Skills, Ability and Education", *The Economic Journal,* Vol. 117, No. 519, Blackwell Publishing.

Bradley, S. and J. Taylor (2002), "The Effect of the Quasi-market on the Efficiency-equity Trade-off in the Secondary School Sector", *Bulletin of Economic Research*, Vol. 54, No. 3, Blackwell Publishing.

de Bruijn, H. (2007), *Managing Performance in the Public Sector*, Routledge, London.

Carneiro, P. and J. Heckman (2003), "Human Capital Policy", *NBER Working Paper, No.* 9495, National Bureau of Economic Research, Cambridge MA.

Coelli, M., D. Green and W. Warburton (2007), "Breaking the Cycle? The Effect of Education on Welfare Receipt among Children of Welfare Recipients", *Journal of Public Economics*, Vol. 91, No. 7-8, Elsevier BV.

Dearden, L. *et al.* (2006), "Education Subsidies and School Drop-out Rates", *CEE Discussion Papers*, No. 53, Centre for the Economics of Education, London School of Economics, January.

DfES (Department for Education and Skills) (2005), *14-19 Education and Skills*, White Paper by the Department for Education and Skills, The Stationary Office, London.

DfES (2006a), "Participation in Education, Training and Employment by 16-18 Year Olds in England: 2004 and 2005", *Statistical First Release*, SFR 21/2006, 8 June, Department for Education and Skills and Office for National Statistics.

DfES (2006b), "Trends in Attainment Gaps in Schools: 2005", *Statistical Bulletin*, Department for Education and Skills and Office for National Statistics, June.

DfES (2007), "Raising Expectations: Staying in Education and Training post-16", Green Paper by the Department for Education and Skills, The Stationary Office, London.

DfES and HM Treasury (2005), "Child Poverty: Fair Funding for Schools", available at: *www.teachernet.gov.uk/_doc/9404/ACF9795.doc*.

Dustman, C., N. Rajah and A. van Soest (2003), "Class Size, Education, and Wages", *The Economic Journal*, Vol. 113, No. 485, Blackwell Publishing.

Erikson, R. and J.H. Goldthorpe (2002), "Intergenerational Inequality: A Sociological Perspective", *Journal of Economic Perspectives*, Vol. 16, No. 3, American Economic Association, Nashville TN.

Feinstein, L. (2002), "Quantitative Estimates of the Social Benefits of Learning 1: Crime", *Wider Benefits of Learning Research Report*, No. 5, Centre for Research on the Wider Benefits of Learning, Institute of Education, London.

Gibbons, S., S. Machin and O. Silva (2006), "Choice, Competition and Pupil Achievement", *Discussion Papers*, No. 2214, Institute for the Study of Labour, Bonn.

Gonand, F. (2007), "Public Spending Efficiency: Institutional Indicators in Primary and Secondary Education", *OECD Economics Department Working Papers*, No. 543, OECD, Paris.

Goodman, A. and L. Sibieta (2006), "Public Spending on Education in the UK", prepared for the Education and Skills Select Committee, *IFS Briefing Note*, No. BN71, Institute for Fiscal Studies, London.

Hanushek, E.A. (2003), "The Failure of Input-based Schooling Policies", *The Economic Journal,* Vol. 113, No. 485, Blackwell Publishing.

Hanushek, E.A. and L. Woessmann (2007), "The Role of School Improvement in Economic Development", *NBER Working Paper, No.* 12832, National Bureau of Economic Research, Cambridge MA.

IEA (International Association for the Evaluation of Educational Achievement) (2003), *PIRLS 2001 International Report: IEA's Study of Reading Literacy Achievement in Primary Schools*, Mullis, IVS *et al.* (eds.), International Association for the Evaluation of Educational Achievement and International Study Center, Lynch School of Education, Boston College.

Krueger, A. (2003), "Economic Considerations and Class Size", *The Economic Journal*, Vol. 113, No. 485, Blackwell Publishing.

Leitch, S. (2006), *Prosperity for All in the Global Economy – World Class Skills*, The Stationary Office, London, available at: *www.hm-treasury.gov.uk/leitch.*

Levačić, R. (2004), "Competition and the Performance of English Secondary Schools: Further Evidence", *Education Economics*, Vol. 12, No. 2, Routledge, London.

Levy, F. and R.J. Murnane (2006), "How Computerized Work and Globalization Shape Human Skill Demands", *MIT IPC Working Papers*, MIT Industrial Performance Center, Cambridge MA.

Lochner, L. and E. Moretti (2004), "The Effect of Education on Crime: Evidence from Prison Inmates, Arrests and Self-Reports", *American Economic Review*, Vol. 94, No. 1, American Economic Association, Nashville TN.

Machin, S. (2006), "Social Disadvantage and Education Experiences", *OECD Social, Employment and Migration Working Papers, No.* 32, OECD, Paris.

Machin, S., S. Telhaj and J. Wilson (2006), "The Mobility of English School Children", *Fiscal Studies*, Vol. 27, No. 3, Institute for Fiscal Studies, London.

Micklewright, J. and S.V. Schnepf (2006), "Response Bias in England in PISA in 2000 and 2003", *Research Report*, No. 771, Department for Education and Skills, DfES Publications, Nottingham.

Nickell, S. (2004), "Poverty and Worklessness in Britain", *Economic Journal*, Vol. 114, No. 494, Blackwell Publishing.

OECD (2000), *Literacy in the Information Age: Final Results of the International Adult Literacy Survey*, OECD, Paris.

OECD (2004), *Learning for Tomorrow's World: First Results from PISA 2003*, OECD, Paris.

OECD (2005a), *OECD Economic Surveys: Chile*, OECD, Paris.

OECD (2005b), *OECD Economic Surveys: United Kingdom*, OECD, Paris.

ONS (Office for National Statistics) (2007), "Measuring Quality as Part of Public Service Output: Strategy Following Consultation", UK Centre for the Measurement of Government Activity, Office for National Statistics, London.

PricewaterhouseCoopers (2002), *Study of Additional Educational Needs – Phase II, Final report*, August, available at: *www.dfes.gov.uk/efsg/docs/133.doc.*

Solon, G. (2002), "Cross-country Differences in Intergenerational Earnings Mobility", *Journal of Economic Perspectives*, Vol. 16, No. 3, American Economic Association, Nashville TN.

Sutherland, D. *et al.* (2007), "Performance Indicators for Public Spending Efficiency in Primary and Secondary Schools", *OECD Economics Department Working Papers,* No. 546, OECD, Paris.

Vignoles, A. *et al.* (2000), "The Relationship between Resource Allocation and Pupil Attainment: A Review", *CEE Discussion Paper,* No. 2, Centre for the Economics of Education, London School of Economics.

ISBN 978-92-64-03772-4
OECD Economic Surveys: United Kingdom
© OECD 2007

Chapter 3

Improving work prospects for the least skilled

The United Kingdom has had a good record of job creation over the past two decades with the aggregate unemployment rate and related expenditures falling, and employment rates at close to record levels. Although most disadvantaged groups including older workers, lone parents and ethnic minorities have enjoyed significant improvements over the past decade, unqualified workers and younger people continue to fare less well. Moreover, while it has reduced significantly in recent years, there is still a considerable flow of people, including prime working age males, into disability benefits. The government has taken a number of positive steps to address these issues including tightening eligibility criteria, offering income supplements and providing personalised counselling. However more could be done, particularly in the area of skills training both prior to employment and while in employment, and in tackling distortions in work incentives that arise from the high cost of child care and through the interface of the tax and social security systems.

The net gains from globalisation are closely related to how smoothly resources can be re-allocated from declining to expanding sectors, while the extent to which the country competes with the emerging markets influences the overall pressures for adjustment. In turn, the adjustment capacity depends to a large extent on policies affecting the labour market, as well as on the general skill level of the population. Compared with most other OECD countries, the United Kingdom has relatively few distorting regulations in the labour market. This suggests that the potential benefits from globalisation should be large. Indeed, re-employment appears to be smoother than in most continental European economies. Long-term unemployment is relatively low, real wages tend to be flexible and outflows from unemployment are fairly high (although lower than in North America and Scandinavia), indicating that displaced workers can find a new job relatively quickly (Figure 3.1). Average job tenure, which provides a broad indicator of overall turnover in the labour market, is relatively low, also suggesting that the labour market is quite flexible. Finally, the United Kingdom also has relatively high "job-to-job" mobility between similar industries, which is of particular importance when the structure of the economy is changing (Kongsrud and Wanner, 2005).

Despite this relatively positive backdrop, wage dispersion has increased over the past decade in the United Kingdom, as elsewhere, as the wages of those at the top of the distribution have increased much faster than those of the rest of the population. The introduction of the minimum wage in 1999 and the subsequent increases in its rate may have helped mitigate an underlying deterioration in relative wages for those at the lower end of the wage distribution. However, low-skilled workers have experienced a relative deterioration in their employment rates, and inactivity among this group has risen; in 2004 the employment rate of low-skilled prime-age workers was just 53%, below the OECD average. Explanations of this phenomenon have focused largely on the impact of globalisation and skill-biased technical change, though supply developments of different types of labour have also played a role. In addition, as pointed out in the previous chapter, there are still many young people leaving school who are ill-equipped to enter the labour force and end up in neither employment, nor in education or training.

In general, a broad consensus has emerged that although globalisation creates aggregate gains, it also entails adjustment and thus creates both winners and losers. This suggests a potential role for governments to ensure that the gains from globalisation are more evenly spread across the population, while continuing to promote economic policies that support structural change and adjustment. Broadly speaking, this can be done through a combination of income support in the short run, and by re-training and providing incentives for individuals to up-skill and progress in work in the medium term. This chapter first reviews recent labour market developments and then evaluates whether current policies get the balance right between these short-term and medium-term goals.

Figure 3.1. **Indicators of labour mobility**

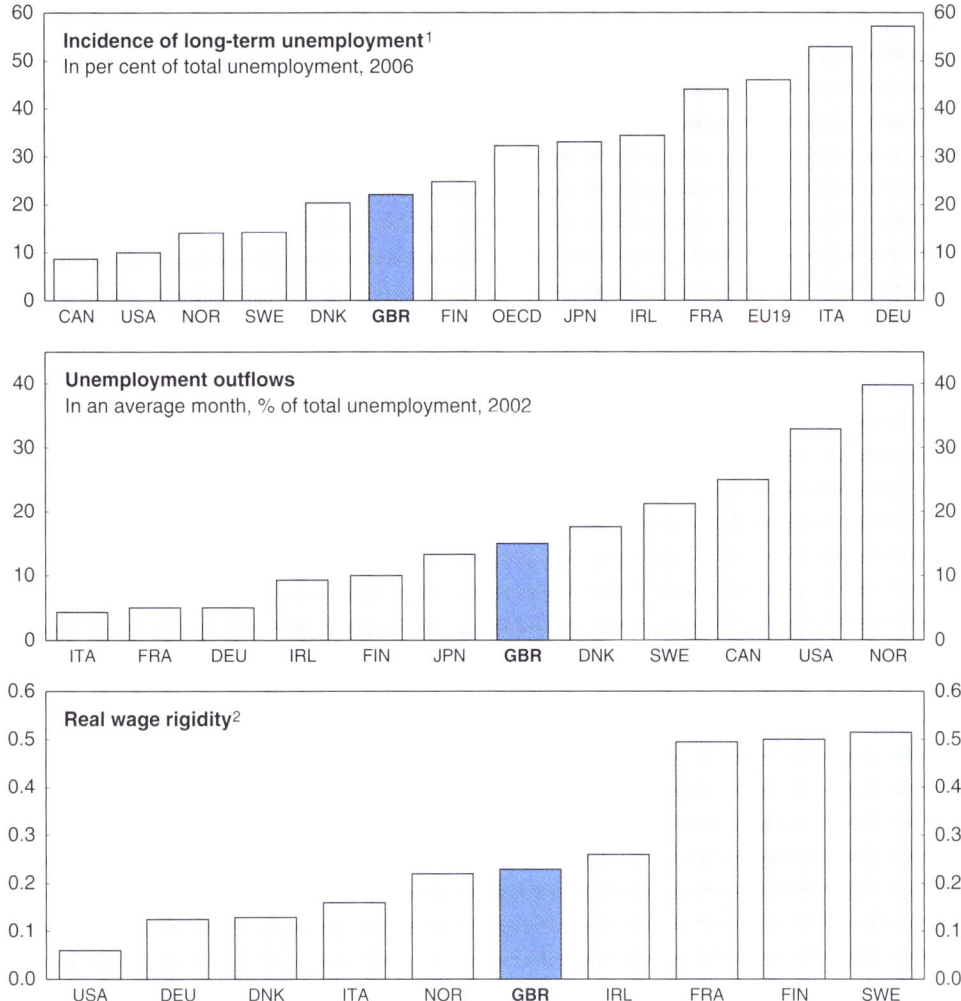

1. Defined as those unemployed continuously for 12 months or more.
2. The measure ranges from 0: no one is subject to the rigidity, to 1: all workers are potentially affected. It estimates the fraction of workers affected by downward wage rigidity in each country (averaged over time) and is based on panel data on individual earnings.

Source: OECD (2007), *OECD Employment Outlook*; Kongsrud, P.M. and I. Wanner (2005), "The Impact of Structural Policies on Trade-Related Adjustment and the Shift to Services", *OECD Economics Department Working Papers*, No. 427; Dickens *et al.* (2006), "The Interaction of Labor Markets and Inflation: Micro Evidence from the International Wage Flexibility Project", *www.brookings.edu/es/research/projects/iwfp.htm*.

StatLink ᴍˢ🔗 *http://dx.doi.org/10.1787/116063254004*

Recent labour market developments

As discussed in Chapter 1, in the United Kingdom, like in most other OECD countries, production has shifted towards knowledge-intensive industries, which has pushed up demand for skilled workers relative to that for unskilled workers and resulted in the "hollowing out" of many moderately skilled jobs. Consistent with this, earned income dispersion in the United Kingdom has widened most toward the upper end of the wage distribution – again, as in most other OECD countries. Such compositional changes in the demand for skill-types have been widely attributed to both offshoring and skill-biased technical change, although a number of studies have argued that skill-biased technical change is relatively more important than globalisation in explaining rising wage inequality (Feenstra and Hansen, 1999; Hijzen, 2004). Rather than attempt to disentangle the effects directly related to globalisation, this chapter simply reviews the overall effects of rising inequality and the relative shift towards highly skilled labour.

Wage dispersion has risen

Wage dispersion has increased in many OECD countries over the past couple of decades and this has often been associated with a decline in unemployment (OECD, 2006a).[1] Wage inequality has risen particularly sharply in the United Kingdom, the United States, and in some Scandinavian countries – economies that have experienced falls in unemployment. However, it has also increased in some other European countries, for instance in Germany, where unemployment started to fall only recently (Figure 3.2). In the United Kingdom, the rise in wage dispersion mainly reflects the fact that the earnings of those in the top income percentile increased much more rapidly than those of the rest of the population; changes at the middle and lower end of the distribution were much smaller (Table 3.1).

Figure 3.2. **Trends in earnings inequality**

Ratio between earnings percentiles, index, 1985 = 100

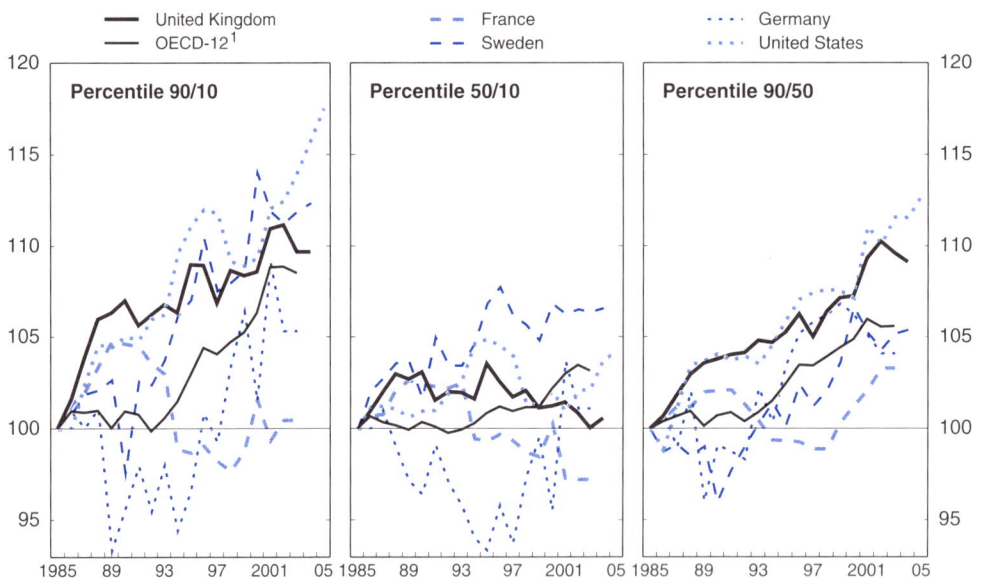

1. Unweighted average of data for Australia, Denmark, Finland, France, Germany, Japan, Korea, Netherlands, Poland, Sweden, United Kingdom and United States. Includes some estimated data points.

Source: OECD (2007), *OECD Employment Outlook.*

StatLink ᴹˢᴾ *http://dx.doi.org/10.1787/116080747147*

Table 3.1. **Wage dispersion in the United Kingdom**

Gross full-time earnings, ratio between two percentiles

	1997	2000	2003	2006
90th/10th	3.46	3.50	3.57	3.63
50th/10th	1.85	1.83	1.81	1.83
90th/50th	1.87	1.91	1.97	1.98

Source: Calculations based on ONS (2006), *Annual Survey of Hours and Earnings (ASHE) – 2006 Results*, on-line edition, Office for National Statistics, *www.statistics.gov.uk.*

Growing concerns have been voiced in the United States and some other countries that "middle-class" workers have not shared in the benefits of growth. In these countries growth in real median wages has been modest in recent years (Table 3.2). In contrast, this has not happened in the United Kingdom, where growth in real median wages has been on average stronger than in the other large OECD economies and has remained broadly in line with labour productivity growth.[2] There is some evidence that changes in the wage distribution in OECD countries are related to the variation in the skill distribution rather than greater variation in the returns to skills themselves (Andersson, 2006; Nickell, 2004).

Table 3.2. **Growth in real median wages in selected OECD countries**
Average growth rate[1]

	1998-2001	2002-05	1998-2005
United Kingdom	**2.05**	**2.09**	**2.07**
Canada	1.06	0.31	0.68
France	0.74	0.84	0.79
Japan	0.87	0.21	0.54
United States	2.59	−0.04	1.28

1. Real growth in median earnings is proxied for by subtracting the growth in the private consumption deflator from the growth in median earnings.
Source: OECD, *Earnings database* and OECD (2006), *OECD Economic Outlook*, No. 80.

Minimum wage increases and tax-benefit changes have cushioned low-income households

Those in the lowest wage deciles have not seen their gross earnings increase as fast as those of the top earners but, at least until the most recent years, they have kept up with or outpaced median earnings growth (Figure 3.3). The introduction of the national minimum wage in 1999 is important in this context. The government has raised it rapidly, thus helping to prevent a decline in relative earnings for the lowest earners. Indeed, since its introduction in 1999 the minimum wage has increased by nearly 50%, compared with an increase in median earnings of 30%. Despite this, the earnings growth of low-skilled workers slowed in the most recent years. This may be the result of the massive inflow of

Figure 3.3. **Earnings growth by income percentiles**
Full-time gross weekly earnings, per cent

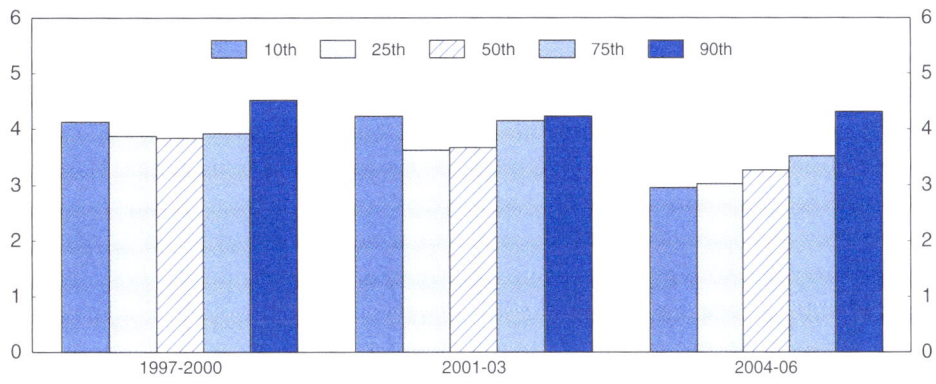

Source: ONS (2006), *Annual Survey of Hours and Earnings (ASHE) – 2006 Results*, on-line edition, Office for National Statistics, *www.statistics.gov.uk.*

StatLink http://dx.doi.org/10.1787/116116126634

migrant workers, who have eased labour market shortages in certain occupations and industries. Consistent with this, wage growth has slowed by relatively more in some industries, such as hotels and restaurants, which have seen a large inflow of migrant workers.[3]

When assessing changes in labour market outcomes for different groups one needs to take into account not only *market income* (as above), which is the sum of wages, self-employment and capital income, but also *disposable income*, since public transfers and taxes affect the "money in the pocket" of households.[4] In most OECD countries, the disposable income share received by the bottom quintile has remained broadly unchanged or has fallen, while it has tended to increase for those at the top (Table 3.3). In the United Kingdom the bottom quintile has maintained its disposable income share. This is likely to reflect minimum wage increases, together with changes to the tax and benefit system, policies that aim at reducing poverty among low-income families.

Table 3.3. **Changes in disposable income shares by quintile**[1]

Entire population, mid-1990s to early 2000

	Bottom quintile	Middle quintile	Top quintile
United Kingdom	+	-	+
Canada	=	-	+
Finland	-	-	+++
France	=	=	=
Germany	=	+	=
Ireland	-	+++	–
Japan	-	-	+
Sweden	-	-	+++
United States	=	=	=

1. Household equivalent disposable income includes gross earnings, gross capital and self-employment incomes, transfers from the general government less income taxes and social security contributions paid by households. The equivalisation adjusts for different household size. The table shows percentage point changes in the shares of equivalised disposable income received by each quintile of the population.

   +++ : an increase of more than 1.5 percentage points in the share of disposable income received by the quintile group.

   +   : increase of between 0.5 and 1.5 percentage point.

   =   : changes between –0.5 and +0.5 percentage points.

   -    : decrease between 0.5 and 1.5 percentage point.

   –   : decrease of more than 1.5 percentage points.

Source: Förster, M. and M. Mira d'Ercole (2005), "Income Distribution and Poverty in OECD Countries in the Second Half of the 1990s", *OECD Social, Employment and Migration Working Papers*, No. 22.

These data on income distribution suggest that the government's policies to reduce poverty have been successful as they have helped to mitigate the underlying downward pressures on the household disposable income of low income households. Nonetheless, even though the minimum wage may have helped to reduce poverty in some cases for those with a low-paid job, it may at the same time have had negative employment effects. Looking ahead, if underlying market income inequality continues to rise, the cost of offsetting it (both political and economic) will also rise. Eventually it may not be possible to prevent a widening in disposable income inequality by raising the minimum wage or redistribution of income *via* the transfer system. This therefore puts the onus on the up-skilling of the workforce.

Low-skilled workers are more affected by low employment rates

Low-skilled workers have experienced a relative deterioration in employment rates, and a significant rise in inactivity. While employment rates tend to rise with educational attainment in all countries, this is particularly so in the United Kingdom. Compared with graduates of upper secondary school, the 2004 employment rate for graduates of tertiary education was around 10 percentage points higher, whereas the employment rate of those with little education was more than 30 percentage points lower. Moreover, the employment rate of 25-64-year-olds with education below the upper-secondary level fell from 61% in 1991 to 53% in 2004, below the OECD average of 56% (Figure 3.4). Measured relative to the employment rate of workers with an upper-secondary education, the employment rate of workers with less than upper-secondary education has been falling over the past decade and is now among the lowest in the OECD. The large gap between the employment rates of the low educated and those with medium levels of education suggests that further efforts to improve the levels of education of the unemployed and inactive is likely to yield positive results.

Figure 3.4. **Employment rate for low-skilled workers**[1]

Per cent

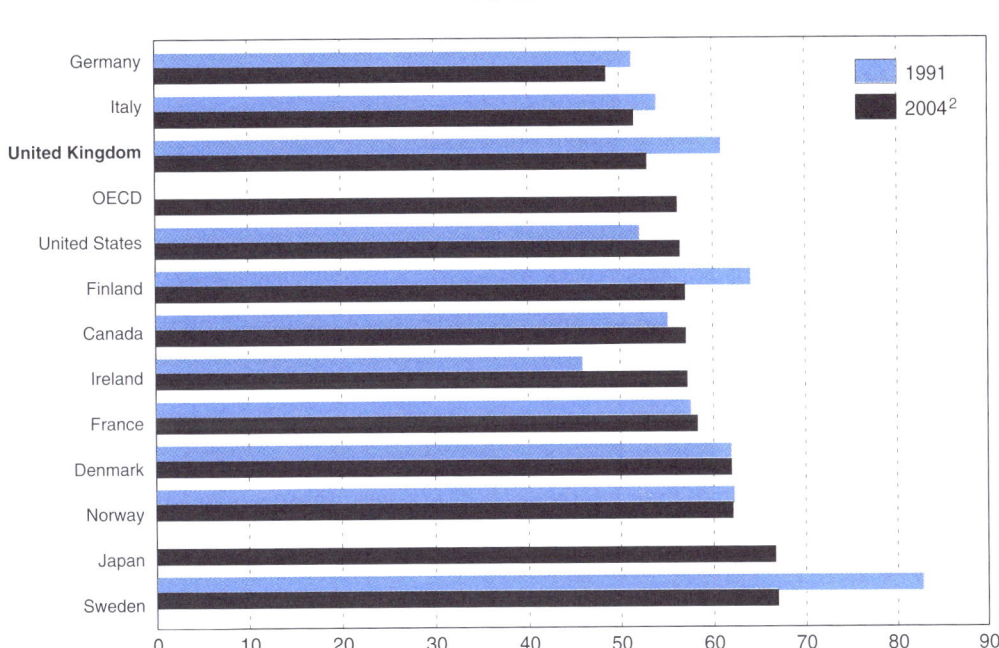

1. Employment rate for persons with less than an upper secondary level of education. Age group 25-64.
2. 2003 for Japan.
Source: OECD (2006), *Education at a Glance.*

StatLink 🔗 http://dx.doi.org/10.1787/116135167132

The inactivity rate among less skilled workers has also increased significantly. In the mid-1980s the difference in inactivity rates between unskilled males and other employees was fairly small. But by 2002 the inactivity rate of unskilled prime-age males was 18.8%, roughly five times the average inactivity rate of 3.7% (Nickell, 2004).[5] Most of the upward trend in the male inactivity rate is due to the growing number of men reporting long-term sickness or disability (ONS, 2006a; OECD, 2007a); around 36% of all inactive men were inactive due to long-term sickness in 2006.[6] The number of incapacity benefit recipients has risen in many OECD countries, but the United Kingdom stands out as having a high concentration of persons on incapacity benefits (Figure 3.5) particularly among prime-age male workers (OECD, 2005a).

Figure 3.5. **Share of working-age population receiving disability benefits**
Per cent of population aged 20-65

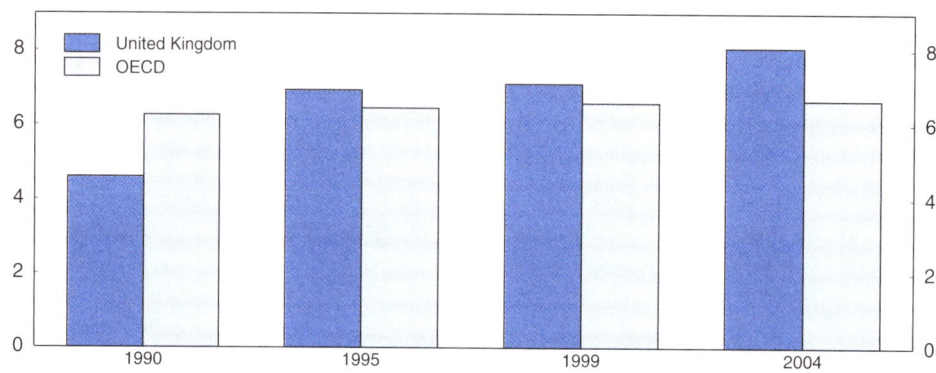

Source: OECD (2007), *Going for Growth*, Economic Reforms.

StatLink ᴹᴵˢᴸ *http://dx.doi.org/10.1787/116146238043*

Recent immigrants tend to work in low-skilled, low-paid jobs despite fairly high educational levels

Although the data on migrants have many limitations, the best estimates suggest that there are currently up to around half a million migrant workers from the new EU member countries in the United Kingdom, roughly equivalent to 1.6% of the labour force (Annex 3.A1; Blanchflower *et al.*, 2007). Most of these new immigrants are young and the majority are male workers and relatively well-educated in comparison with natives (Blanchflower *et al.*, 2007; Saleheen and Shadforth, 2006). Estimates based on the age at which migrants left full-time education suggest that 45% of the accession country immigrants have degrees, compared with 27% of the UK working-age population (Saleheen and Shadforth, 2006).[7] Despite their relatively high skill level, these workers predominantly work in the least skilled occupations in the less productive industries such as administration, hospitality and catering, and agriculture (Annex 3.A1; Home Office, 2006). One explanation for this might be a lack of English language skills in which case it is likely that they will move on to better and more skill-intensive jobs as they improve their language skills.

A number of positive labour market effects of migration have been observed. For example, since immigrant workers are often more responsive than local workers to labour market conditions, they help to iron out regional differences (European Commission, 2005) and alleviate bottlenecks by taking jobs natives do not want. In absolute numbers the largest inflow of immigrants from the new EU accession countries is to London and the South East, but it has increased in all regions since 2004 and the increase has tended to be larger in areas with lower unemployment rates (Annex 3.A1 and Blanchflower *et al.*, 2007).

Unemployment among native youths has risen more than the overall unemployment rate

While the increased inflow of fairly skilled young immigrants has coincided with an increase in the unemployment rate of younger workers, leading some to argue that immigrant workers may have displaced some school leavers in the labour market, the evidence does not support this. The most recent UK analysis, based on claimant count data, has found no support for the argument that accession country immigrants have contributed to the recent rise in overall unemployment or that of younger workers (Gilpin *et al.*, 2006). However, ongoing analysis in this area is warranted.

Policies to improve labour market outcomes for the least skilled

Slow the future pace of increase in the minimum wage

Since it was introduced in 1999 the statutory national minimum wage has risen by almost 50% (representing an average increase of 5.2% per annum) while median earnings have risen by only around 30% (3.8% per annum on average) (Figure 3.6).[8] A minimum wage can play an important role in improving the incomes of low-skilled workers, particularly if the tax/benefit treatment of low wages is also favourable (as it is in the United Kingdom, see Box 3.1), as long as it does not price them out of work. A moderate minimum wage can also be a useful supplement to in-work benefits, since it limits the extent to which employers can appropriate these benefits by lowering pay levels (Gregg, 2000; OECD, 2006a).

Figure 3.6. **Comparison of minimum wages and median earnings**

Index, 1999 = 100

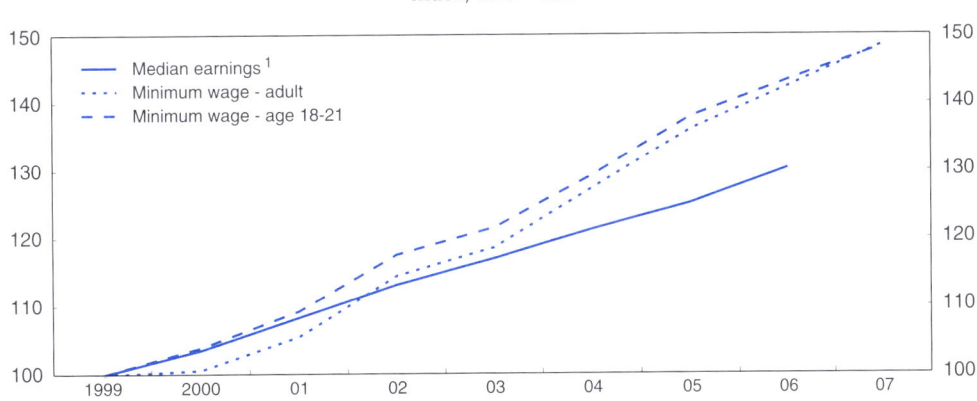

1. Median gross hourly earnings for a full-time worker.

Source: ONS (2006), *Annual Survey of Hours and Earnings (ASHE) – 2006 Results*, on-line edition, Office for National Statistics, *www.statistics.gov.uk*.

StatLink ⟶ *http://dx.doi.org/10.1787/116168422601*

Nevertheless, the minimum wage can only play a supporting role in a broader anti-poverty and make-work-pay programme, due to the need to avoid setting it at a level that would price low-skilled workers out of jobs and reduce employment for this group (OECD, 2006a).

The empirical literature on the link between the minimum wage and employment is mixed, with many studies finding little empirical evidence for employment losses due to minimum wages (OECD, 2006a; Dolado *et al.*, 1996), while other studies find a significant negative effect, particularly for young adults (Neumark and Wascher, 1999; OECD, 1998).[9] At

Box 3.1. **Take-home pay for minimum wage earners**

In the United Kingdom the tax burden on low pay has eased slightly since 2000 and is among the lowest in the OECD. The average tax rate for a full-time worker employed at the minimum wage was 13% in 2006, *versus* 27% for a person working at the average wage (OECD, 2006b). The progressivity of the tax system, together with the available benefits for low-paid workers, boosts the "take home pay" of low wage earners relative to that of the median wage earner. In absolute terms, the annual "take home" pay from working full-time in a minimum wage job, after adjusting for purchasing power, is now among the highest in the OECD (Figure 3.7, upper panel). The United Kingdom also ranks above average in terms of the level of the minimum wage relative to the median wage (Figure 3.7, lower panel) Between 2001 and 2005, the "take-home" pay for a single person grew by about 18% (4.2% per annum on average) and for a one-earner couple with two children by 15% (3.6% per annum on average).* During the same period the nominal minimum wage increased by some 29% (or on average 6.6% per annum). This implies that as the minimum wage increases and the person moves up the earnings distribution, relatively less of the gross minimum wage increase translates into a net increase as benefits begin to be withdrawn and average tax rates increase.

Figure 3.7. **Take-home pay for a minimum wage earner:**
selected OECD countries

For a single person, 2004

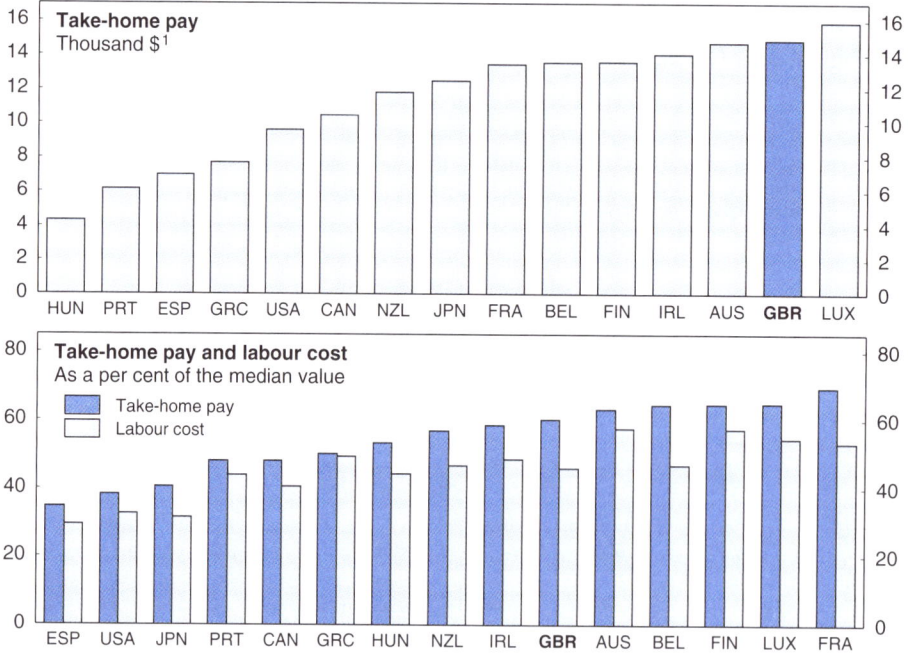

1. Using 2004 purchasing power parities.

Source: Calculations based on the OECD *Taxing Wages* and *Minimum Wage databases*; and the OECD Tax-Benefit Models, May 2006.

StatLink 🔗 *http://dx.doi.org/10.1787/116171883226*

---

* At the beginning of 2001, approximately 1.2 million families were receiving the Working Families' Tax credit (the predecessor of Working Tax Credit and Child Tax Credit). By the beginning of 2006 this had increased to 1.9 million families receiving the Working Tax Credit (HM Revenue and Customs, Child and Working Tax Credits Statistics).

42% of median earnings, the minimum labour cost in the United Kingdom (the minimum wage plus employers' social security contributions at that wage level) is around the OECD average. But this ratio varies significantly across industries: from 34% in financial intermediation to 78% in low-pay (low-skill) industries such as hotels and restaurants. Thus the minimum wage is more likely to "bite" and cause adverse employment effects in those sectors that have traditionally been more sensitive to wages at the low end. Machin *et al.* (2003) found some evidence of this "bite" in another sector: the disability-care and retirement home sector, where there was a reduction in employment and hours after the introduction of the minimum wage in 1999. Among the workforce as a whole however, research has not identified any significant negative employment effect of the minimum wage.

Given the sectoral differences, it is difficult to judge the point at which the minimum wage begins to "bite" and cause adverse employment effects. However, the indicators listed below suggest that this point may now have been reached in some sectors, suggesting that the minimum wage should be raised more slowly in future. This concern was shared by the Low Pay Commission which recently recommended that the 2007 minimum wage be raised by slightly less than expected average earnings growth (Low Pay Commission, 2007):[10]

● The share of all adult jobs paid less than the minimum wage rate increased slightly to 1.2% in the spring of 2006, up from 0.9% in 2000. For workers aged 18-21 the corresponding share in 2006 was 2.5%, up from 2.2% in 2000 (ONS, 2006b). As a measure of "non-compliance" with minimum wage regulations, such measures can be used as a proxy indicator for the extent to which the minimum wage is binding.

● As the 10th percentile earnings premium[11] over the minimum wage has fallen over time it has turned negative in a few industries (*e.g.* hotels and restaurants, other services, manufacturing of wearing apparel), suggesting that the minimum wage is increasingly binding in these sectors (Figure 3.8). The 10th percentile earnings premium for 18-21-year-old workers over the reduced minimum wage is also close to zero in some industries.[12]

Figure 3.8. **Tenth percentile earnings premium over the minimum wage**

Hourly gross wages for a full-time worker relative to the hourly adult minimum wage, in £

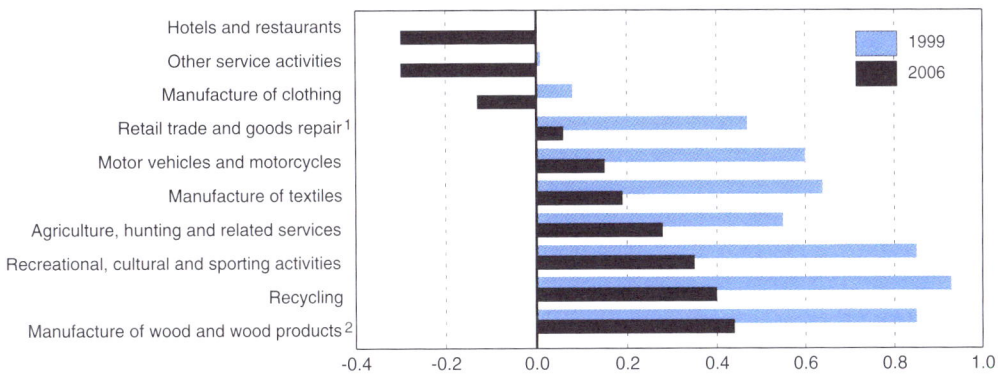

1. Excluding motor vehicles and motorcycles.
2. Excluding furniture.

Source: ONS (2006), *Annual Survey of Hours and Earnings (ASHE) – 2006 Results*, on-line edition, Office for National Statistics, *www.statistics.gov.uk*.

StatLink ᵐˢᴾ *http://dx.doi.org/10.1787/116188338028*

The "bite" of the minimum wage also varies geographically across regions, as does the unemployment rate. Compared with other OECD countries, regional unemployment disparities in the United Kingdom, measured by the coefficient of variation, are fairly high: the disparity in regional unemployment was the third highest among the G7 economies in 2003 and it increased between the mid-1990s and 2003 (OECD, 2005b). Since the minimum wage is set nationwide in nominal terms, its real value is much higher outside London where it is more likely to "bite" because it enters at a higher point of the wage distribution and is thus more likely to cause negative employment effects (Stewart, 2002).

Ensure a balance between alleviating poverty and ensuring incentives to up-skill and progress in work

A key aim of the current government has been to alleviate child, pensioner and in-work poverty. But it has also placed emphasis on minimising welfare traps by making work pay. In attempting to achieve these two goals the government has substantially increased the use of means-tested tax and benefit programmes. The Working Families Tax Credit for low-income families and single-parent households was introduced in April 1999 and has been replaced by a number of other programmes that target support where the need is greatest, such as to families with young children. Less attention has been paid to ensuring that low-skilled workers have good incentives to progress in work and to up-skill. In the medium-term, however, such incentives have the potential to significantly impact poverty rates. Putting more emphasis on a "work strategy" rather than a "benefits strategy" is likely to yield better results both in terms of the fiscal burden and addressing poverty in the longer term (Whiteford and Adema, 2007).

Among the means-tested programmes, the most important is the Working Tax Credit: an employment contingent in-work benefit that tops-up the earnings of low income earners (Box 3.2).[13] Other means-tested benefits which do not depend on the claimant's employment status include:

● The Child Tax Credit – this supports families with children and young people aged 16-19 in full-time education.

● The Housing Benefit – the current housing benefit (based largely on the beneficiary's rent) is due to be replaced with the Local Housing Allowance (LHA) in March 2009. Currently piloted in nine local areas, the LHA will pay a fixed benefit based on family size and local housing costs.

● The Council Tax Benefit – which reduces the tax levied by local authorities.

These policies have had some success in raising the labour supply of some groups and in reducing child poverty. Incentives to re-enter the labour market after a period of unemployment – at least into part-time work – are now stronger for some groups than they were in the mid-1990s, reducing the risk of "unemployment traps" and "inactivity traps". For example, the average effective tax rate (AETR) faced by an unemployed lone parent or (one-earner) married couples with children, who takes up a part-time (third of full time) average paid job, is now around 60%. These AETRs exclude the impact of child-care costs, which can push up effective AETRs significantly – particularly for second income earners, as discussed in more detail below. Nevertheless, a recent study evaluating the Working Families' Tax Credit found that it had increased the labour supply of lone mothers by around 5 percentage points compared with the earlier programme (Brewer *et al.*, 2007).

Box 3.2. **The Working Tax Credit and other means-tested benefits**

The Working Tax Credit (which replaced the Working Families Tax Credit in 2003) is an in-work means-tested benefit that tops up the earnings of people on low-incomes working more than 16 hours per week who are responsible for children, disabled, or persons aged 50+ and are returning to work after a period on the unemployment benefit. A person over 25 years of age and working more than 30 hours per week is also eligible for the Working Tax Credit. The size of the Working Tax Credit depends on the family situation and has different elements (Table 3.4).

Table 3.4. **Working Tax Credit elements**
Maximum amounts per tax year, in £

	2006/07	2007/08
Basic element paid to everyone who is entitled to receive Working Tax Credit	1 665	1 730
Additional elements		
Second adult if claiming as a couple	1 640	1 700
Lone parent	1 640	1 700
Working 30 hours or more per week (or jointly if claiming as a couple)	680	705
Disability	2 225	2 310
Severe disability	945	980
Aged 50 or over and returning to work after a period on benefit		
• Working 16-29 hours per week	1 140	1 185
• Working over 30 hours per week	1 705	1 770
Child-care element covering up to 80% of costs for eligible child care		
• Weekly maximum for one child	175	175
• Weekly maximum for two or more children	300	300
Gross income earnings threshold where phasing out begins	5 220	5 220
Withdrawal rate	37%	37%

Source: HM Revenue and Customs.

In addition, workers looking after children under the age of 16 are eligible for the Child Tax Credit regardless of whether the claimant is in work or not. All families with children can claim the Child Tax Credit if their income is no more than £58 175 a year (up to £66 350 if the child is under one-year-old). The payment is made up of two elements: first, a *family element* paid to any family with at least one child and worth up to £545 per annum (2007/08 tax year); and second, a *child element* paid for each child in the family and worth up to £1 845 per annum (2007/08 tax year). Additional benefits are payable for disabled children.

The benefit value of the Working Tax Credit is calculated by adding up all the elements the person/household is entitled to. At the same time, if eligible, the amount of Child Tax Credit is added. Then 37% of the difference between the claimant's gross income and the threshold amount of £5 220 per year is deducted. Gross income is defined as earned income plus all relevant benefits before the deduction of taxes and social security contributions. Income from other benefits such as the Child Benefit, the Housing Benefit, the Disability Allowance and the Council Tax Allowance are not included in the gross income calculation. The Working Tax Credit and the Child Tax Credit are subject to a single means test applied at the family level. Families with annual incomes below £5 220 (£14 495 for families eligible only for the Child Tax Credit) are entitled to the maximum credits. The main elements in the Working Tax Credit are withdrawn first, followed by the child-care element and finally the child and disability elements of the Child Tax Credit.

> **Box 3.2. The Working Tax Credit and other means-tested benefits** *(cont.)*
>
> The family element of the Child Tax Credit is not withdrawn until the family's income exceeds £50 000 and then at a rate of 6.67%. In April 2006, approximately 1.9 million families were receiving the Working Tax Credit and out of those 1.6 million were also receiving the Child Tax Credit. This suggests that just under one fifth of the Working Tax Credit recipients had no dependent children (Phillips and Sibieta, 2006).
>
> In addition to the Working Tax and the Child Tax Credits, persons on low income are eligible for the Housing Benefit if their savings are less than £16 000, or if they are aged 60 or over and receiving the Guarantee Credit of the Pension Credit. If a person lives with a partner only one person qualifies for the benefit and a single person under the age of 25 is only entitled to a Housing Benefit for bed-sit accommodation or one room in shared accommodation. The maximum amount is the "eligible rent" which may not be the same as the full rent. The eligible rent is based on the rent plus charges for water, heating and other services. The Housing Benefit is assessed at the same time as the Council Tax Benefit and does not affect any other benefits. Since November 2003, a new housing benefit system called the Local Housing Allowance (LHA) is being piloted in nine local areas. The LHA bases the maximum amount paid to tenants on the household size and the area. Therefore, two households in similar circumstances in the same area will be entitled to a similar amount of benefits. This system creates individual choice for each tenant on how to spend their income/benefit as they can choose whether to rent a larger property, or spend less on housing and more on other consumption items (or savings). The pilots are planned to be rolled out nationwide in March 2008.

The combination of higher parental employment and large increases in tax credits and benefits paid to low income families has also reduced child poverty. Between 1998/99 and 2004/05 the number of children living in poverty fell from 4.4 million children to 3.6 million.[14] This constitutes a fall from 33% to 25% of all children but while it represents progress, it is not full achievement of the government's goal of reducing child poverty by a quarter by 2004-06 (see also Hirsch, 2006). The government's longer-term target is that child poverty should be halved by 2010 and eliminated by 2020. These targets could prove to be ambitious given that the child poverty numbers have remained flat for the past three years. Similarly, poverty among working-age adults has remained unchanged at 19% (Palmer *et al.*, 2006).

Marginal effective tax rates are highest for low income single-earner households who are moving into higher wage jobs or work additional hours

Despite some progress towards meeting the government's poverty goals, the means-tested tax and benefit programmes have often worsened the incentives of those in part-time work to increase hours and to progress in work by up-skilling and by education. Thus the two main ways the government can help people on low-incomes – by providing them with direct income support and by encouraging them to earn more – are in conflict with one another (Adam *et al.* 2006a; 2006b). As well, the interaction between the tax and benefit systems often creates "low-wage traps" whereby an increase in gross in-work earnings fails to translate into a net income increase, because of higher taxation and lower benefit payments.[15]

The marginal effective tax rate (METR) measures the percentage of additional earnings that is taxed away by the combined tax and benefits system.[16] METRs arising from moving from a full-time job paying the minimum wage to a higher paid job are particularly high (close to 90% in some cases) for lone parents and one-earner couples with children (Table 3.5). But the METR is also fairly high (60-80%) for single persons or one-earner couples without children wishing to increase their pay from the minimum wage to two-thirds of the average wage. The influence of each policy instrument and its contribution to the overall METR is important in understanding the factors influencing incentives to move into higher paid, more skilled jobs. For lone parents and one-earner married couples with children a large part of the METR faced when moving from working at the minimum wage to a job paying 67% of the average wage is explained by the withdrawal of in-work and housing benefits together with increased income tax (Figure 3.9). For a single person the withdrawal of housing benefits and increased income tax account for about two-thirds of the METR while the withdrawal of in-work benefits contributes less.

Table 3.5. **Marginal effective tax rates for different earnings transitions**[1]

Holding hours worked constant at full-time hours, 2005

	Minimum wage to 67% of average worker earnings		Minimum wage to 100% of average worker earnings		67% to 100% of average worker earnings	
	2001	2005	2001	2005	2001	2005
No children						
Single person	59	59	46	46	32	33
One-earner married couple	71	76	52	54	32	33
Two-earner married couple (2nd earner)	32	33	32	33	32	33
Two children						
Lone parent	89	90	77	75	65	61
One-earner married couple	89	90	78	77	66	65
Two-earner married couple (2nd earner)	32	33	32	33	32	33

1. Calculations based on the OECD Tax-Benefits Models by varying the earnings levels assuming full-time work. In the case of a married couple it is assumed that the second earner varies his/her earnings level while the principal earner makes 67% of average worker earnings. Social assistance and any other means-tested benefits are assumed to be available subject to relevant income conditions. Neither child-care benefits nor child-care costs are considered in these calculations.

Source: Calculations based on OECD (2007), *Benefits and Wages*, forthcoming.

Figure 3.9. **Contributions to marginal effective tax rates**

Moving from earnings at the minimum wage level to 67% of the average wage, per cent, 2005

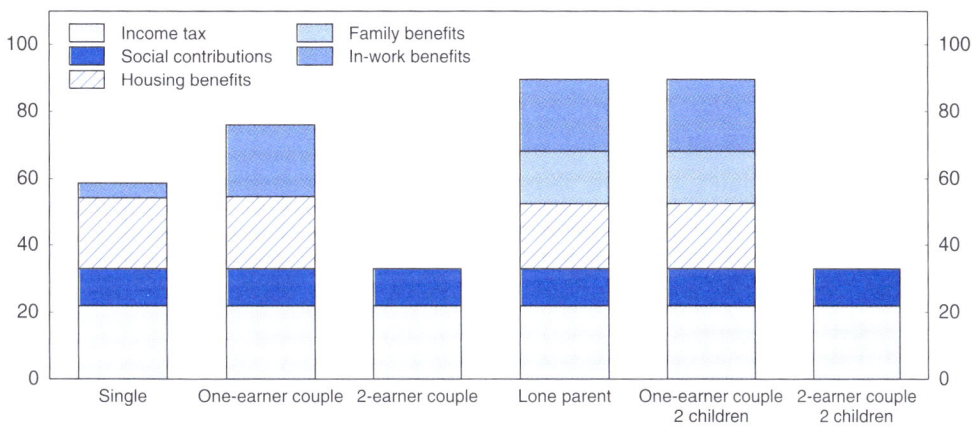

Source: OECD (2007), Tax-Benefit Models, forthcoming, *www.oecd.org/els/social/workincentives*.

StatLink ᴍꜱᴘ *http://dx.doi.org/10.1787/116218386526*

The combination of tax increases and benefit withdrawal also affects workers' financial incentives to increase the number of working hours at a given wage. In particular high METRs are observed for workers who double their working hours from either half to full-time or from a third to two-thirds of full-time, particularly for lone parents and one-earner married couples with children. Thus, while unemployment traps and inactivity traps are minimised by providing incentives to take up at least some work (OECD, 2005a) low-skilled workers often end up in "low-wage traps" with part-time jobs instead (Table 3.6). Since the higher income of a two-earner couple makes them ineligible for the tax credits, low-skilled one-earner couples have significantly worse incentives than dual-income couples to progress in work either by moving into a better paid job or by working more hours. This reflects the policy trade-off between providing poverty relief for single-income families *versus* improving their incentives to progress in work (Draper, 2006).

Table 3.6. **Marginal effective tax rates for part-time employees**
Different working hours transitions in per cent, 2005[1]

| | Half to full-time | | | | | | One-third to two-thirds | | | | | |
| | No children | | | Two children | | | No children | | | Two children | | |
	Single person	One-earner married couple	Two-earner married couple	Lone parent	One-earner married couple	Two-earner married couple	Single person	One-earner married couple	Two-earner married couple	Lone parent	One-earner married couple	Two-earner married couple
United Kingdom	**35**	**43**	**33**	**69**	**72**	**33**	**58**	**69**	**33**	**84**	**84**	**33**
Canada	34	36	31	60	60	39	32	39	29	44	52	39
Finland	42	58	42	61	76	42	64	93	34	63	100	34
France	39	29	35	34	33	33	34	35	36	55	55	31
Germany	54	45	53	60	58	53	51	58	50	81	78	51
Ireland	30	44	30	80	56	30	49	91	25	53	74	25
Italy	37	40	37	34	31	43	35	25	34	3	−7	49
Japan	21	20	21	40	45	24	19	52	19	86	94	26
Sweden	35	45	35	51	54	35	57	82	35	52	92	35
United States	29	23	29	46	47	30	32	37	29	41	44	38

1. Hourly earnings correspond to the average worker level throughout so that a half-time employee would have earnings equal to 50% of the average worker. Social assistance and any other means-tested benefits are assumed to be available subject to the relevant income conditions. Children are aged 4 and 6 and neither child-care benefits nor child-care costs are considered. In-work benefits that depend on a transition from unemployment into work are not available since the person changing working-hours is already in employment prior to the change. For married couples the percentage of average worker relates to one spouse only; the second spouse is assumed to be "inactive" with no earnings in a one-earner couple and to have full-time earnings equal to 67% of the average worker in a two-earner couple.

Source: OECD (2007), *Benefits and Wages* forthcoming.

High child-care costs reduce incentives for many low-skilled second income earners and lone parents to return to work

There is good evidence that the UK labour market is relatively flexible particularly in regard to accommodating flexible working hours for women. In 2002 close to 35% of female workers in the United Kingdom worked less than 30 hours per week, in contrast to around 18% for Sweden, 13% for Finland and 22% for Canada (OECD, 2005c). While this might be related to legal arrangements and employer flexibility, it might also be related to the availability and cost of child care. Child care, which is more expensive in the United Kingdom than in most other OECD countries (OECD, 2005c), can be a major cost for families, particularly low-income families. Thus child care also has a big impact on incentives to participate in the labour market, in particular deterring second-earners from entering the labour market or returning to work in low-paid jobs, thereby contributing to "inactivity traps". Abstaining from the labour market also hinders the person from later progressing in work and reduces future earnings potential.

Three main child-related benefits are available. First, the child-care element in the Working Tax Credit refunds 80% of child-care costs for low-income families, up to a ceiling which depends on the number of children with the taper beginning at roughly £19 500 for families with one child and £24 500 with two children. These thresholds apply to total family income. Second, the Child Tax Credit is a general income supplement paid to families with children regardless of whether they are in work or not. Third, the Child Benefit is paid for each child in the family under the age of 16, or under the age of 19 if the person is still in full-time non-advanced education or training (A-level or equivalent).[17] This benefit is not affected by income or savings, so most people bringing up a child obtain the Child Benefit. The amount is £18.10 a week for the eldest child and £12.10 a week for each additional child.

Once child-care costs as well as taxes and benefits are taken into account, the average marginal tax rate (AETR) or the implicit tax on returning to work increases significantly for some parents. For example, OECD estimates are that a lone parent returning to full-time work at two-thirds of the average wage faced an AETR of 101.3% in 2004, compared with an AETR of just 69.8% when child-care costs are excluded. For a second-earner, where the principal earner receives two-thirds of the average wage, the corresponding implicit tax on returning to work was 89.5%, *versus* just 23.1% excluding child-care costs (Figure 3.10).[18] In other words, child-care costs add roughly 16 percentage points to the AETRs faced by low-income lone parents and roughly 70 percentage points to the AETRs faced by second-income earners. Compared with other OECD countries these implicit tax rates are among the highest.

Possible reforms to improve work prospects for the low-skilled may, therefore, include the following:

- Changing the tax and benefit system that would improve the incentives for low-income (often part-time) lone parents and one-earner couples to move up the earnings distribution.

- Considering ways to mitigate the impact of child-care costs and subsidies on incentives to participate in the labour force, particularly for second earners.

- Making the child-care element of the Working Tax Credit available to those participating in approved courses of study, as well as to those who are working. This would have the potential to alleviate poverty in the future by improving the longer-term employment prospects of lone parents and second income earners.

- Introducing more work-testing for lone parents. At present lone parents are not required to work until the youngest child is 16 years old. This dependent child cut-off age is high in comparison to other OECD countries where the average is around 6 years of age. However, the government's recent Green Paper "*In Work, Better Off: next steps to full employment*" (DWP, 2007) which followed up on the recommendations of the report by Freud (2007) on reforming the welfare system, set out proposals to reduce this age to 7 years by October 2010, or as resources allow. The consultation period ends in October 2007.

Not only does the interface between the social security system and the tax system present a formidable challenge to policy makers in a static sense, there is also a dynamic dimension. While someone moving from unemployment into employment might be

Figure 3.10. **Implicit tax on returning to work**[1]

Per cent of gross earnings in new job, 2004

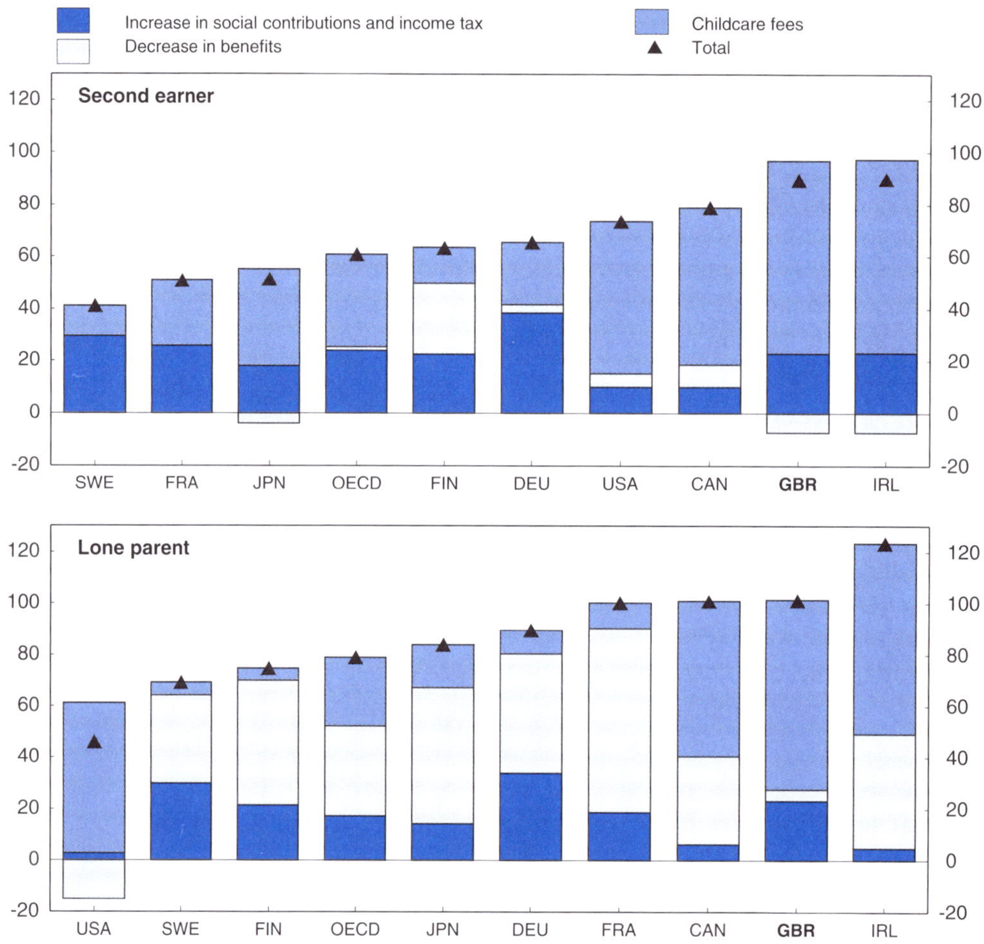

1. Taking into account child-care fees and changes of taxes and benefits in case of a transition to a job paying two-thirds of average worker earnings.

Source: OECD (2007), *Benefits and Wages*, forthcoming.

StatLink http://dx.doi.org/10.1787/116232817078

confronted by unfavourable marginal effective tax rates, meaning that the increase in their disposable income may be small (particularly in light of the leisure-time trade off) for those with good prospects in the labour market this may only be a transitory phase. For someone with a good level of core skills, work experience will assist advancement leading eventually to higher take home pay. This is a reason why investment in education and skills is so important as it is instrumental in shortening the low productivity transition period. If the unemployed, the low-skilled and youth invest in their own futures through education and training then they have a stake in that future and will be more prepared to participate in a system that entails a mutual obligation. Meghir and Phillips (2007) make the point that while labour supply elasticities with respect to income are generally found to be low in empirical studies, these tend to be short run analyses. Longer-run adjustments to the tax and transfer system might be more important particularly in how they affect human capital accumulation behaviour.

Active labour market policies

Helping those on incapacity benefits back to work

For those with health conditions and disabilities, getting back into employment is one of the effective routes out of poverty. However, this group faces significant additional hurdles in joining the workforce and those on incapacity benefits can face weak work incentives (OECD, 2007b), suggesting that active labour market programmes can play an important role in assisting this transition. This is particularly important in the United Kingdom where the biggest increase in inactivity rates has been recorded for prime age males reporting long-term sickness or disability as the main reason for inactivity.

The New Deal programmes for disadvantaged groups are part of the active labour market programmes (introduced in 1998) that offer tailored individual help with a focus on work as the best way out of poverty.[19] The long-run goal of the government is to raise the overall employment rate to 80% of the working-age population from its current level of 74.5% and it is recognised that this goal will not be achieved without tackling inactivity among key groups such as people on incapacity benefits. Rather than being spread evenly among the population, the majority of incapacity benefit recipients are concentrated in some of the poorest and most disadvantaged areas and among the least skilled workers. The piloted Pathways to Work programme, which was developed to deal with this problem, has so far produced promising results, although there are concerns about how well it will continue to perform when extended on a compulsory basis (Box 3.3).

Box 3.3. **Pathways to Work**

Under the Pathways to Work programme most new or repeat incapacity benefit claimants are required to attend an initial work-focused interview with a trained personal adviser. Most then go on to attend another five work-focused interviews with the same adviser at monthly intervals. During the initial interview an action plan is agreed detailing the activities the benefit-claimant has identified to undertake, and this is reviewed at each meeting. The benefit claimant has access to Jobcentre Plus support – such as the New Deal for Disabled People – plus some extra support developed especially for Pathways to Work. Finally, a "Return to Work Credit" of £40 a week is available up to 52 weeks for people starting work for at least 16 hours a week and earning no more than £15 000 per year.

The first pilot covered around 9% of the country at the beginning of 2005 and was gradually extended to cover around 40% of the United Kingdom by December 2006. By April 2008 it will be available on a mandatory basis to all new claimants and on a voluntary basis to the existing stock of claimants.

The Welfare Reform Act 2007 has put in place reforms to incapacity benefits with the introduction of a new integrated and simplified Employment and Support Allowance (ESA), in place of the current system of incapacity benefits. ESA will be introduced in 2008. The reformed benefit will provide enhanced financial security for the most severely sick and disabled as well as more money than at present for all claimants who take part in work-focused activity.[1] The medical assessments for receiving the Incapacity Benefit (Personal Capability Assessment, PCA) will also be changed so that the focus is on the capacity that people have to move towards work, rather than on their incapacity to work at present. It will also include a mental health test. A new assessment called the "work-focused health-related assessment" will be introduced to assess what skills and abilities the claimant has, as well as to identify equipment or other special assistance that would

---

Box 3.3. **Pathways to Work** (*cont.*)

be required by people judged to be able to move back to work. During the assessment phase (lasting 3 months) the recipient will receive the Job Seekers Allowance. Once the person fulfils the PCA assessment they become eligible for the additional Employment Support, conditional upon drawing up a personal action plan focused on work-related activities. People with the most serious disabilities and health conditions would not be required to undergo work-related activities in order to receive the top-up of the allowance, but they could participate on a voluntary basis.

Early results from the Pathways to Work pilots were encouraging with around an 8 percentage point increase in the Incapacity Benefit six month off-flow rate in the pilot districts (Blyth, 2006).[2] More recently (in the second half of 2005), the off-flow rates in the pilot areas fell back to just 5 percentage points above the control group (Figure 3.11). One weakness with the Pathways to Work pilots is that most are provided on a voluntary basis and mostly to new benefit claimants, rather than to the stock of claimants. The Pathways to Work programme should also put more emphasis on mental health to be able to better help the large and growing number of incapacity benefit claimants with mental and behavioural disorders. Nevertheless, if the pilots continue to be successful and cost efficient, the programme should be extended to cover all new claimants (except those with the most serious disability and health problems) as planned and also to the stock of claimants on a mandatory basis.

Figure 3.11. **Pathways to Work increases the off-flow from incapacity benefit**[1]

Six-month off-flow rate, per cent

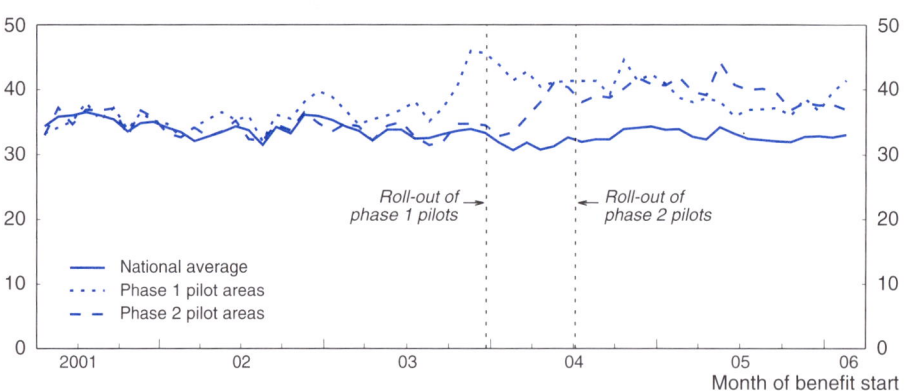

1. The off-flow rates presented are produced from the Working Age Statistical Database (WASD). WASD does not include a proportion of short-term incapacity benefit claims, therefore the off-flows presented will be lower than actual rates; however trends over time will be consistent.

Source: Department for Work and Pensions.

StatLink ⫘⫘ *http://dx.doi.org/10.1787/116255041581*

1. Those who completely refuse to engage – failing even to attend interviews – will receive the Job-Seekers Allowance, which is lower than the incapacity benefit.
2. There is typically some positive selection bias in these results because voluntary participants tend to be those who are most active in seeking work (Carcillo and Grubb, 2006).

More could also be done to prevent people from moving on to incapacity benefits in the first place. Many claimants receive incapacity benefits before a medical assessment is carried out and many also transfer automatically onto incapacity benefits after exhausting their statutory sick pay which lasts for 28 weeks. Similarly, more attention should be paid to the early sickness stage of the large number of people moving onto an incapacity benefit from a non-employment status. Better monitoring of the health status of jobseeker allowance recipients could help to identify the need for support earlier and avoid a transfer onto the incapacity benefit. Another important challenge is long-term benefit claimants: only 22% of people who have claimed an incapacity benefit for a full year move off it within the following year and 29% of them are still receiving the benefit after 8 years (DWP, 2006).

Focus on the most disadvantaged areas

A new initiative focusing on the most disadvantaged areas was introduced in 2006. The City Strategy "pathfinders" include 13 cities that will be given greater flexibility to provide individually tailored programmes to tackle the specific problems that have stopped people from working in that area and improve the attractiveness of that area through employment, skills and health initiatives.[20] The approach is based on the formation of a consortium made up of government agencies, local government and employers who will develop outcome targets negotiated between the government and the municipality. The focus will be, in particular, on the most disadvantaged individuals and is likely to include incapacity benefit claimants, lone parents, older people and those from ethnic minority groups. The consortia will join up with the work of Jobcentre Plus and Learning Skills Councils to ensure that the access to support is less complicated for individuals. It will also ensure that the available help meets the needs of local employers better, offering a clearer route from training and skill development to the workplace. Additional initial funding from the Department of Work and Pensions will be available for these areas and outcome-based funding will then be available against the agreed targets. If this first round of these "pathfinders" is successful the government intends to roll out the programme to other areas.

Box 3.4. Labour market recommendations

1. Reconsider the relative priority that is currently accorded to incentives to up-skill and work *versus* poverty reduction:

   - Consider modifications to the tax and benefit system that would reduce the marginal effective tax rate faced by lone parents and one-earner couples when extending their hours or when progressing in work.

   - Improve incentives for labour force participation by second earners by reducing the high implicit taxes on returning to work caused by high child-care cost.

   - Improve incentives to up-skill by making the child-care element of the Working Tax Credit available to low-skilled people undertaking approved courses of study, as well as those who are working.

   - As proposed in the Green Paper "In Work, Better Off", make the work test for lone parents more stringent, particularly in light of the generous child-care subsidies that are available to single income families.

2. Raise the national adult and the reduced minimum wage by less than median earnings in order to foster employment of the low-skilled. Continue to monitor job developments in low-paying sectors to make sure the minimum wage is not set at a level that reduces employment.

Box 3.4. **Labour market recommendations** (cont.)

3. Continue to extend the Pathways to Work scheme to cover all new claimants as planned and make sure that the implementation is effective.

- Extend the scheme on a mandatory basis to the stock of existing claimants if the pilots are successful and cost efficient. More public sector resources are likely to be required to implement this.

- Improve the monitoring of the health status of people reaching the end of their entitlement to sickness pay and benefits and make the medical assessment of benefit claims earlier.

- Pay more attention to the early sickness stage of the large number of people claiming incapacity benefit from a non-employment status. Better monitoring of the health status, *e.g.* of jobseeker allowance recipients, would help identify the need for support earlier and avoid a transfer onto the incapacity benefit.

- If the first round the City Strategy "pathfinders" is successful in bringing disadvantaged groups (for instance low-skilled workers) back into work in a cost-effective way then consider rolling out the programmes on a wider basis. Also since programmes tend to become less effective over a period of successful implementation, new approaches should be developed and evaluated.

4. Improve statistical monitoring of the stock of migrant labour by "cross-checking" registered workers on the Worker Registration Scheme against other databases (*e.g.* taxpayers). In addition, make registration on the Worker Registration Scheme mandatory for the self-employed as well. Consider reducing the registration fee which may deter some workers from registering.

Notes

1. Where income inequality is measured by the ratio of the 90th to the 10th percentile earnings, full-year and full-time workers.

2. Weaker real wage growth in the United States may be related to rapid growth in non-wage labour costs (*e.g.* health care costs).

3. Between 2001-03 and 2004-06 overall annual gross median full-time earnings growth slowed by just 0.1 percentage point. However, the deceleration was much larger at 3.3 percentage points in hotels and restaurants and 0.8 percentage points in other community, social and personal service activities. These industries have seen a relatively large inflow of migrant labour (calculations based on *Annual Survey of Hours and Earnings*, 2006).

4. There are a number of other factors influencing disposable income that are significant in the United Kingdom, including family formation dynamics.

5. Based on the General Household Survey the inactivity rate among prime-age males in the bottom skill quartile rose by 7.7 percentage points between 1987-91 and 2000-01, while it has only increased by 2.9 percentage points since then. For older low-skilled male workers the inactivity rate rose by 8.8 percentage points and 5.7 percentage points for the remainder. Using Labour Force Survey data, between 1987-91 and 2002 the prime-male low-skilled inactivity rate rose by 9.9 percentage points while for the remainder it increased by 0.7 percentage points. For older male workers the corresponding figures are 5.7 percentage points and 1.4 percentage points respectively (Nickell, 2004).

6. Other common reasons for reporting inactivity are studies, short-term sickness and taking care of the family.

7. According to OECD data on educational attainment, in 2004 26% of the total working-age population in the United Kingdom had a tertiary education and 31% of workers aged 25-34 years.

8. Between the introduction of the minimum wage in April 1999 and its latest rise in October 2006, the hourly rate for adult workers increased from £3.60 to £5.35 and the hourly youth rate (for 18-21-year-olds) from £3 to £4.45. In the latest round the government has agreed to raise the adult minimum wage by 3.2% to £5.52 per hour and the reduced youth rate by 3.4% to £4.60 per hour from October 2007.

9. Although there is a differentiation of the minimum wage for younger workers (aged 18-21 years), there is evidence that employers tend to pay them the full adult national minimum wage rather than the reduced rate (DTI, 2006).

10. The Commission's present view is that they will recommend increases in the minimum wage for 2008 at around the pace of average earnings growth (Low Pay Commission, 2007).

11. The 10th percentile earning premium is the difference between the average wage paid to the lowest paid 10% of full time adult workers in a sector relative to the minimum wage itself.

12. For instance, compared with the reduced minimum wage for 18-21-year-olds of £4.45 per hour, the 10th percentile earnings for 18-21-year-olds is only £4.49 per hour in construction, £4.54 per hour in sales, maintenance and repair of motor vehicles and £4.54 per hour in other community, social and personal service activities (ONS, 2006b).

13. Recent figures show that a significant proportion of those eligible have not taken up the Working Tax Credit, particularly childless working couples.

14. These data are from the Department of Work and Pensions' *Households Below Average Income (HBAI) 1994/95-2005/06 (Revised)* publication using the number of children living in households earning less than 60% of average earnings after housing costs.

15. In the United Kingdom, an increase in earnings due to a rise in hours worked is not always equivalent to the same increase coming from a higher hourly wage since there is a minimum number of hours that must be worked to be eligible for in-work benefits (the thresholds are 16 hours and 30 hours).

16. METR = 1 - (change in net income from a given earnings transition)/(change in gross income from a given earnings transition) while holding hours worked constant.

17. The Child Benefit is paid to young people under the age of 20, provided the course began before their 19th birthday.

18. The increase in the reimbursement ceiling for eligible child care from 70% to 80% of costs is not yet included in the calculation as it is based on the Tax and Benefit rules as of 2004.

19. The disadvantaged groups are: disabled people, lone parents, minority ethnic groups, older workers, the less-skilled and those living in the 30 most deprived local authority districts.

20. The cities are Birmingham, Blackburn, Dundee, Edinburgh, Glasgow, Heads of the Valleys, Leicester, Liverpool, Manchester, Nottingham, Rhyl, Sheffield, Tyne and Wear.

References

Adam, S., M. Brewer and A. Shephard (2006a), "Financial Work Incentives in Britain: Comparison over Time and between Family Types", *IFS Working Paper*, No. W06/20, Institute for Fiscal Studies, London.

Adam, S., M. Brewer and A. Shephard (2006b), *The Poverty Trade-off: Work Incentives and Income Redistribution in Britain*, Jospeh Rowntree Foundation, New York.

Andersson, T. (2006), "Globalisation Challenges for Europe – Labour Market Perspectives", *Globalisation Challenges for Europe*, Prime Minister's Office Publications, No. 18/2006, Helsinki.

Blanchflower, D.G., J. Saleheen and C. Shadforth (2007), "The Impact of the Recent Migration from Eastern Europe on the UK Economy", *Discussion Paper*, No. 17, Bank of England, London.

Blyth, B. (2006), "Incapacity Benefit Reforms – Pathways to Work Pilots Performance and Analysis", *Working Paper*, No. 26, Department for Work and Pensions, London.

Brewer, M. *et al.* (2007), "Did Working Families' Tax Credit Work? The Impact of In-work Support on Labour Supply in Great Britain", *Labour Economics*, Vol. 13, No. 6, Elsevier BV.

Carcillo, S. and D. Grubb (2006), "From Inactivity to Work: The Role of Active Labour Market Policies", *OECD Social, Employment and Migration Working Papers*, No. 36, OECD, Paris.

Dolado, J. et al. (1996), "The Economic Impact of Minimum Wages in Europe", *Economic Policy, No. 23.*

Draper, D. (2006), "Families Compared 2006/07", *CARE Research Paper,* Christian Action Research and Education, London.

DTI (Department of Trade and Industry) (2006), *Government Evidence to the Low Pay Commission on the the National Minimum Wage,* Department of Trade and Industry, London.

DWP (Department for Work and Pensions) (2006), *A New Deal for Welfare: Empowering People to Work,* Welfare Reform Green Paper, Department for Work and Pensions, The Stationary Office, London.

DWP (2007), *In Work, Better off: Next Steps to Full Employment,* Green Paper, Department for Work and Pensions, The Stationary Office, London.

European Commission (2005), *The EU Economy: 2005 Review,* European Economy, No. 6, Office for Official Publications of the European Communities, Luxembourg.

Feenstra, R. and G. Hansen (1999), "The Impact of Outsourcing and High-Technology Capital on Wages: Estimates for the United States", *Quarterly Journal of Economics,* Vol. 114, No. 3, The MIT Press, Cambridge MA.

Freud, D. (2007), "Reducing Dependency, Increasing Opportunity: Options for the Future of Welfare to Work", Independent Report to the Department for Work and Pensions, available at: *www.dwp.gov.uk/publications/dwp/2007/welfarereview.pdf.*

Gilpin, N. et al. (2006), "The Impact of Free Movement of Workers from Central and Eastern Europe on the UK Labour Market", *Working Paper,* No. 29, Department for Work and Pensions, London.

Gregg, P. (2000), "The Use of Wage Floors as Policy Tools", *OECD Economic Studies,* Vol. 2000/2, No. 31, OECD, Paris.

Hijzen, A. (2004), "Trade in Intermediates and the Rise in Wage Inequality in the UK: A GNP Function Approach", *GEP Research Paper,* No. 04/03, Leverhulme Centre for Research on Globalisation and Economic Policy, University of Nottingham.

Hirsch, D. (2006), *What Will it Take to End Child Poverty? Firing on All Cylinders,* Joseph Rowntree Foundation, New York.

Home Office (2006), *Accession Monitoring Report, May 2004 – September 2006,* Joint on-line report by the Home Office, Department for Work and Pensions, HM Revenue and Customs, and Department for Communities and Local Government, available at: *www.ind.homeoffice.gov.uk/aboutus/reports/accession_monitoring_report.*

Kongsrud, P.M. and I. Wanner (2005), "The Impact of Structural Policies on Trade-Related Adjustment and the Shift to Services", *OECD Economics Department Working Papers,* No. 427, OECD, Paris.

Low Pay Commission (2007), *National Minimum Wage. Low Pay Commission Report 2007,* The Stationary Office, London.

Machin, S., A. Manning and L. Rahman (2003), "Where the Minimum Wage Bites Hard: Introduction of Minimum Wages to a Low Wage Sector", *Journal of the European Economic Association,* No. 1, The MIT Press, Cambridge MA.

Meghir, C. and D. Phillips (2007), "Labour Supply and Taxes", draft paper prepared for the IFS Conference on "Reforming the Tax System for the 21st Century: The Mirrlees Review", Cambridge, 12 April, available at: *www.ifs.org.uk/mirrleesreview/publications.php.*

Neumark, D. and W. Wascher (1999), "A Cross-National Analysis of the Effects of Minimum Wages on Youth Employment", *NBER Working Papers,* No. 7299, National Bureau of Economic Research, Cambridge MA.

Nickell, S. (2004), "Poverty and Worklessness in Britain", *The Economic Journal,* Vol. 114, No. 494, Blackwell Publishing.

OECD (1998), *Employment Outlook,* OECD, Paris.

OECD (2005a), *OECD Economic Surveys: United Kingdom,* OECD, Paris.

OECD (2005b), *OECD Employment Outlook,* OECD, Paris.

OECD (2005c), *Babies and Bosses: Reconciling Work and Family Life,* Vol. 4, OECD, Paris.

OECD (2006a), *OECD Employment Outlook,* OECD, Paris.

OECD (2006b), *Taxing Wages,* OECD, Paris.

OECD (2007a), *Going for Growth*, Economic Reforms, OECD, Paris.

OECD (2007b), *Sickness, Disability and Work: Breaking the Barriers. Australia, Luxembourg, Spain and the United Kingdom,* Vol. 2, OECD, Paris, forthcoming.

ONS (Office for National Statistics) (2006a), "Over 500 a Day Gained Through Migration to the UK", *News Release*, 2 November, Office for National Statistics, London.

ONS (2006b), *Annual Survey of Hours and Earnings (ASHE) – 2006 Results*, on-line edition, Office for National Statistics, available at: *www.statistics.gov.uk*.

Palmer, G., T. MacInnes and P. Kenway (2006), *Monitoring Poverty and Social Exclusion 2006*, Joseph Rowntree Foundation, New York.

Phillips, D. and L. Sibieta (2006), "A Survey of the UK Benefit System", *IFS Briefing Note*, No. BN13, Institute for Fiscal Studies, London.

Saleheen, J. and C. Shadforth (2006), "The Economic Characteristics of Immigrants and their Impact on Supply", *Quarterly Bulletin*, Vol. 46, No. 4, Bank of England, London.

Stewart, M.B. (2002), "Estimating the Impact of the Minimum Wage Using Geographical Wage Variation", *Oxford Bulletin of Economics and Statistics*, Vol. 64, Blackwell Publishing.

Whiteford, P. and W. Adema (2007), "What Works Best in Reducing Child Poverty: A Benefit or Work Strategy", *OECD Social, Employment and Migration Working Papers*, No. 51, OECD, Paris.

ANNEX 3.A1

Migration data

Nationals from the eight new EU member countries (A8) that joined the Union in 2004,[*] who wish to work for more than one month for an employer in the United Kingdom need to register under the Worker Registration Scheme (WRS) which provides a source of the inflow of immigrants. Once a worker has been working legally in the United Kingdom for 12 months without a break he/she has full rights of free movement and will no longer need to register on the Worker Registration Scheme administered by the Home Office. Workers who are self-employed do not need to register and are therefore not included in these figures. The cost to register is £70 for the first application. Failure to register within a month of starting to work implies that the employment is illegal. One important caveat with the WRS data is that it measures gross flows only since there is no need to de-register if a worker leaves the country. Thus, the total number of registrations is not a good measure for the stock of A8 immigrants in the United Kingdom. The data used in this survey refers to applicants rather than applications to WRS. Applicants have to register more than once if they are employed by more than one employer and they have to re-register if they change employer. Thus each application to the WRS measures one job, not one applicant. To avoid counting each applicant more than once each applicant is represented only once in the data with information relating to his/her first employment and since May 2004 until September 2006 a total number of 487 000 applicants registered in the WRS (Home Office, 2006).

The International Passenger Survey (IPS) is a voluntary survey (random sample) of passengers entering and leaving the United Kingdom by main air and sea ports and the Channel Tunnel. The IPS questions annually a quarter of a million passengers passing through the United Kingdom. The survey is based on the respondent's planned length of stay and considers a migrant a person who changes her/his country of residence for at least a year. The survey includes questions about age, gender, marital status, citizenship and country of last residence. The advantage of the IPS is that it provides an estimate of net

---

[*] Czech Republic, Estonia, Hungary, Latvia, Lithuania, Poland, Slovak Republic and Slovenia. Cyprus[1, 2] and Malta also joined the EU in 2004 but their nationals have full rights of free movement and work.

  1. Footnote by Turkey: The information in this document under the heading "Cyprus" relates to the southern part of the Island. There is no single authority representing both Turkish and Greek Cypriot people on the Island. Turkey recognises the Turkish Republic of Northern Cyprus (TRNC). Until a lasting and equitable solution is found within the context of the United Nations, Turkey shall preserve its position concerning the "Cyprus" issue.

  2. Footnote by all the European Union Member States of the OECD and the European Commission: The Republic of Cyprus is recognised by all members of the United Nations with the exception of Turkey. The information in this document relates to the area under the effective control of the Government of the Republic of Cyprus.

flows since it measures those who leave as well as those who enter the United Kingdom. The estimated net number of A8 citizens migrating into the United Kingdom for a period of at least a year was 132 000 in 2005 (based on International Passenger Surveys) which is considerably lower than the estimate from the WRS (Blanchflower *et al.*, 2007). But the exclusion of short-term visitors from the number of long-term migrants may account for the lower estimate compared to the WRS data. According to the Office for National Statistics the number of short-term travellers who intended to stay less than 3 months from the A8 countries accounted for 89% of all A8 travellers coming into the United Kingdom through 2006 (Blanchflower *et al.*, 2007; ONS 2006).

National Insurance number allocation to overseas nationals is another source of migration data. National insurance numbers (NINos) are required for employment and self-employment and to claim benefits and tax credits. The Department for Work and Pensions (DWP) is responsible for allocating NINos to overseas nationals who apply for their number through their local Job Centre Plus office. An interview is held at the local office where an application form is completed and documentation examined. This may include checking the authenticity of passports and visas with ultra-violet lighting (DWP, 2006). The DWP controls the evidence supplied at the interview and checks that the employer is genuine and has made a job offer and also controls that a NINo has not already been allocated to the applicant. Registrations of A8 nationals increased from 111 000 to 271 000 between 2004/05 and 2005/06. This estimate is closer to the WRS data than the IPS data and the difference may be due to different time periods covered and the inclusion of self-employed in the NINos (Blanchflower *et al.*, 2007).

The Labour Force Survey (LFS) provides a large range of data on labour market statistics and related topics. It is feasible to obtain estimates of the stock of accession county migrants resident in the United Kingdom from the LFS. However, the LFS is likely to underestimate the stock of immigrants in the United Kingdom, particularly those who have been there for less than 6 months and those living in communal households (Gilpin *et al.*, 2006). Estimates by Blanchflower *et al.* (2007) and Gilpin *et al.* (2006) suggest that around 375 000 nationals from A8 countries were resident in the United Kingdom in September 2006 and around 265 000 had arrived since 2004.

Thus, the actual number of migrants that have entered the United Kingdom since the opening up of the borders seems quite uncertain given the available data. Estimates trying to reconcile the differences in the coverage of data, both in the terms of migrants captured and time conclude that 500 000 is likely to be an upper bound of the number of A8 migrants that could potentially be in the United Kingdom in late 2006 (Blanchflower *et al.*, 2007).

Characteristics of the immigrants

Between the opening up of the border and September 2006 the number of people registering on the WRS was almost 500 000 out of which the majority were Polish (63%), followed by Lithuanians (11%) and Slovaks (10%) (Home Office, 2006). Precisely the same A8 nationality proportions are recorded registering for a national insurance in 2005/06. Most workers who register in the WRS are young and the majority are male workers. Of all registered workers in the WRS 82% were aged 18-34 with more than 40% in the younger 18-24 age bracket. NINo registrations confirm that most immigrants are young and male (DWP, 2006). Based on the 2005 LFS data Saleheen and Shadforth (2006) found that new immigrants are younger than earlier waves of immigrants suggesting that they have few years of work experience. This suggests that immigrant workers may be substitutable for younger native workers. It also appears that the A8 immigrants have relatively high levels of education or qualifications in comparison with natives (Blanchflower *et al.*, 2007; Saleheen and Shadforth, 2006). Estimates on the basis of the age at which they left full-time education using LFS data suggest that 45% of the accession country immigrants have degrees while only 17% of the UK born population has a degree and 66% of the UK population have only completed upper-secondary school while the corresponding number for recent immigrants is 52% (Saleheen and Shadforth, 2006).

The number of applicants in the WRS has increased over time in all regions and was largest in the East followed by the Midlands and London (Tables 3.A1.1 and 3.A1.2). Also

Table 3.A1.1. **Number of registrations in the worker registration scheme**

	Total number of registrations							Unemployment rate[1] (%)	Change between 2005 and 2006 (% points)	
	Thousands				Percentage share					
	2004	2005	2006	Total (2004-06)	2005	2006	Total (2004-06)	2006	Unemployment rate[1]	Registrations
East	21.9	29.9	31.2	83.0	14.6	13.9	15.0	4.8	0.8	−0.7
Midlands	11.7	26.8	32.6	71.0	13.1	14.5	12.8	5.6	1.0	1.5
London	25.5	23.5	21.2	70.1	11.4	9.5	12.6	7.9	0.9	−2.0
Yorkshire and Humber	13.9	20.6	21.0	55.5	10.1	9.4	10.0	5.8	1.0	−0.7
North East	9.1	21.4	25.0	55.4	10.4	11.1	10.0	6.5	0.1	0.7
North West	7.7	19.1	23.5	50.3	9.3	10.5	9.1	5.3	0.6	1.2
South West	9.7	18.2	21.1	48.9	8.9	9.4	8.8	3.8	0.2	0.5
Scotland	8.2	15.9	18.8	42.8	7.8	8.4	7.7	5.2	−0.2	0.6
South East	11.2	13.7	13.1	38.0	6.7	5.9	6.8	4.5	0.6	−0.8
Northern Ireland	3.7	8.8	8.8	21.3	4.3	3.9	3.8	..	..	−0.4
Wales	2.4	5.5	6.8	14.7	2.7	3.0	2.6	5.3	0.6	0.3
Not stated	1.0	1.6	1.3	3.9	0.8	0.6	0.7	..	..	−0.2
Total	**125.9**	**205.0**	**224.2**	**555.0**	100.0	100.0	100.0	..	..	..

1. Total unemployment rate for each region.
Source: National Statistics website, *Labour Market Statistics*, *www.statistics.gov.uk* and Home Office (2007), *Accession Monitoring Report, May 2004-December 2006.*

Table 3.A1.2. **National insurance number registrations**

	Total number of registrations					Unemployment rate[1] (%)	Change (% points)	
	Thousands			Percentage share			Unemployment rate[1]	Registrations
	2002/03	2004/05	2005/06	2004/05	2005/06	2006	2005-06	2004/05-2005/06
North East	5.4	7.3	11.1	1.7	1.7	6.5	0.1	0.0
North West	21.8	30.7	48.9	7.0	7.4	5.3	0.6	0.4
Yorkshire and Humber	17.9	20.2	36.6	4.6	5.5	5.8	1.0	0.9
East Midlands	13.4	23.5	38.5	5.3	5.8	5.4	1.0	0.5
West Midlands	23.4	28.1	41.7	6.4	6.3	5.9	1.0	−0.1
East	26.2	34.1	52.8	7.8	8.0	4.8	0.8	0.2
London	148.0	167.2	235.6	38.0	35.6	7.9	0.9	−2.4
South East	37.5	50.7	79.9	11.5	12.1	4.5	0.6	0.5
South West	15.4	22.6	33.7	5.1	5.1	3.8	0.2	−0.1
Wales	5.4	9.9	16.4	2.3	2.5	5.3	0.6	0.2
Scotland	14.5	22.9	41.4	5.2	6.3	5.2	−0.2	1.0
Northern Ireland	2.5	5.5	16.3	1.3	2.5	..	..	1.2
Not stated	17.8	17.1	9.4	3.9	1.4	..	..	−2.5
Total	**349.2**	**439.8**	**662.4**	100.0	100.0	..	..	..

1. Total unemployment rate for each region.
Source: National Statistics website, *Labour Market Statistics*, *www.statistics.gov.uk* and DWP (2006), *National Insurance Number Allocations to Overseas Nationals Entering the UK.*

according to the NINo registrations immigration has increased in all regions but the numbers were especially high in London and the South East. It appears that the increase in immigration is largest in regions with lower unemployment. The dominant occupations among recent immigrants are less skilled occupations such as factory workers which was the most common occupation registered in the WRS followed by warehouse operatives and kitchen and catering assistants. The top five industries registered in the WRS were administration, business and management (35%), hospitality and catering (21%), agriculture (12%), manufacturing (7%) and food, fish and meat processing (5%). The majority of workers, 78%, were earning between £4.50 and £5.99 per hour (Home Office, 2006). Thus, the new immigrants appear to have a relatively high level of education but they are more likely to be working in low-skilled, low-paid jobs.

References

Blanchflower, D.G., J. Saleheen and C. Shadforth (2007), "The Impact of the Recent Migration from Eastern Europe on the UK Economy", *Discussion Paper*, No. 17, Bank of England.

DWP (Department for Work and Pensions) (2006), *A New Deal for Welfare: Empowering People to Work*, Welfare Reform Green Paper, Department for Work and Pensions, The Stationary Office, London.

Gilpin, N. *et al.* (2006), "The Impact of Free Movement of Workers From Central and Eastern Europe on the UK Labour Market", *Working Paper*, No. 29, Department for Work and Pensions, London.

Home Office (2006), *Accession Monitoring Report, May 2004 – September 2006,* Joint on-line report by the Home Office, Department for Work and Pensions, HM Revenue and Customs, and Department for Communities and Local Government, available at: *www.ind.homeoffice.gov.uk/aboutus/reports/ accession_monitoring_report*.

ONS (Office of National Statistics) (2006), "Labour Market Statistics", *First Release*, November, Office for National Statistics, London.

Saleheen, J. and C. Shadforth (2006), "The Economic Characteristics of Immigrants and their Impact on Supply", *Quarterly Bulletin*, Vol. 46, No. 4, Bank of England, London.

ISBN 978-92-64-03772-4
OECD Economic Surveys: United Kingdom
© OECD 2007

Chapter 4

Addressing the productivity gap

The United Kingdom has recorded strong productivity growth over the past decade, surpassing the performance of many continental European countries and thereby narrowing the productivity gap. However, despite narrowing substantially in the early 1990s, the productivity gap with the United States has remained unchanged more recently. While overall the United Kingdom has some of the least restrictive product and labour market regulations, it needs to guard against increasing red tape and tax complexities which can raise the costs of doing business. Restrictive planning regulations make entry of new firms in retailing difficult and inefficient land use raises property prices. Poor transport infrastructure is another potential factor reducing productivity growth, while R&D spending and adult training are relatively low.

The United Kingdom has enjoyed strong productivity growth over the past decade. With its relatively free product and labour markets, the country has been in a good position to benefit from the opportunities offered by globalisation. In general, globalisation is seen as an opportunity to promote productivity growth through greater competition and by permitting firms to specialise in areas where they have a comparative advantage. However, despite the UK's recent good performance, it must go further in a number of areas to ensure it continues to reap the benefits from globalisation. First, restrictive planning and land usage regulations may be holding back entry of new firms, thus hindering adjustment that can promote productivity growth; second, the increasing regulatory burdens on businesses from increasing tax complexities and red tape can raise the costs of doing business; third, there is evidence of underinvestment by both government and business in a number of areas including investment in research and development and transport infrastructure, as well as investment in the skills of the labour force. Research and development may be insufficient for moving up the value-added chain while poor transport infrastructure may be slowing productivity growth by raising transportation costs and by making the labour market less flexible. The relatively low skill level of the workforce could hamper the re-location of labour from declining to expanding sectors and hinder the workforce from fully absorbing new technologies and making the most of knowledge spillovers. Finally, there is also some evidence that lower management skills in the United Kingdom may be hampering faster improvements in productivity. This chapter first highlights recent trends in productivity performance and then discusses potential improvements to policies in these areas.

Labour productivity growth has slowed down slightly

The UK's average labour productivity growth, as measured by the OECD and calculated on a per hour basis, slowed slightly during 2000-05 compared to the previous five-year period (Table 4.1) although cyclical factors may have played a role.[1] Even so productivity grew faster than in many continental European economies, narrowing the gap in productivity levels with the leading European countries. On the other hand, productivity growth accelerated in the United States. Since 2000, the UK's average growth in output per hour is estimated to have been 0.6 percentage points lower than that in the United States (Figure 4.1).

Table 4.1 also illustrates that most labour productivity growth in the United Kingdom since the mid-1980s has been generated by multifactor productivity (MFP) growth and that the most significant explanation for the recent shortfall in the UK's average labour productivity growth relative to that in the United States is a deficit in MFP growth. Similar conclusions are drawn by Escolano (2003). Nonetheless, in comparison with most other G7 economies the UK's MFP growth was fast.

Table 4.1. **Output and productivity growth and the components of output growth**

Per cent

	United Kingdom	United States	Canada	France	Germany[1]	Italy	Japan
GDP growth							
1985-90	**3.2**	3.2	2.8	3.2	. .	3.1	4.7
1990-95	**1.6**	2.4	1.7	1.2	1.5	1.3	1.5
1995-00	**3.1**	4.1	4.0	2.8	2.0	1.9	1.0
2000-05	**2.4**	2.4	2.5	1.5	0.6	0.7	1.3
Labour productivity per hour worked (A + B)							
1985-90	**1.4**	1.3	0.4	2.7	. .	2.1	4.2
1990-95	**2.8**	1.2	1.4	2.0	2.4	2.4	2.3
1995-00	**2.3**	2.2	2.3	2.1	2.0	0.9	2.1
2000-05	**1.9**	2.5	1.1	1.5	1.3	0.0	2.2
Multifactor productivity growth (A)							
1985-90	**0.8**	0.8	−0.4	1.9	. .	1.4	3.2
1990-95	**1.6**	0.7	0.6	1.1	1.4	1.5	1.0
1995-00	**1.5**	1.3	1.5	1.4	1.3	0.3	0.8
2000-05	**1.3**	1.8	0.4	0.8	0.7	−0.7	1.4
Contribution of factor inputs to labour productivity growth (B)[2]							
1985-90	**0.6**	0.5	0.8	0.8	. .	0.8	1.0
1990-95	**1.2**	0.5	0.9	0.9	0.9	0.9	1.3
1995-00	**0.8**	0.8	0.7	0.7	0.7	0.6	1.2
2000-05	**0.6**	0.7	0.6	0.7	0.6	0.7	0.8

1. 1991-95 instead of 1990-95.
2. The factor shares are the share of labour and capital in total factor costs measured at current prices. Compensation of labour corresponds to the compensation of employees and the compensation of capital input is the value of capital services (measured by the user cost of capital services times the quantity of capital services).
Source: OECD (2007), Productivity database, April, www.oecd.org/statistics/productivity.

There is a productivity gap in most industries, but it is largest in the service sectors

The sizeable productivity gap relative to the United States is due largely to poor performance in a few service sectors, notably wholesale and retail trade, business services, and to a lesser extent financial intermediation (Figure 4.2, upper panel).[2] Together they account for almost 60% of the total productivity gap. While the service sectors account for the majority of the productivity gap, manufacturing also accounts for around 20% of the total gap. Other studies have similarly emphasised the importance of the service sectors in this regard; Griffith et al. (2003) found that about one-third of the total productivity gap in 2001 relative to the United States was accounted for by wholesale and retail trade and financial intermediation, and Basu et al. (2003) found that wholesale and retail trade accounted for about three quarters of the acceleration in US MFP growth in the late 1990s and one-third of the UK's deceleration. Moreover, despite the lower level of productivity in these sectors the evidence below suggests that they have not been catching up. Indeed, labour productivity growth per employee has lagged behind that of the United States in most industries during the past decade (Figure 4.2, lower panel), particularly in manufacturing and in low-skilled services such as wholesale and retail.

Figure 4.1. **Labour productivity**

Measured by the gap in GDP per hour worked relative to the United States[1]

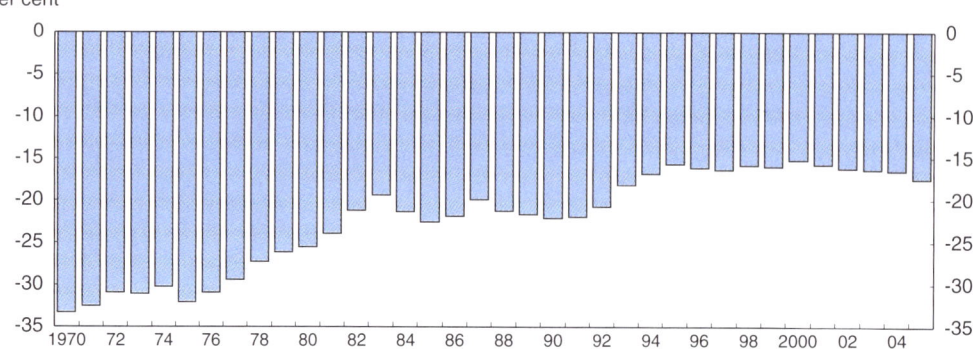

Evolution of the United Kingdom gap
Per cent

International comparison

Average % growth,[2]
1995-2005

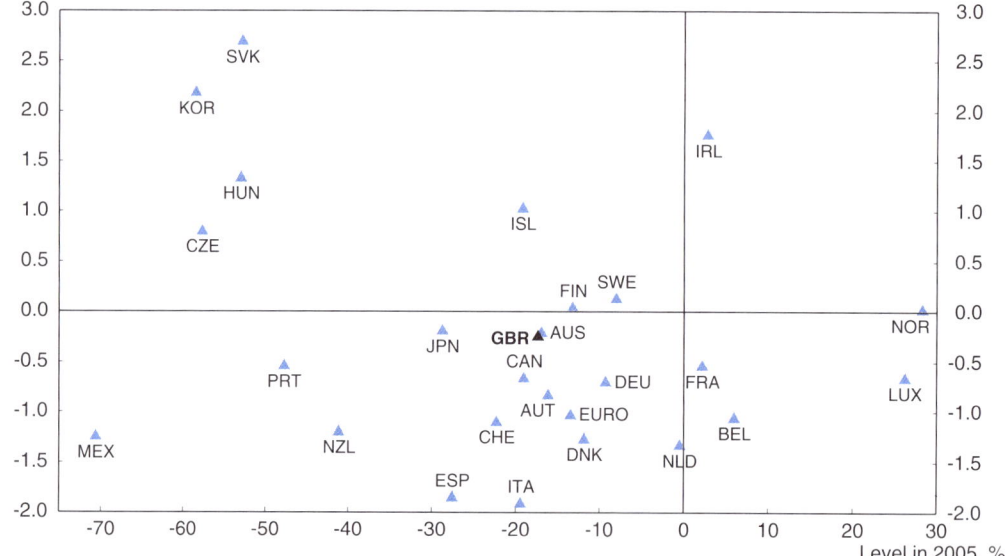

Level in 2005, %

1. GDP in volume converted to US dollars using constant purchasing power parities.
2. Compound annual rate.

Source: OECD (2007), *Productivity database*, March, *www.oecd.org/statistics/productivity*.

StatLink ⚙ *http://dx.doi.org/10.1787/116363005347*

Restrictive planning regulations hinder productivity growth by limiting new firm entry

There is evidence that a large fraction of labour productivity and total factor productivity growth at the industry level is accounted for by the reallocation of outputs and inputs from less productive to more productive firms (Disney *et al.*, 2003) (Figure 4.3, upper panel).[3] Indeed, firm turnover, which is a good proxy for the reallocation of resources, is higher in most UK sectors than in the majority of European countries (Figure 4.3, middle panel). However, within the United Kingdom, firm turnover in retail and wholesale trade is low compared with other sectors (Figure 4.3, lower panel).[4] Foster *et al.* (2002) found that productivity growth in US retailing has been largely due to the entry and exit of new stores,

Figure 4.2. **Productivity gap relative to the United States**
Per cent

Contribution to the overall productivity gap[1]
In selected industries

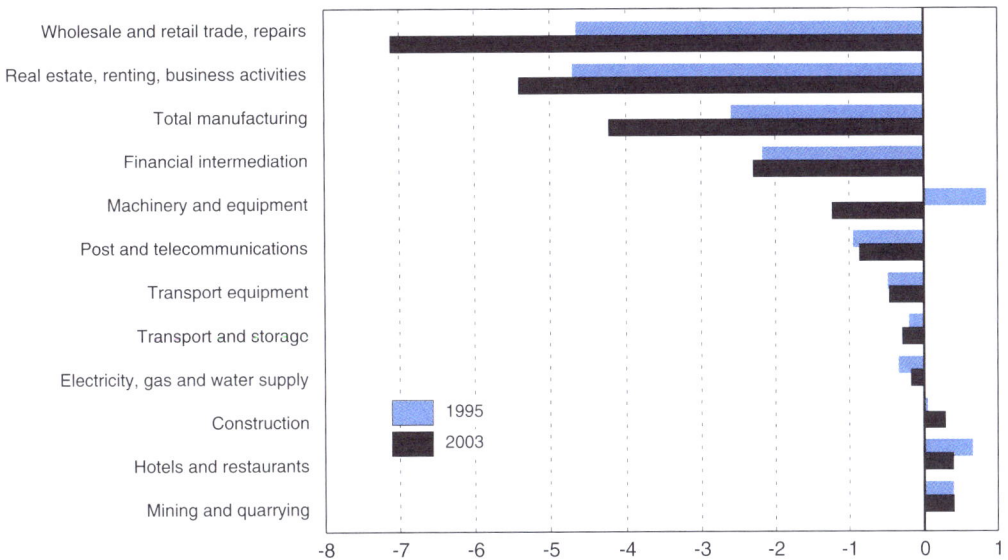

Labour productivity growth per employee [2]
In selected sectors, 1995-2003

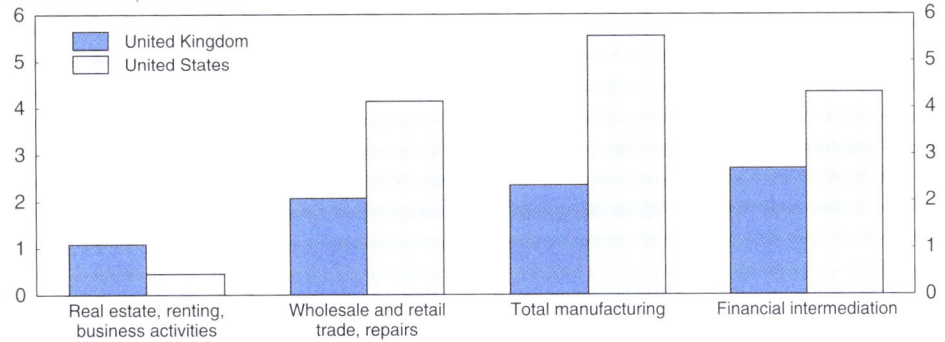

1. Productivity measured as value added per employee, converted to US dollars using 2000 purchasing power parities and weighted by employment share.
2. Using current purchasing power parities.

Source: Calculations based on the OECD (2006), *Structural Analysis (STAN) database, www.oecd.org/sti/stan.*

StatLink 🔗 *http://dx.doi.org/10.1787/116364431428*

rather than productivity growth in incumbent stores, suggesting that low turnover in retail could be a factor explaining low productivity in this sector in the United Kingdom.

Previous *Economic Surveys* have identified restrictive planning regulations as a key factor curtailing the entry of new businesses, particularly large-format operators, in the wholesale and retail sector. For example, the World Bank *Doing Business* database ranks the United Kingdom 24th in the OECD in terms of the number of procedures required for a construction business to build a standard warehouse (Figure 4.4). These procedures include those required to obtain all necessary licenses and permits, receive all required inspections, complete all required notifications and submit the relevant documents (for example, building plans and site maps) to the authorities.

Figure 4.3. **Firm turnover and labour productivity**[1]

Firm turnover and average labour productivity

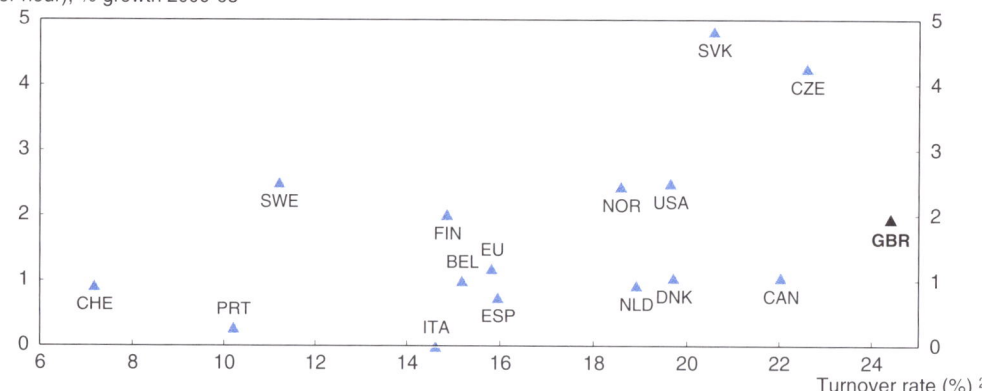

Comparison of turnover: United Kingdom and EU

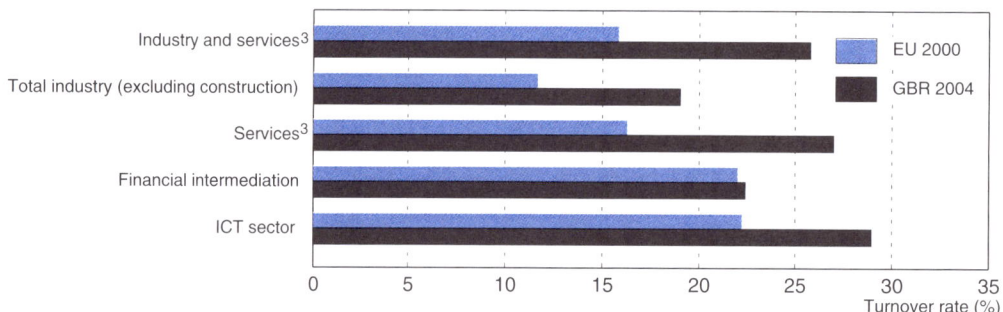

Turnover in the United Kingdom

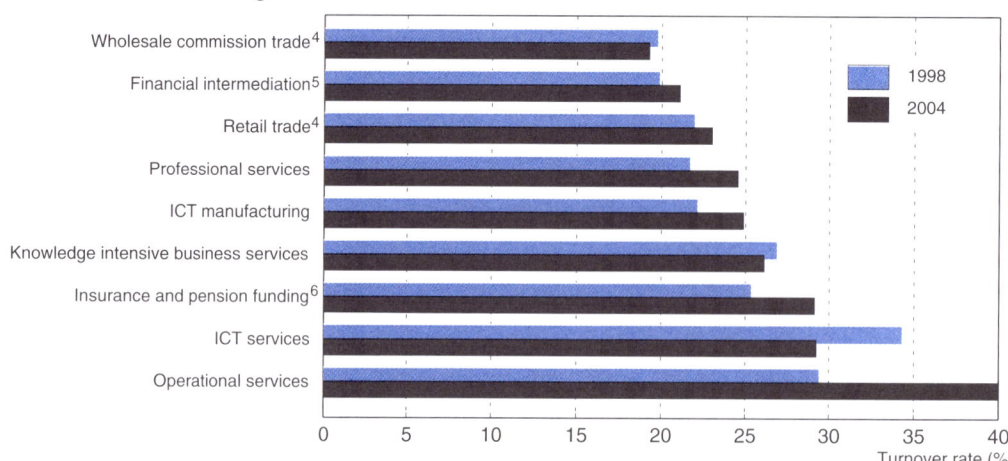

1. The turnover rate is calculated as the sum of births and deaths of firms over the total number of active firms.
2. 2003 or latest year available: United States 1996; Canada 1997; Belgium 1998; Denmark, EU and Norway 2000; Netherlands and Portugal 2002.
3. Excluding public administration and management activities of holding companies.
4. Excluding motor vehicles and motorcycles. Retail trade also excludes repair of personal and household goods.
5. Excluding insurance and pension funding.
6. Excluding compulsory social security.

Source: Eurostat database, Structural Business Statistics, September 2007; OECD Firm-Level Data Project, *www.oecd.org/eco/firmleveldataproject*; OECD (2007), *Productivity database*, March, *www.oecd.org/statistics/productivity*.

StatLink 🔗 *http://dx.doi.org/10.1787/116410527078*

OECD ECONOMIC SURVEYS: UNITED KINGDOM – ISBN 978-92-64-03772-4 – © OECD 2007

Figure 4.4. **Procedures for a business in the construction industry**

Number of procedures for building a warehouse, 2006[1]

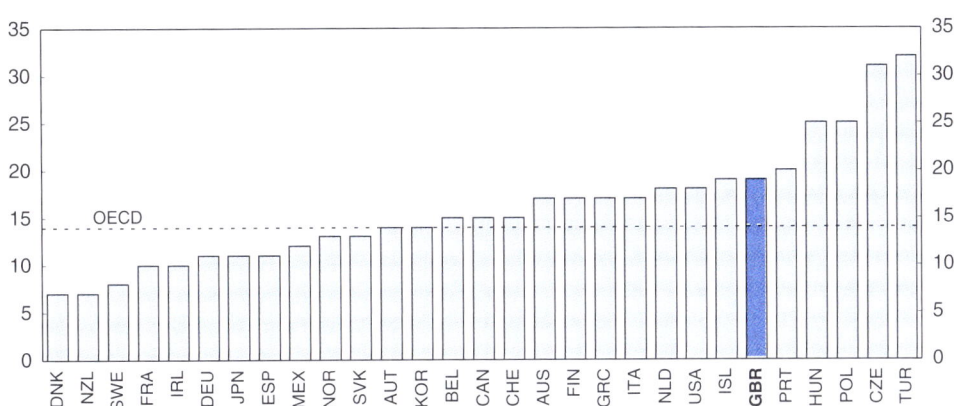

1. All procedures required to build a standardised warehouse as an example of dealing with licenses. No data is available for Luxembourg.

Source: World Bank and International Finance Corporation (2007), *Doing Business* – online database, *www.doingbusiness.org.*

StatLink 🔍 *http://dx.doi.org/10.1787/116432484314*

Firm entry in the retail and wholesale sector is also impeded by the "town-centre first" policy which is intended to protect the vitality and viability of town centres by giving planning preference to town centre sites. Since the introduction of this policy in 1996 the percentage of retail floorspace constructed in town centres has steadily increased; the percentage of small shops has increased by 8 percentage points; and the median size of stores belonging to a large supermarket chain fell from 75 employees in 1997/98 to 56 employees in 2002/03 (Haskel and Sadun, 2007). By contrast, large store formats and edge-of-town or out-of-town developments, which tend to be lower cost, have suffered (Griffith and Harmgart, 2005; Haskel and Sadun, 2007).

Within the "town centre first" policy, applications for retail outside the town centre that have not been previously anticipated in local plans are subject to both a "needs test" and a "sequential test". The needs test assesses the future market demand for additional retail floor space based on population levels, forecast expenditure on specific goods and retail space productivity growth. The sequential approach implies that preference should first be given to town centre sites, followed by edge-of-centre and then out-of-centre sites. In addition, in the 2005 government guidance for planning (Planning for Town Centres), local authorities are instructed to include in their development plans policies on maximum gross floorspace for different types of centres. All of these policies are likely to have reduced outlet size, adversely affecting productivity. Indeed, there is evidence showing that larger retailers have higher labour productivity in the United Kingdom (Haskel and Khawaja, 2003) and a recent study by Haskel and Sadun (2007) suggests that the fall in within-chain shop size in UK retailing was associated with a lowering of total factor productivity (TFP) growth by about 0.4% (corresponding to about 40% of the post-1995 slowdown in UK retail TFP growth of about 1%). Since firm turnover appears to be relatively low in UK retailing, restrictive regulation may also have hindered the opening of new stores and the closing of older less productive stores.

The Barker Review of Land Use Planning (Barker, 2006) (Box 4.1) recommended that planning should give more weight to economic issues in its decision making and that a

---

Box 4.1. **The Barker Review of Land Use Planning**

The Barker Review was an independent review of the land use planning system of England, focusing on the link between planning and economic growth. The review looked into how, in the context of globalisation, planning policy and procedures can better deliver economic growth and prosperity alongside other sustainable development goals. In particular it assessed ways of further improving the efficiency and speed of the system and ways of increasing the flexibility, transparency and predictability that businesses require. Another goal was to assess the relationship between planning and productivity and the relationship between economic and other sustainable development goals in the delivery of sustainable communities.

The recommendations targeting flexibility and responsiveness aim to ensure that regional and local plan documents are as timely as possible and that they take full account of the requirements of economic growth alongside social and environmental needs. The second set of recommendations focuses on the efficiency of the process with the aim of achieving an improved framework for the delivery of major infrastructure projects, a simpler national policy framework and decision-making processes focused on outcomes. The final set of recommendations deals with the more efficient use of land. Two important suggestions are for changes to encourage business property to be kept in use and to provide incentives for the use of vacant previously developed land, and for a review of green belt boundaries to ensure that they remain appropriate given sustainable development needs, including regeneration.

---

more positive approach to development should be taken in cases where local plans were indeterminate or out-of-date. In relation to retail development, it also concludes that the needs test has most likely limited retail choice and resulted in higher prices while restricting the expansion of stores beyond the town centre that could enter the market without harming the town centre itself. Thus it recommended removing the needs test for market demand, which can add up to £50 000 to planning fees, from the town-centre-first policy.

The government has recently released a White Paper in response to the Barker Review (HM Government, 2007). Like the Barker Review, the White Paper makes explicit reference to the desirability that planning policy be formulated with a view to its potential to promote productivity. The major recommendation of the White Paper is the implementation of a new single planning regime for major infrastructure projects with the view to streamlining the planning approval process. Additionally, while supporting a town centre first policy, the White Paper foreshadows the removal of the requirement for applications to meet a town centre "impact test" and a "needs test" which inhibit competition and consumer choice.

Policies to encourage a more efficient use of land

Inefficient land use has probably contributed much to the long-term upward trend in real house and property prices, exacerbating problems of affordability. In 2004, the cost of living in London (based on prices and/or rents of inner-city apartments typically bought or rented) was the highest among the major large cities in the OECD, reducing London's strong position as an attractive business location (OECD, 2006a).[5] The Barker Review suggested that the re-development of low-productivity agricultural land would have the least environmental or wider social impact. While this land is often located close to cities and towns, much of it is currently classified as part of the green belt, leading to the recommendation that regional and local planning bodies should review their green belt boundaries. This recommendation makes a lot of sense, although strong political leadership and a change in public perception may be required to confront opposition from environmental lobbyists and from rural residents, especially in light of a widespread misconception of the scale of current development. Although only 17% of respondents in a survey conducted for the review think that it is important to protect low-productivity agricultural land from development, about half the population thinks that at least half of all land in England is developed, even though it actually is only 13%, the same size as the green belts (EUI, 2007; Barker, 2006). However the government's White Paper response to the Barker Review explicitly rules out a change to the government's current "green belt" policy.

In the 2007 Budget the government announced steps to reform tax exemptions on vacant and unused commercial land by shortening the exemption period and by applying the shortened exemption period more uniformly across different types of properties. The government has also signalled its intention to examine whether other rates and charges should apply to vacant and derelict land.[6] These changes should go some way towards increasing the productive utilisation of land and reducing speculative behaviour. While good early progress has been made in tackling these issues, the government needs to formulate an explicit strategy outlining how it plans to implement the balance of the Barker Review's recommendations particularly with regard to freeing up land for active commercial use, as well as for housing.

Low overall product market restrictions but growing tax complexities and red tape

Since the mid-1990s, business sector labour productivity growth seems to have increased by less in countries where the regulatory stance was more restrictive (Figure 4.5). A recent OECD study suggests that this is largely because competition-restraining regulations slow the rate of catch-up with the technological frontier (Conway *et al.*, 2006). In the United Kingdom, product market regulation is among the least restrictive in the OECD. However, the United Kingdom must be vigilant against increasing complexities in the tax system (see Chapter 5) and more red tape. While these factors add to the regulatory burden of businesses, they are not captured by the OECD indicator of product market regulation.

Tax complexities and "red tape" may hinder productivity

Tax administration and compliance can be a significant cost to businesses. While the statutory corporate tax rate is the lowest among the G7 economies, many European countries have cut the tax rate in recent years, so that the United Kingdom has lost tax competitiveness. Chapter 5 discusses tax competition issues, including the rising complexity of the UK corporate tax system.

Although a large proportion of business legislation now has its origins in Brussels,[7] businesses have voiced their concern that the UK government has "over-implemented" or "gold-plated" EU directives by adding unnecessary burdens, when EU-wide legislation is implemented in the United Kingdom.[8] While there is some debate about the prevalence of such over-implementation, it is agreed that it may have had an adverse impact upon

Figure 4.5. **Product market regulation and labour productivity**

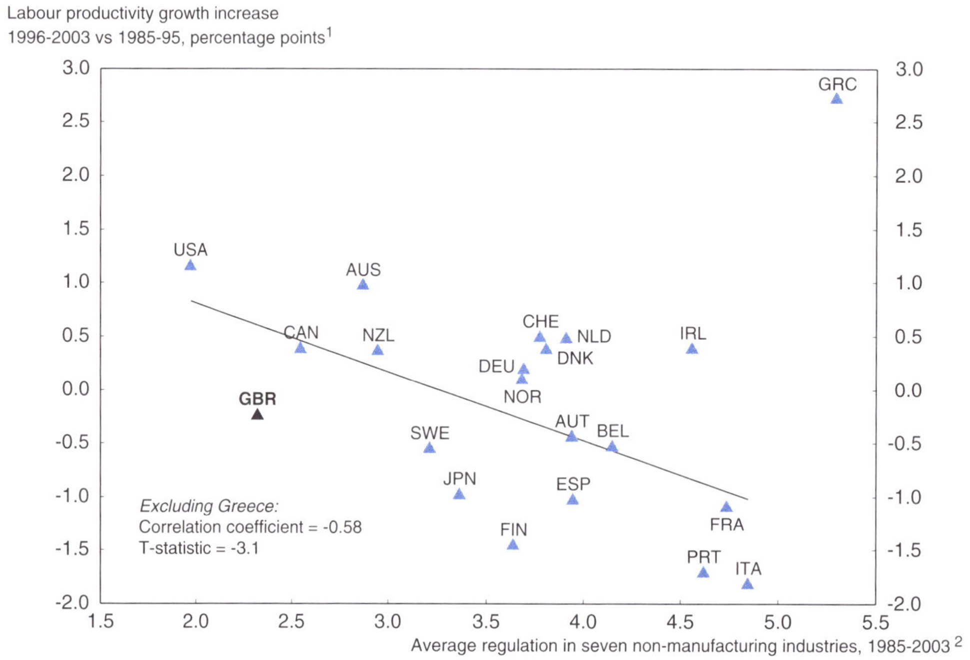

Labour productivity growth increase
1996-2003 vs 1985-95, percentage points[1]

1. Labour productivity is defined as output per hour worked.
2. The scale of the indicators is 0-6 from least to most restrictive of competition.

Source: Conway, P. *et al.* (2006), "Regulation, Competition and Productivity Convergence", *OECD Economics Department Working Papers*, No. 509.

StatLink ⟨⟨⟨ http://dx.doi.org/10.1787/116443084630

competitiveness and growth. In response to these concerns, the Davidson Review (Davidson, 2006) looked at this issue and concluded that it was not as widespread in the United Kingdom as is sometimes claimed. Nonetheless, the Review recommended legislative simplification in a number of areas (*e.g.* consumer sales, financial services, transport, food hygiene and waste legislation) and it made a number of additional recommendations to help spread best practice in the implementation of European legislation across departments and regulators.

With respect to domestic regulations, the Legislative and Regulatory Reform Act 2006 introduced a number of measures to improve the quality and effectiveness of the regulatory system. The government also committed all departments and major regulators to publish rolling programmes of simplification of regulation as a key part of making progress on the better regulation agenda.

Is investment in R&D and adult learning too low?

The United Kingdom has a low level of business investment but ICT investment is high

Business investment is an important driver of labour productivity growth, both through capital deepening and through embodying technical progress. The OECD growth study found a robust cross-country correlation between physical capital and productivity (OECD, 2003). Past OECD *Economic Surveys* have pointed to the relatively low level of business investment per worker in the United Kingdom (OECD, 2004). For example, growth in real business investment fell from an average rate of 7% per annum over 1995-99 to an average 2% per annum over 2000-05. However, there is some debate about whether or not this is holding back productivity. Escolano (2003) finds that higher productivity could be achieved without a higher capital-output ratio and Koeva (2003) argues that it is investment in machinery and equipment which matters most for productivity growth and this component of UK investment is comparable to that in other OECD countries. Another encouraging sign is that the share of information and communication technology (ICT) investment in business fixed investment doubled to more than 20% between 1985 and 2003. The United Kingdom now has one of the highest shares of ICT investment in the OECD (Figure 4.6, upper panel). Among OECD countries there appears to be a positive correlation between ICT investment and MFP growth (Figure 4.6, lower panel) and there is

Figure 4.6. **ICT investment in OECD countries**[1]

Per cent

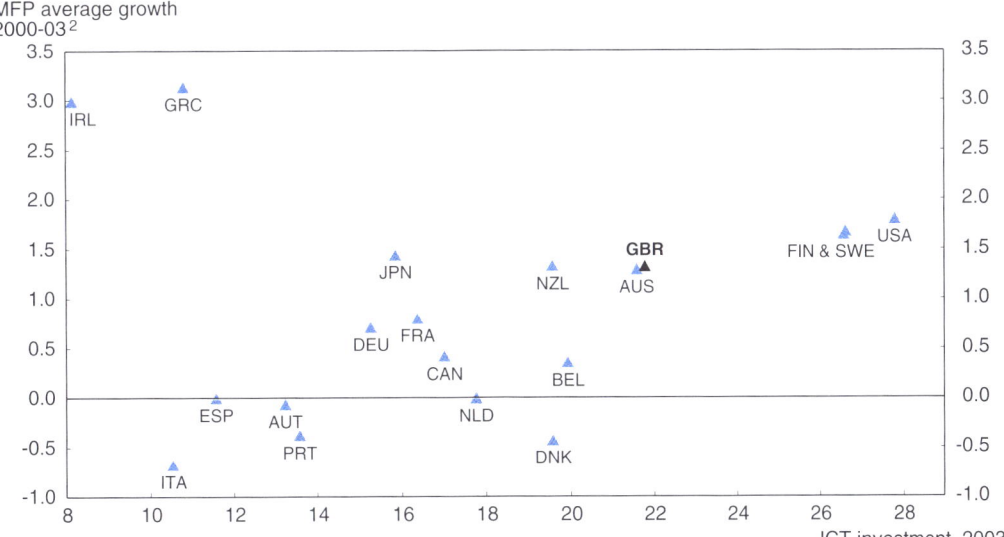

1. Information and communication technology (ICT) investment as a per cent of non-residential gross fixed capital formation for the total economy.
2. Or latest year available: 2005 for Canada, France, Germany, Italy and the United States; 2004 for Australia, Japan, Korea and Spain; 2002 for New Zealand and Norway.
3. Multifactor productivity. The correlation excluding Greece and Ireland is 0.77.

Source: OECD (2007), *Productivity database*, April, *www.oecd.org/statistics/productivity.*

StatLink *http://dx.doi.org/10.1787/116476034147*

evidence of a positive productivity effect of ICT investment in computers and software by firms and of internet use by employees in the United Kingdom (Clayton, 2005; Basu et al. 2003).[9] Moreover, recent work by Marrano et al. (2007) suggests that investment in intangibles is important in the United Kingdom, reflecting its industrial structure, and that its inclusion in the measure of aggregate investment improves the UK's record of investment growth.

Some of the productivity benefits from the high ICT share may be yet to come. For example, Basu et al. (2003) stress the role of ICT as a "general purpose technology" which may require reorganisation and learning and so only raises MFP in ICT-using sectors with a time lag. Thus, the finding that MFP growth has not yet picked up despite strong increases in ICT investment may reflect such lags. In turn, this raises questions about whether the UK's complementary investment in human capital is sufficient to realise these productivity gains (Keep et al., 2006). For instance, if a firm undertaking significant computer investment fails to complement this with sufficient organisational change, it may fail to realise productivity gains. At the same time, productivity growth may temporarily slow during the process of organisation change as these investments divert resources from current production (Crespi et al., 2006).

The 2007 Budget included a package of reforms intended to enhance productivity. These changes included the introduction of an annual investment allowance and changes to remove distortions in the tax treatment of business investment. In addition, the corporate tax rate is to be lowered from 30% to 28% from April 2008. These changes should improve incentives for businesses to invest.

Innovation performance

Research and development (R&D) is another important driver of productivity growth. The previous *Economic Survey* reported that on traditional measures of innovation performance, such as spending on R&D and patenting activity, the United Kingdom ranks close to the OECD average, but poorly relative to the G7. However, also as discussed in the previous *Economic Survey,* one possible explanation is that the industrial mix of the UK economy is concentrated in sectors that are not traditionally R&D intensive.

In addition to industry structure, there are several further possible explanations for the UK's mediocre performance on traditional R&D measures. First, it can be argued that a large share of innovation activities in the UK service sectors are changes in process, organisation and marketing, which are not recorded as R&D spending (OECD, 2006a; OECD, 2005). According to the latest *R&D Scoreboard* by the Department of Trade and Industry, spending on R&D rose by £2 billion in 2006 and around two-thirds of the increase was accounted for by service sector companies.

Second, there is some evidence from the Third Community Innovation Survey that although the most innovative firms in the United Kingdom have a comparable R&D intensity to firms in other countries, a relatively smaller proportion of UK firms are innovative in the first place (Abramovsky et al., 2005a).[10] More recent survey data covering the period 2002 to 2004 suggests that there has been an increase in this proportion. The government's 10-year plan for science and innovation aims to raise R&D intensity from around 1.7% of GDP in 2004 to 2.5% by 2014. This appears to be an ambitious target as it involves a reversal of the trend decline in R&D spending as a share of GDP that has been in place since the early 1980s.

The United Kingdom is well-placed to benefit from knowledge spillovers from multinational enterprises and FDI

Foreign multinational enterprises make up an important part of R&D investment. In 2000, multinational enterprises (MNEs) accounted for about a third of all business R&D performed, with that proportion rising to nearly half of all R&D in the mechanical engineering and electrical machinery industry (Table 4.2). Compared with other OECD countries, a particularly large (and rising) share of UK R&D is being financed from abroad – close to one-quarter of all business sector R&D (Figure 4.7). At the same time, UK multinationals are undertaking an increasing amount of R&D abroad (Abramovsky *et al.*, 2005a).

Table 4.2. **Proportion of R&D performed by multinational enterprises**

2000

	Total R&D spending (billion £)	Percentage share performed by		
		Domestic firms	UK multinational enterprises	Foreign multinational enterprises
Pharmaceuticals and chemicals	3.42	16	52	32
Mechanical engineering and electrical machinery	2.36	16	36	48
Transport equipment and aerospace	1.85	10	52	38
Other manufacturing	1.08	42	38	21
Services	2.25	39	43	17

Source: Griffith, R., S. Redding and H. Simpson (2004), "Foreign Ownership and Productivity: New Evidence from the Service Sector and the R&D Lab", *IFS Working Papers*, No. W04/22, Institute for Fiscal Studies, London.

Figure 4.7. **Share of research and development financed from abroad**

Business sector, per cent

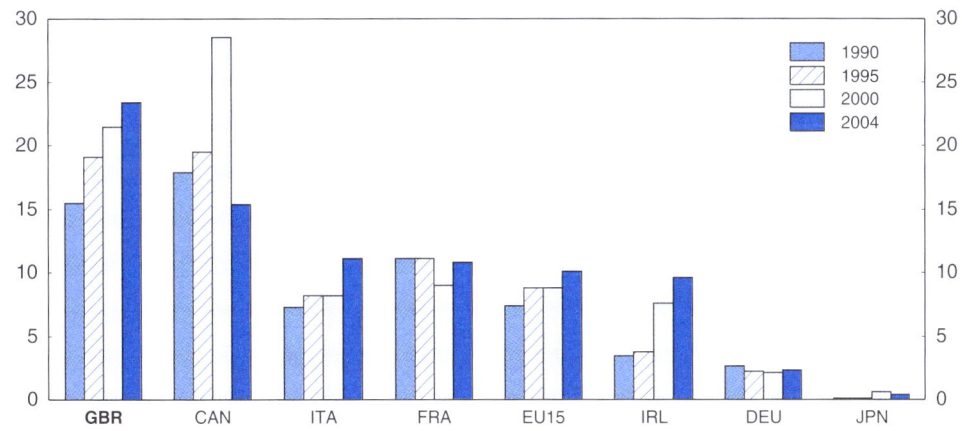

Source: OECD (2007), *Main Science and Technology Indicators*, Vol. 2007/1.

StatLink ⟨ᴍˢᴸ⟩ *http://dx.doi.org/10.1787/116478465788*

The increasingly footloose nature of R&D investment and the importance of knowledge spillovers suggest that domestic rates of R&D investment are not the only way of benefiting from innovation. Other important channels include the presence of multinational enterprises and foreign direct investment (FDI), both of which play an important role in the United Kingdom in generating knowledge spillovers to domestic firms within the same industry as well as to upstream or downstream industries. The way in which FDI generates knowledge spillovers is not well understood. One hypothesis is that it works through pure demonstration effects and *via* the mobility of skilled workers across production facilities. Another potential mechanism is through MNE demand for higher product quality and better technology from suppliers. There is some empirical evidence of such positive knowledge spillovers from inward FDI benefiting the productivity of British firms. For example, Haskel *et al.* (2002) suggested that a 10 percentage point increase in the foreign presence in a UK industry raises total factor productivity of that industry's domestic plants by about 0.5%.

Tax credits may play a less important role in boosting R&D investment than general framework conditions

A recent OECD study found that tax incentives could help to raise R&D expenditure, but with long time lags and a relatively modest overall impact (Jaumotte and Pain, 2005). However, the increasingly footloose nature of investment suggests that R&D spending in one country is also likely to respond to a change in incentives in other countries (Abramovsky *et al.*, 2005a; Bloom and Griffith, 2001). Thus if tax credits that attract R&D to one country lead other countries to offer similar benefits, the overall tax cost may be pushed up without commensurate benefits in R&D investment itself.

R&D tax incentives were introduced in 2000 for small and medium-sized enterprises (SMEs)[11] and extended to larger firms in 2002. For larger companies the tax credits take the form of a tax relief which can reduce a company's tax bill although for some small or medium-sized companies they can provide a direct cash payment.[12] By early 2006 about 23 000 claims had been made, with around 20 000 of these qualifying under the SME scheme. The total amount of support claimed was almost £1.8 billion (HMRC, 2007). The sectoral distribution of the productivity gap, with a large negative contribution from services, may have implications for the effectiveness of the tax credit. Since a large share of formal research and development is undertaken in manufacturing industries, tax credits to raise R&D may have little effect on productivity in service sectors. On the other hand, there is some evidence that R&D is becoming more important in services (Abramovsky *et al.*, 2005b; DTI, 2006).

The previous *Economic Survey* emphasised the importance of general framework conditions. Among other things it pointed to the importance of raising general skills, improving the funding of universities which have a good record of collaboration with business, reducing red tape, and lowering the overall tax burden on business. It also recommended improved monitoring of the number of students studying science and technology, and improved evaluations of fiscal measures to support R&D.[13] Since the last *Survey* the government has commissioned and released several reviews which aim to improve such framework conditions. However, it is yet to be seen to what extent the recommendations of these reviews will be implemented.

Poor transport infrastructure may hinder productivity

It is often argued that decades of insufficient investment in public transport infrastructure may be holding back productivity growth (OECD, 2005; IoD, 2007). There is a perception of a deficiency in this area with the United Kingdom ranked sixth in the G7 and fifteenth in the OECD on measures of infrastructure according to the Global Competitiveness Report (World Economic Forum, 2006). However, the cross-country evidence on the effects of public infrastructure investment on productivity is mixed. While a survey of the empirical evidence by the European Commission concluded that most studies found a positive impact of public infrastructure investment on output or productivity, in most cases the effect was weak and in some cases insignificant (European Commission, 2003). Similarly, a more recent study of road investment in western European countries, found that, although an increase in investment in road infrastructure improved productivity growth, the rate of return on investment was not high (Kopp, 2007). UK-specific studies tend to find clearer results. For example, a recent study established that proximity to economic mass has statistically significant productivity effects and estimated that a 10% reduction in all travel times would raise overall productivity by 1.2% (Rice et al., 2006).

Not only is transport infrastructure important for the efficient movement of both intermediate inputs to production and final goods, it also plays an important role in the labour market, with rail and road networks influencing workers' labour supply, via decisions on where to live, as well as the demand for labour, via firms' business location decisions. Well-functioning transport systems also support labour market efficiency and flexibility by facilitating the matching of labour supply and demand (Gibbons and Machin, 2006). Good transport links can be important in attracting and retaining business activities. For example, in a survey asking senior European executives what factors were perceived as "absolutely essential" for business location, transport links with other cities and international links were ranked as the third most important factor (Cushman & Wakefield, 2006).

The publication in 2000 of the government's Ten Year Plan for Transport represented a turning point for public spending on transport. It established a long-term investment programme with £180 billion of public and private expenditure over a 10 year period. The plan set out to reduce congestion and pollution, which were identified as the main priorities in the 1998 Integrated Transport White Paper ("A new deal for transport: Better for everyone"). The main focus of the plan was on large scale infrastructure projects with only brief references to policies on transport pricing, car dependence, land use and travel behaviour. Indeed, the plan was subsequently criticised for only being a capital investment programme, for not taking into consideration pricing decisions, for being "built" around inadequate indicators on congestion and pollution and for not setting out any visions for transport beyond 2010 (House of Commons, 2002). The subsequent 2004 White Paper ("The future of transport – A network for 2030") revised the Ten Year Plan and set out the government's transport vision for the next 30 years. It took a more balanced approach between expanding transport capacity and making existing transport networks more efficient. Road pricing was acknowledged as one possible solution.

The Hatfield accident in October 2000 consolidated the view that immediate action needed to be taken to end decades of under-funding in railway infrastructure and coincided with a surge in funding. Total (public and private) investment in railway infrastructure increased from 0.3% of GDP in 2000 to a peak of 0.5% of GDP in 2003 (Figure 4.7). However, while this constituted a notable increase in the level of spending on improving and expanding rail capacity, the United Kingdom was towards the bottom of the ranking on inland transport infrastructure spending over the period 2000-05 despite this period including the spike in railway spending (Figure 4.8).[14] Another notable feature is the dramatic decline in road infrastructure funding, down from around 0.8% of GDP in the early 1990s to around 0.4% of GDP in 2004 which has meant that total spending on inland transport infrastructure has declined as a proportion of nominal GDP since the early 1990s although indications are that public expenditure on roads has risen more recently.[15] Total expenditure on transport infrastructure over the first four years covered by the Ten Year Plan suggests that spending will have to be lifted very considerably if the Plan's expenditure projections are to be met.

Figure 4.8. **Transport infrastructure spending**
Road and rail investment in per cent of GDP

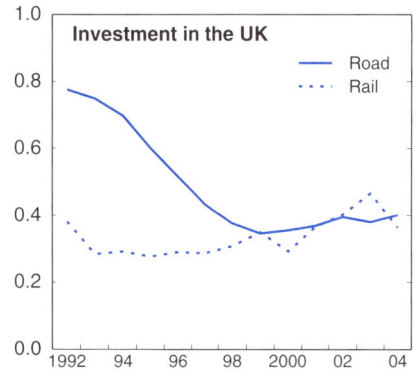
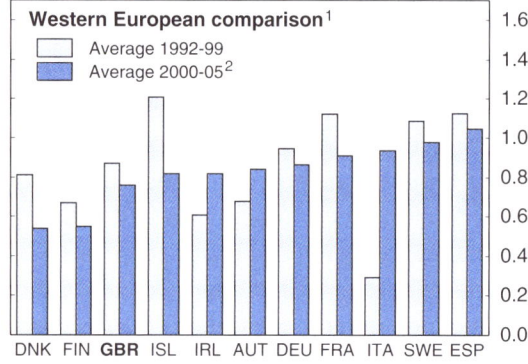

1. No data is available for railways for Ireland from 2002 and there are no railways in Iceland.
2. To 2004 instead of 2005 for Austria, Italy and the United Kingdom.
Source: European Conference of Ministers of Transport (ECMT).

StatLink ⊞ *http://dx.doi.org/10.1787/116483708207*

The government recognised that improving transport infrastructure remains an important challenge by commissioning the Eddington Review (Eddington, 2006) to look into the long-run links between transport and productivity and growth. The main recommendations from the report are to:

● Improve the capacity and the performance of the existing transport network by focusing investment on easing bottlenecks rather than new large scale projects.

● Identify future strategic economic priorities and target future growth-focused investment on congested and growing city catchments, and the key inter-urban corridors and key international gateways that are showing signs of increasing congestion and unreliability.

● Accelerate progress towards a widespread road pricing scheme.

● Preserve a systematic and transparent approach to policymaking and funding and ensure that the delivery system can support these policies. This should include reform of the planning system to speed up the approval of major infrastructure projects.

The recommendation to focus investment on bottlenecks in the transport system makes a lot of sense. However, the fact that it implies increased spending in London and the affluent South-East at the expense of other areas of the country suggests that it may meet with political resistance.

The proposal for a widespread road pricing scheme is consistent with the recommendation in the previous *Survey*. It would also provide another source of funding for road infrastructure, spending on which had declined substantially over the past decade and a half (Figure 4.8). Current plans suggest that regional pilots on road-pricing could be underway shortly with the possibility of a national scheme being introduced in about a decade.[16] The success of the London congestion charge might provide useful lessons in the design, introduction and operation of a nationwide system.

The government has welcomed the Eddington Review, agreed with the strategic analysis and committed to taking steps to implement its advice. It plans to report on progress sometime in 2007. The Comprehensive Spending Review may include plans to bolster transport infrastructure spending. To date aggregate spending seems to have been below what would be required to achieve the projections outlined in the Ten Year Plan.

Job-related education and training does little to fill skill gaps

A significant share of the UK population has not completed upper secondary education and a large proportion of adults has relatively low literacy and numeracy skills (Chapter 2). Low investment in the general skills of the workforce is widely cited as a factor holding back productivity growth, by reducing the potential for knowledge spillovers and by slowing the uptake of new technologies.

Not only is initial education important, but changing demand for skills makes non-formal continuing education and training important. In the United Kingdom around 27% (OECD, 2006b) of employees participate in non-formal job-related education and training – well above the OECD average. However, the intensity of participation in non-formal job-related training is comparatively low. The expected number of hours of training per worker is only 315 over the course of a normal working life – considerably below the OECD average. Perhaps most importantly, job-related training and education in the United Kingdom is particularly low among the low-skilled and older workers; for persons who have not reached upper secondary qualifications the intensity of participation is only 103 hours and for older workers it is just 28 hours (Figure 4.9). This suggests that continuing education and training do not succeed in filling in skill gaps.

Figure 4.9. **Time spent on professional training**[1]

By level of educational attainment, number of hours, 2003[2]

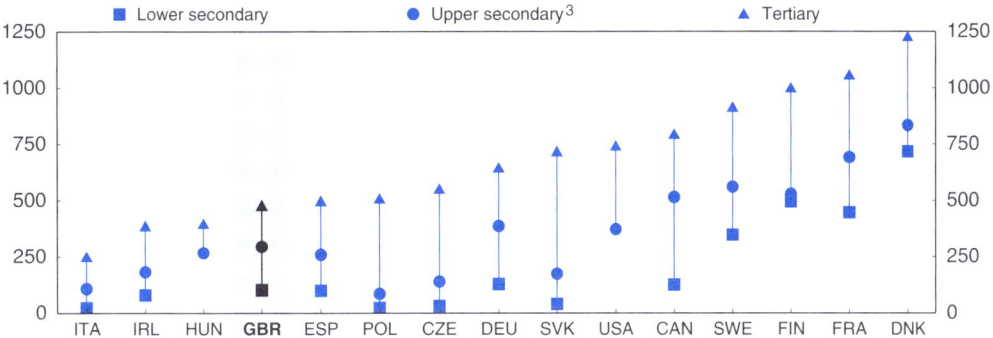

1. Expected hours spent in non-formal job-related education and training over a forty-year period for persons aged 25-64.
2. 2002 for Canada.
3. Includes post-secondary non-tertiary education.

Source: OECD (2006), *Education at a Glance.*

StatLink ⟶ *http://dx.doi.org/10.1787/116500551877*

In recognition of these weaknesses the government commissioned the Leitch Review which published its report ("Prosperity for All in the Global Economy – World Class Skills") in December 2006. The Leitch report acknowledged the UK's poor performance in this area and concluded that even if the existing targets to improve attainment were met, the United Kingdom would continue to fall further behind. In July the government published its response, "World Class Skills" (DIUS, 2007) in which it set out new targets across the range of education levels and made a number of announcements including greater employer involvement in the design and direction of training. Key elements of the plan include:

● Setting an adult literacy target of 95% by 2020, increasing the proportion of adults with level 2 qualifications up to 90% and increasing the numbers with higher education qualifications to 40%.

- Substantially increasing in the *Train to Gain* programme aimed at increasing funding available to employer-directed training schemes.

- Expanding the apprenticeship programme including the introduction of an entitlement for young apprentices.

Even if these targets are met, there are questions about how well these targets reflect the true skill level of the population. As discussed in the previous *Economic Survey*, it is not clear to what extent national vocational qualifications offer a significantly positive return on investment.[17] A better metric than volumes of domestic qualifications may be provided by internationally recognised surveys of adult cognitive skills or by measuring the impacts of acquiring skills in terms of employment and pay progression. Thus, the results of the next adult skills survey (PIAAC), due to be implemented in 2011 will be important, as it will document the extent to which current initiatives are successfully improving adult cognitive skills.

British firms may have a management deficit

One final possible factor contributing to the productivity gap with respect to the United States is that UK firms may be less well managed than US firms. Recent empirical work finds evidence that better managerial practices are associated with higher productivity growth (Bloom and van Reenen, 2006; Bloom *et al.*, 2005). Poor management practices seem to be more prevalent when product market competition is weak and when management of family-owned firms is passed to the eldest son, a practice which is more common in the United Kingdom. These studies conclude that poor management practices could account for one-third of the productivity gap with the United States. Better management practices in the United States are consistent with the fact that foreign affiliates, particularly US affiliates, are more productive than British multinationals. There is also evidence that US-owned firms are more likely to introduce organisational change than British firms (Crespi *et al.*, 2006). Since the skills required of managers are very broad, one somewhat controversial explanation for poor management skills in the United Kingdom is that the current system of A-levels forces specialisation at a too early stage, limiting the breadth of skills of future managers. The Tomlinson Review suggested a new broader diploma for senior high school, although public support for the current system led the government to reject this proposal (Tomlinson, 2002).

Box 4.2. Recommendations on enhancing productivity

- In implementing the Barker recommendations the government should facilitate the entry of new businesses by reforming and simplifying planning regulations, especially in the area of retail trade; abolish the "needs test" for market demand; and put in place strategies that ensure that more weight is given to economic issues in the planning process.

- Free-up more land for development by reconsidering the boundaries of the "green belts" in fast-growing areas.

- Consider further incentives for land development particularly those with the potential to contribute to the funding of local infrastructure.

- Make sure that best practices are followed to avoid "over-implementing" or "gold-plating" EU directives.

Box 4.2. **Recommendations on enhancing productivity** *(cont.)*

● Ensure that infrastructure investment does not fall short of that envisaged in the government's Ten Year Plan for Transport. Follow through with targeted spending in key strategic growth areas.

● Continue to examine the options for addressing road congestion and environmental impacts including the implementation of a road-pricing system on a national scale.

● Raise the general skill level of the workforce by focusing adult training on the most disadvantaged groups. In terms of evaluating progress, focus more on broader measures rather than on simple volumes of qualifications. For example, more focus should be given to international measures of adult cognitive skills as well as assessments of employment outcomes that result from acquiring skills and qualifications.

● Assess the efficiency of fiscal support to R&D, such as the R&D tax credit, over the longer term.

Notes

1. International comparisons of productivity are hampered by measurement difficulties, such as the treatment of government output, the measurement of various inputs and the choice of a common denominator, but the OECD has developed a *Productivity Database*, which overcomes most, though not all comparability issues. These issues are covered in detail in Ahmad *et al.* (2003).

2. An important limitation when using industry data from the OECD's industrial Structural Analysis Database (STAN) is that productivity is only available per employee instead of per hour. Another limitation is that the conversion to a common currency is done by assuming the same price structure (*i.e.* by using the overall purchasing power parities) in all industries instead of using sector-specific purchasing power parities.

3. Disney et al. (2003) show that during the 1980-92 period external restructuring accounted for around 50% of plants' labour productivity growth and 80-90% of total factor productivty growth.

4. Turnover is calculated as the sum of the birth and death rate. The birth rate is the number of enterprise births divided by the number of enterprises active over the period. The death rate is number of enterprise deaths divided by the number of active enterprises.

5. The cities included were: Amsterdam, Dublin, Frankfurt, London, Madrid, Milan, New York, Paris, Stockholm, Sydney, Tokyo and Toronto.

6. The changes are set out in the Empty Property Rates Bill.

7. Some estimates suggest that this proportion is close to 80%: Open Europe (2005) estimates that 77% of the major regulations passed in the UK since 1998 were wholly or partly driven by EU legislation. However, more conservative estimates are that some 50% of UK legislation has its origin in EU law.

8. Gold-plating includes extending the scope of EU-directives by including extra pieces of legislation, widening the scope of the EU-directives to cover extra requirements and introducing targets and deadlines.

9. Clayton (2005) finds that an extra 10% of employees using computers in manufacturing firms raises productivity by 2.2%, with this effect rising to 4.4% in newer firms.

10. The response rate in the UK survey was low so that there are concerns about it being representative.

11. A SME is defined as a company with fewer than 250 employees and either turnover not exceeding £50 million or a balance sheet totalling less than £43 million.

12. The 2007 Budget announced increases from April 2008 in some elements of the SME R&D tax credit from 150% to 175% and the large company R&D tax credit from 125% to 130%.

13. HM Treasury has recently commissioned a feasibility study for an econometric assessment of the impact of the R&D tax credit on R&D expenditure (*www.hmrc.gov.uk/research* – Report 19). The

conclusion was that there is currently insufficient data for any firm conclusions to be drawn. This is consistent with the long lags found in Jaumotte and Pain (2005).

14. The 30 Year Plan White Paper (entitled "The Future of Transport" published in 2004) proposed extra funding for the Department of Transport. This was provided in the 2004 Spending Review which included additional spending of £1.6 billion over 2006/07 and 2007/08 to meet the expenditure set out in the Ten Year Plan combined with an additional permanent annual level increase of £0.5 billion from 2006/07 onwards. Additionally a £1.7 billion transport reform package over 2005/06 and 2006/07 was funded to meet immediate exigencies.

15. Inland transport is road, rail and inland waterways, and excludes airports and sea ports.

16. The Department for Transport is currently examining a number of options to address road congestion. These include assessing the use of road hard shoulders in conjunction with reduced speed limits, offering funding support for regional road-pricing pilots and tendering for proof of concept submissions for nationwide road pricing strategies and technologies.

17. See Box 8.1 in OECD (2005).

References

Abramovsky, L., R. Griffith and R. Harrisson (2005a), "Background Facts and Comments on 'Supporting Growth in Innovation: Enhancing the R&D Tax Credit'", *IFS Briefing Note*, No. BN68, Institute for Fiscal Studies, London.

Abramovsky, L. *et al.* (2005b), "Productivity Policy", *IFS Briefing Note*, No. BN60, Institute for Fiscal Studies, London.

Ahmad, N. *et al.* (2003), "Comparing Labour Productivity Growth in the OECD Area: The Role of Measurement", *OECD STI Working Papers*, No. 2003/14, OECD, Paris.

Barker, K. (2006), *Delivering Stability: Securing our Future Housing Needs*, Barker Review of Housing Supply – Final Report, available at: *www.barkerreview.org.uk*.

Basu, S. *et al.* (2003), "The Case of the Missing Productivity Growth: Or, Does Information Technology Explain Why Productivity Accelerated in the United States but not in the United Kingdom?", *Working Paper*, No. 03-08, Federal Reserve Bank of Chicago.

Bloom, H. and R. Griffith (2001), "Internationalisation of UK R&D", *Fiscal Studies*, Vol. 22, No. 3, Blackwell Publishing.

Bloom, N. *et al.* (2005), "Management Practices across Firms and Nations", *CEP Special Reports*, No. 17, Centre for Economic Performance, London School of Economics.

Bloom, N. and J. van Reenen (2006), "Measuring and Explaining Management Practices Across Firms and Countries", *CEPR Discussion Paper*, No. 5581, Centre for Economic Policy Research, London.

Clayton, T. (2005), "IT Investment, ICT Use and UK Firm Productivity", *Non-journal articles*, Vol. 169Kb, No. 625, Office for National Statistics, London.

Conway, P. *et al.* (2006), "Regulation, Competition and Productivity Convergence", *OECD Economics Department Working Papers*, No. 509, OECD, Paris.

Crespi, G., C. Criscuolo and J. Haskel (2006), "Information, Technology, Organisational Change and Productivity Growth: Evidence from UK Firms", *Working Papers*, No. 558, Department of Economics, Queen Mary, University of London.

Cushman & Wakefield (2006), *European Cities Monitor 2006*, available at: *www.cushmanwakefield.com*.

Davidson, N. (2006), *Davidson Review of the Implementation of EU Legislation*, Cabinet Office, The Stationary Office, London, available at: *www.cabinetoffice.gov.uk/regulation/reviewing_regulation/davidson_review*.

Disney, R., J. Haskel and Y. Heden (2003), "Restructuring and Productivity Growth in UK Manufacturing", *The Economic Journal*, Vol. 113, No. 489, Blackwell Publishing.

DIUS (Department of Innovation, Universities and Skills) (2007), *World Class Skills: Implementing the Leitch Review of Skills in England*, Department of Innovation, Universities and Skills, The Stationary Office, London.

DTI (Department of Trade and Industry) (2006), *The R&D Scoreboard 2006*, Department of Trade and Industry, available at: *www.innovation.gov.uk/rd_scoreboard*.

Eddington, R. (2006), *The Eddington Transport Study*, HM Treasury and Department for Transport, available at: *www.dft.gov.uk/about/strategy/eddingtonstudy*.

EIU (Economist Intelligence Unit) (2007), *Country Report, United Kingdom,* Economist Intelligence Unit, London.

Escolano, J. (2003), "Cross-Country Overview of Growth Patterns 1970-2000", *United Kingdom: Selected Issues,* IMF Staff Country Report, No. 03/47, International Monetary Fund, Washington DC.

European Commission (2003), *Public Finances in EMU – 2003*, European Economy, No. 3, Office for Official Publications of the European Communities, Luxembourg.

Foster, L., J. Haltiwanger and C. Krizan (2002), "The Link Between Aggregate and Micro Productivity Growth: Evidence from Retail Trade", *NBER Working Paper*, No. 9120, National Bureau of Economic Research, Cambridge MA.

Griffith, R. *et al.* (2003), "The UK Productivity Gap and the Importance of the Service Sectors", *IFS Briefing Notes*, No. BN42, Institute for Fiscal Studies, London.

Griffith, R. and H. Harmgart (2005), "Retail Productivity", *IFS Working Paper*, No. W05/07, Institute for Fiscal Studies, London.

Gibbons, S. and S. Machin (2006), "Transport and Labour Market Linkages: Empirical Evidence, Implications for Policy and Scope for Further UK Research", background paper for the Eddington Report to the Department of Transport.

Haskel, J., S. Pereira and M. Slaughter (2002), "Does Inward Foreign Direct Investment Boost the Productivity of Domestic Firms?", *NBER Working Paper*, No. 8724, National Bureau of Economic Research, Cambridge MA.

Haskel, J. and N. Khawaja (2003), "Productivity in UK Retailing: Evidence from Micro Data", draft working paper, Centre for Research into Business Activity (CeRIBA).

Haskel, J. and R. Sadun (2007), "Regulation and UK Retailing Productivity: Evidence from Microdata", Centre for Research into Business Activity (CeRIBA).

HM Government (2007), *Planning for a Sustainable Future: White Paper*, The Stationary Office, London, available at: *www.communities.gov.uk*.

HMRC (HM Revenue and Customs) (2007), "Research and Development Tax Credits", HM Revenue and Customs, available at: *www.hmrc.gov.uk/randd/index.htm*.

House of Commons (2002), *Ten Year Plan for Transport*, Transport, Local Government and the Regions Committee, Eighth Report of Session 2001-02, The Stationary Office, London.

IoD (Institute of Directors) (2007), "UK Transport Policy for the 21st Century", *IoD Policy Paper*, Institute of Directors, London.

Jaumotte, F. and N. Pain (2005), "From Ideas to Development: The Determinants of R&D and Patenting", *OECD Economics Department Working Papers*, No. 457, OECD, Paris.

Keep, E., K. Mayhew and J. Payne (2006), "From Skills Revolution to Productivity Miracle – Not as Easy as it Sounds?", *Oxford Review of Economic Policy*, Vol. 22, No. 4, Oxford University Press.

Koeva, P. (2003), "UK Investment: Is There a Puzzle?", *United Kingdom: Selected Issues,* IMF Staff Country Report, No. 03/47, International Monetary Fund, Washington DC.

Kopp, A. (2007), "Macroeconomic Productivity Effects of Road Investment – A Reassessment for Western Europe", *Transport Infrastructure Investment and Economic Productivity*, ECMT Round Tables, No. 132, OECD/ECMT, Paris.

Marrano, G., J. Haskel and G. Wallis (2007), "What Happened to the Knowledge Economy? ICT, Intangible Investment and Britain's Productivity Record Revisited", *Working Papers*, No. 603, Department of Economics, Queen Mary, University of London, June.

OECD (2003), *The Sources of Economic Growth in OECD Countries*, OECD, Paris.

OECD (2004), *OECD Economic Surveys: United Kingdom*, OECD, Paris.

OECD (2005), *OECD Economic Surveys: United Kingdom*, OECD, Paris.

OECD (2006a), *Going for Growth*, Economic Policy Reforms, OECD, Paris.

OECD (2006b), *Education at a Glance*, OECD, Paris.

Open Europe (2005), "Less Regulation: 4 Ways to Cut the Burden of EU Red Tape", available at: *www.openeurope.org.uk/research/regs.pdf*.

Rice, P., A.J. Venables and E. Patacchini (2006), "Spatial Determinants of Productivity: Analysis for the Regions of Great Britain", *Regional Science and Urban Economics*, Vol. 36, No. 6, Elsevier BV.

Tomlinson, M. (2002), "Inquiry into A-level Standards: Final Report", Department for Education and Skills, available at: *www.dfes.gov.uk.alevelsinquiry*.

World Economic Forum (2006), *Global Competitiveness Report 2006-2007*, Palgrave Macmillian.

ISBN 978-92-64-03772-4
OECD Economic Surveys: United Kingdom
© OECD 2007

Chapter 5

Tax competition:
How to remain competitive?

Statutory corporate tax rates have been lowered in the United Kingdom and elsewhere, while tax bases have been broadened. This has rendered corporate tax systems more efficient. Falling tax rates are not a proof of tax competition, but consistent with it. While the United Kingdom was early in cutting tax rates and had strong tax competitiveness, others have caught up. And some countries now have considerably lower tax rates, even after the recent announcement to cut the UK statutory corporate tax rate from 30% to 28% in 2008. This chapter assesses options to preserve international competitiveness.

Statutory corporate tax rates in the OECD have shown a remarkable trend decline, from 50% at the beginning of the 1980s to close to 30% today (Figure 5.1). The fall in tax rates was more than offset by a broadening of the tax base and other factors,[1] and revenue from corporate income tax has increased as a share of GDP in the OECD on average. There were two distinct tax rate cut phases: a sharp fall in statutory rates in the mid-1980s, and a new push downwards since the turn of the century, especially in the EU countries. In the United Kingdom, the first major rate-cutting cum base-broadening reform was in the early 1980s, when the rate was slashed from more than 50% to 35%. The rationale for the reform was to reduce distortions, by lowering the dispersion in effective marginal tax rates across different forms of investment and sources of finance. This was probably also the motive for tax reforms in other countries at this time, while tax competition played only a minor role.

Figure 5.1. **Corporate tax rates and revenues**[1]

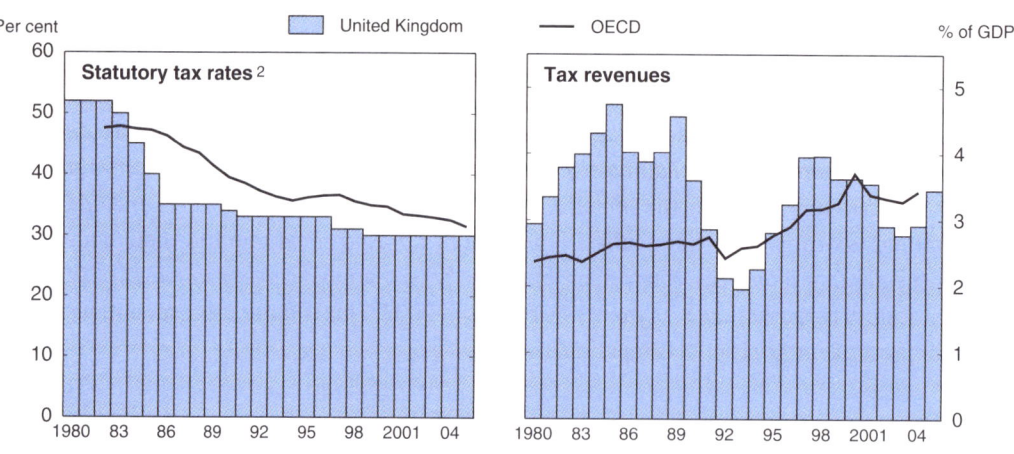

1. The OECD aggregate is an unweighted average of available data.
2. Long time series are only available for 19 OECD countries.

Source: Institute for Fiscal Studies (2005), *Corporate Tax Rate Data* – online dataset; Devereux, M.P., R. Griffith and A. Klemm (2002), "Corporate Income Tax Reforms and International Tax Competition", *Economic Policy*, Vol. 17, No. 35, Blackwell Publishing; OECD (2006), *OECD Tax Statistics: Revenue Statistics 1965-2005* on CD-ROM, Vol. 2006/1.

Tax competition has become a more dominant factor in recent years. International trade and financial market liberalisation and the creation of a single financial market in Europe have raised capital mobility considerably and thereby made the tax base more mobile. Moreover, the recent drop in tax rates in the EU is related to the enlargement of the EU in 2004. The average tax rate in the new member states at 20% in 2006 is substantially lower than in the old member states (29%). With the exception of Ireland and Austria, virtually all the new member states have lower statutory rates than the old ones.[2] The United Kingdom, which had lost tax competitiveness, as the rate had come down only little since the 1980s, recently announced a cut in the corporate tax rate from 30% to 28%, to take effect from April 2008. One motivation was to enhance international competitiveness.

Other objectives for corporate tax reform are: to ensure neutrality, by not favouring some investment at the expense of another, potentially more productive, investment; to provide flexibility by not impeding new types of transactions, nor giving them an unfair advantage; to aim at consistency, by treating transactions that have the same commercial result the same way for tax purposes; and to use the tax system to tackle market failures (HM Treasury and Inland Revenue, 2003). While this chapter focuses on corporate taxation, tax competition issues arise also in the sphere of the personal income tax (Box 5.1).

Box 5.1. Tax competition for personal income tax revenues

Tax competition issues also arise in the sphere of personal income taxation. Highly skilled people tend to be mobile, often demanding a specific disposable income after taxes, when they choose among job offers. The employer has to compensate for taxes payable. Compensation thus comprises disposable income, which is the same in all locations, plus the tax arising at the specific location. In terms of the effective average tax rate, the United Kingdom is very competitive in international comparison for single employees, but less so for married couples (Elschner *et al.*, 2006). There is one aspect of the UK tax system that leads to personal income tax shifting: foreign nationals residing but not domiciled in the United Kingdom are only liable for UK tax payments on foreign income and capital gains when these funds are brought into the United Kingdom. This means non-domiciled people can transfer any excess funds they have into a savings account offshore and leave it to accumulate income tax-free for as long as they like.

Employees who are not resident in the United Kingdom are not liable for UK taxes on overseas earnings. Expatriate workers, for example, can have non-resident status in the United Kingdom for up to three years and reduce tax liabilities by declaring part of their income overseas. The same rules apply to those who are resident in the United Kingdom but not domiciled. A person is domiciled in the country in which they have a permanent home and domicile status is decided by the tax administration. Hence, for longer-term residents who remain foreign domiciled it is possible to set up dual contracts for work in the United Kingdom and overseas, where the overseas portion of income is not taxable unless remitted to the United Kingdom. Moreover, capital gains generated outside the United Kingdom are only subject to UK tax once remitted to the country. This system gives wealthy individuals an incentive to settle in the United Kingdom. According to the Treasury, about 105 000 non-domiciled individuals declared £8.9 billion in taxable income in 2003/04. Estimates by the Treasury in 2003 suggest that it could have raised between £1 and £1.5 billon through a reform of the tax rules. The latest information available from HM Revenue and Customs, which takes into account late tax returns, indicates that there were 112 000 individuals claiming non domiciled tax status in 2004/05.

The UK tax system is also attractive for partners in private equity funds since returns, in the form of carried interest, are taxed as a capital gain and not as income. Moreover, capital gains on business assets attract generous tax relief. Private equity partners thus typically pay tax at an effective rate of just 10%, whereas the tax rate for high income earners is 40%. The rationale for the introduction of this relief was to encourage risky business start-ups. However, the taper relief is estimated to have cost about £6 billion in revenue forgone in 2006/07. While the low taxation of partners in private equity funds has recently hit the headlines and is seen as inequitable, there may still be a case for taxing highly mobile professionals at a lower rate so as to prevent them from moving on to greener tax pastures. Indeed, several OECD countries have special tax arrangements for people staying temporarily in the country to work, especially for highly skilled immigrants (OECD, 2005).

Box 5.2. **Which tax rate matters for what?**

Taxation differences across countries can lead to the shifting of real economic activity and profits across jurisdictions with subsequent implications for tax revenues. Multinational corporations are able to influence the location of profit either by changing the location of production or by just moving profits between countries. Even though a factory, once set up, is difficult to move and is therefore not mobile in the short run, localisation decisions are an ongoing process. Profit shifting also occurs *via* the manipulation of the prices of cross-border intra-group transactions. Tax avoidance is particularly easy for intangible assets such as patents, where reference prices do not exist, but can also apply to intermediate goods trade between establishments of the same company. Profit shifting may also be linked to debt-shifting within groups. By placing equity capital in a subsidiary located in a low tax country and by allocating debt to a subsidiary in a high tax country a multinational can offset the interest payments against tax at a high rate, while the equity-using subsidiary pays tax on the return to equity at a low tax rate. This reduces the overall amount of tax the multinational has to pay.

As a basis for the analysis of activity and profit shifting, Devereux (2007) provides a decision tree for multinational companies. The first two levels represent discrete choices: first is the choice of whether to export or produce abroad; second, if the company decides to move production it has to choose the location for the new plant. The impact of taxation on these decisions can be measured by the extent to which the pre-tax profit is reduced by taxation. This is captured by the effective average tax rate – essentially the proportion of the pre-tax income which is taken in tax. The third and fourth levels of the decision tree represent continuous choices: conditional on being present abroad the multinational will choose the optimal level of investment between jurisdictions, and finally, reallocate profits among locations or repatriate them to the parent. Investment will be undertaken until the marginal product of capital equals the cost of capital. The impact of the tax on the cost of capital is measured by the effective marginal tax rate. As companies will take advantage of tax allowances in different jurisdictions in which they operate, the incentive to transfer profits between jurisdictions will depend on differences in the statutory tax rate. The sharp fall in statutory rates supports the notion that competitive pressure has driven down this rate. The effective tax rate – both average and marginal – depends on both the tax rate and the tax base and both have declined by much less (Figure 5.2). This is mainly because the tax base has been broadened by lowering depreciation rates.

Figure 5.2. **Average and marginal effective tax rates**
Unweighted average of 19 OECD countries, per cent

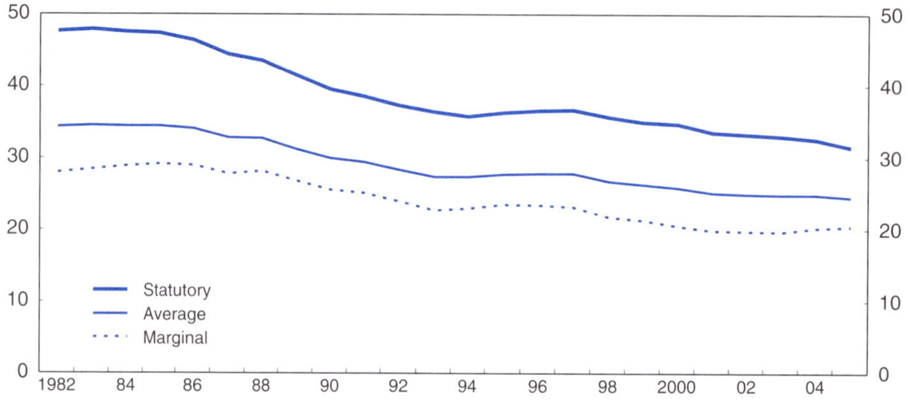

Source: Institute for Fiscal Studies (2005), *Corporate Tax Rate Data* – online dataset and Devereux, M.P., R. Griffith and A. Klemm (2002), "Corporate Income Tax Reforms and International Tax Competition", *Economic Policy*, Vol. 17, No. 35, Blackwell Publishing.

It is often argued that tax competition – a non-cooperative tax setting by governments competing for a mobile tax base – could lead to a "race to the bottom" in tax rates and leave the competing jurisdictions with too little revenue to provide public services at a socially-optimal level.[3] The conclusion that tax competition lowers welfare crucially depends on the assumption that the policymaker is benevolent, and hence aims at maximising the welfare of the whole economy. But governments may also behave as a self-serving "Leviathan" with the objective of maximising the size of the state, resulting in too high tax rates. In this case tax competition will have positive welfare effects since a fall in the tax rate enhances efficiency by constraining a tendency to spend too much and too wastefully (Krogstrup, 2004).

In a literature review, Nicodème (2006) concludes that a race to the bottom has not occurred, mainly because corporate tax revenues have not plunged with falling tax rates. Yet, the belief that countries are competing over corporate tax bases by cutting rates is supported by other empirical evidence. Among others, Devereux *et al.* (2005) find evidence of strategic interaction between countries in setting tax rates, both to attract profits and investment. Moreover, there is empirical work showing that differences in taxation across countries affect flows of capital and profits, in addition to influencing the decision on where to locate production (Nicodème, 2006 and Devereux, 2007). And work by the OECD suggests that while corporate taxation is only one among many factors that shape firms' location decision, it has a significant impact (Nicoletti *et al.*, 2007; OECD, 2007). Box 5.2 discusses how multinationals might redistribute activity and profits and which tax rates influence their decisions.

Figure 5.3 suggests that the shifting of economic activity and of profits between countries may be important. The figure relates the corporate tax base as a per cent of GDP

Figure 5.3. **Corporate tax rates and taxable corporate income**
Average 2000-04

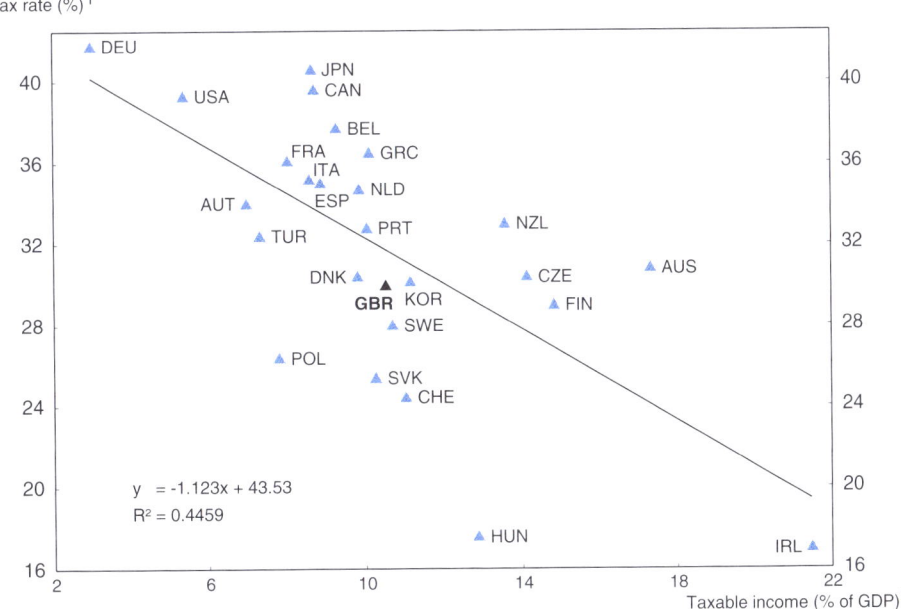

1. Basic combined central and sub-central (statutory) corporate income tax rate.
2. Calculated by grossing up corporate tax revenue by the tax rate.
Source: OECD (2007), *Tax database, www.oecd.org/ctp/taxdatabase* and OECD (2006), *OECD Tax Statistics: Revenue Statistics 1965-2005* on CD-ROM, Vol. 2006/1.

StatLink ⟶ http://dx.doi.org/10.1787/116517601185

to the statutory tax rate. There is a clear negative relationship between the level of the corporate tax rate and corporate income, indicating that real activity and/or profits are being shifted from high to low tax countries. Ireland, for example, which has the lowest tax rate also has the highest taxable corporate income as share of GDP. Germany, on the other hand, has both the highest tax rate and the lowest profit share of GDP.[4]

In recognition of the impact that globalisation is having on tax rates and the tax base there has been increasing international co-operation among the OECD countries (Box 5.3).

Box 5.3. **OECD work on cross-border issues in corporate taxation**

The OECD's Center for Tax Policy and Administration has been at the forefront of developing tax rules that encourage sustainable economic growth while ensuring governments retain their fiscal sovereignty. Moreover, the OECD encourages countries to move towards tax systems with lower tax rates and broader tax bases and supports fair tax competition between countries. Priority areas of work are:

- Working to develop common international tax rules to avoid conflicting practices that distort international trade and investment flows. This work has resulted in important instruments such as the Model Tax Convention on Income and on Capital, and Transfer Pricing Guidelines. The Model Tax Convention serves as the model for the 3 000 bilateral tax agreements now in existence and helps to ensure that returns on cross-border investments are not taxed twice. The Transfer Pricing Guidelines were developed to reflect an international consensus on transfer pricing within multinationals. A large share of trade consists of the transfer of goods, intangibles and services within multinational enterprises. To determine tax liability in each jurisdiction, the right price (arm's length price) has to be applied to allow for the appropriate division of the tax base between the countries in which a multinational enterprise operates.

- Encouraging and facilitating exchange of information between OECD countries. While businesses are increasingly operating at a global level, tax administration is confined to national jurisdictions. The proper exercise of fiscal sovereignty depends upon the development of international co-operation. The OECD's work in this field includes improving access to information, facilitating effective exchange of information while at the same time respecting taxpayer confidentiality, combating corruption, improving co-operation between tax and anti-money laundering authorities, and countering harmful tax practices.

- Providing the mechanisms to resolve tax disputes. In February 2007 the OECD issued recommendations to improve the Mutual Agreement Procedure and for mandatory arbitration so as to encourage countries' competent authorities to resolve disputes in a timely and principled manner.

- Developing best practices in tax administration. Regular exchanges of experiences and approaches to tax administration and the identification of best practices allow for improved administration leading to better services to taxpayers and better compliance. Topics covered include improving tax compliance, the use of modern risk management approaches, improving taxpayer service delivery through the effective use of modern technology and sharing knowledge of the key features of the systems of tax administration in member countries. This work also includes a study of the role of tax intermediaries in compliance and enhancing the relationship between tax administrations and corporate taxpayers.

Source: OECD (2006), Tax in a Borderless World: The Role of the OECD.

The UK corporate tax system in international comparison

The corporate tax system has been subject to two major reforms in the last 25 years: one in 1984 and the second in 1997. In 1984, the main corporate tax rate was cut from 52% to 35% (and further reduced to 33% by 1991/92). At the same time the very generous depreciation allowances were made much less generous. In 1997, the main corporate tax rate was cut to 31% and the small companies' rate from 24% to 19%. The main rate was cut further to 30% in 1998.

In 1999 the advanced corporation tax (ACT) was abolished and the system for corporate tax payments was reformed. ACT was a tax charge that companies faced at the time of paying a dividend and was for most firms credited against corporation tax and thus affected the timing of tax payments only. However, some firms with a small UK corporation tax liability (*i.e.* firms with important foreign operations), were not able to reclaim ACT fully and the ACT might have made the United Kingdom a less attractive place to locate a firm's headquarters.

In 2000 a tax relief on R&D expenditure was introduced for small firms and later, in 2002, extended to large companies. Since then, corporate tax reform has been given almost continuous attention, with three major consultations and a number of smaller more technical ones. The reforms actually implemented, however, have been of relatively minor importance. They have included the introduction of transfer pricing legislation for domestic transactions and changes to the taxation of oil companies on the continental shelf. The introduction of a zero tax rate for companies with less than £10 000 of taxable profit in 2002 was reversed in 2005. Estimates by Hawkins *et al.* (2002) showed that the costs of the zero tax rate potentially could run into billions of pounds as self-employed individuals registered as companies to reduce their tax liabilities. Box 5.4 provides a brief description of the corporate tax system, based on the 2006/07 budget year, and a short summary of the changes announced in the 2007 Budget.

Box 5.4. **The UK's corporate tax system**

Corporation tax is charged on the global profits of UK-resident companies, public corporations and unincorporated associations. Firms not resident in the United Kingdom pay corporation tax only on their UK profits. Taxable profit comprises income from trading, investment and capital gains, less various deductions. Trading losses may be carried back for one year to be set against profits earned in that period or carried forward indefinitely.

The standard rate of corporation tax is 30%, with a reduced rate of 19% on profits under £300 000 (the small companies' rate) (Table 5.1). For firms with profits between £300 000 and £1 500 000, a system of relief on the standard rate operates, such that an

Table 5.1. **Corporation tax rates in the United Kingdom**
2006/07

Profits (£ per annum)	Marginal tax rate (%)	Average tax rate (%)
0-300 000	19	19
300 000-1 500 000	32.75	19-30
1 500 000 and above	30	30

Source: HM Revenue and Customs.

Box 5.4. **The UK's corporate tax system** *(cont.)*

effective marginal rate of 32.75% is levied on profits in excess of £300 000. This increases the average tax rate gradually until it reaches 30%.

Capital allowances provide relief for the consumption or depreciation of capital assets incurred for the purposes of carrying on a trade. Capital allowances may be claimed in the year they accrue, set against future profits, or carried back for up to three years. Different types of assets qualify for different rates of allowances:

- Expenditure on plant and machinery may be written off on a 25% declining basis. Long-life plant and machinery is written off at 6%. A higher, 40%, allowance is available in the first year for expenditure by medium-sized companies; the small companies allowance is 50%.

- Expenditure on industrial buildings and hotels is written down on a straight-line basis of 4% per year.

- Expenditure on commercial buildings may not be written down at all.

- Spending on intangible assets is written down on a straight-line basis at either the accounting depreciation rate or at a rate of 4%, whichever the company prefers.

- Capital expenditure on plant, machinery and buildings for research and development (R&D) is treated more generously: under the R&D allowance, it can all be written off against taxable profits immediately.

Current expenditure on R&D, like current expenditure generally, is fully deductible from taxable profits. Moreover, current R&D expenditure is subject to additional tax relief, if it exceeds a certain limit. For small and medium-sized companies, there is a two-part tax credit. The first part is called R&D tax relief and applies at a rate of 50% (allowing companies to deduct a total of 150% of qualifying expenditure from taxable profits). The second part is a payable tax credit that is only available to loss-making firms, where the firm can give up the right to offset losses equivalent to 150% of their R&D expenditure against future profits, in return for a cash payment of 16% of the losses given up. A R&D credit for larger companies was introduced in 2002. The credit applies at a rate of 25%, allowing 125% of qualifying expenditure to be deducted from taxable profit.

The March 2007 Budget announced a reduction in the corporation tax rate from 30% to 28% to take effect from April 2008. At the same time, the small companies' tax rate will rise in stages from 19% to 22% to reduce incentives for individuals to incorporate to reduce tax payments. Capital allowances will be reformed from 2008, with a new 20% rate (down from 25%) and a new 10% rate for long-lived plant and equipment (up from 6%). Industrial building allowances, hotel allowances and agricultural building allowances are to be phased out. The capital allowance changes will finance the reduction in the main rate. The changes to capital allowances and tax rates do not apply to North Sea oil and gas companies. There will be a new environmental tax credit and the rate of R&D tax credits for small companies will rise to 175% (from 150%); for larger firms they will increase from 125% to 130%. There will also be an annual 100% investment allowance of £50 000.

Source: Adam *et al.* (2007) and HM Treasury, Budget 2007 (available at: *www.hm-treasury.gov.uk/budget/ budget_07*).

Corporate tax revenues are highly correlated with the business cycle but, unlike in the OECD aggregate, it is difficult to spot a trend in UK revenues as a share of GDP (Figure 5.1). Despite falling statutory rates, revenues have hovered around 3.5% of GDP, mainly because of the broadening of the tax base. Moreover, the importance of the financial sector has increased, so that the development in corporate revenues has been strongly correlated with financial market developments.

The United Kingdom was among the first countries to lower the statutory corporate tax rate in the OECD (Figure 5.1),[5] and in 1999 it reached 30%. Figure 5.4 shows that the UK's statutory rate is no longer particularly low, neither in the OECD, nor in the European Union, where it is now the 8th highest. On the other hand, it is striking that all the G7 economies have high statutory rates, with the UK rate the lowest among them. Apparently, economies with a large market potential are able to sustain a higher tax rate than smaller countries, without negative repercussions (Krogstrup, 2004).

Figure 5.4. **Statutory corporate tax rates in international comparison**
Combined rate, per cent[1]

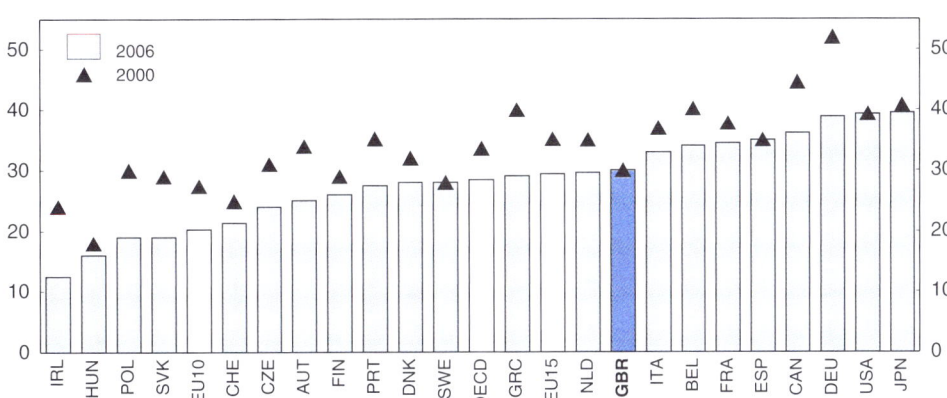

1. Basic combined central and sub-central (statutory) corporate income tax rate. Aggregates are unweighted averages and EU10 covers the new EU member states.

Source: OECD (2007), Tax Database, www.oecd.org/ctp/taxdatabase and European Commission (2006), Structures of the Taxation Systems in the European Union.

StatLink ⬛〓🔗 http://dx.doi.org/10.1787/116518186658

Figure 5.5 shows that both the UK's effective marginal tax rate and the effective average tax rate are close to the OECD average. While the effective average tax rate has come down a little since the mid-1980s, the effective tax rate on a marginal investment has not changed over time, implying that the tax reforms have done little to improve incentives to invest. Given the more recent tax reforms in many other countries, the United Kingdom has lost tax competitiveness, moving from being a low tax country to being close to the OECD average. Taking into account the new EU member countries, which are not included in Figure 5.5, worsens the UK's ranking considerably. The recent lowering of the corporate tax rate in the United Kingdom follows a distinct downward trend in the European Union where 17 out of 25 countries reduced their tax rates between 2002 and 2006 and several plan further cuts (Table 5.2).

The United Kingdom had strong appeal to global investors in Europe. However, the UK's position as the preferred location has been overtaken by Germany (Ernst & Young, 2006). Moreover, while only few headquarters have moved abroad so far, those considering relocating business activities in the future cited their headquarters second only to relocating the financial back office (out of 10 activities) (CBI, 2007). The United Kingdom has also been an attractive location for inward investment. According to Ernst & Young's European Investment Monitor the UK received 31% of foreign investment projects in Europe in 1997.

Figure 5.5. **Effective tax rates**

Per cent

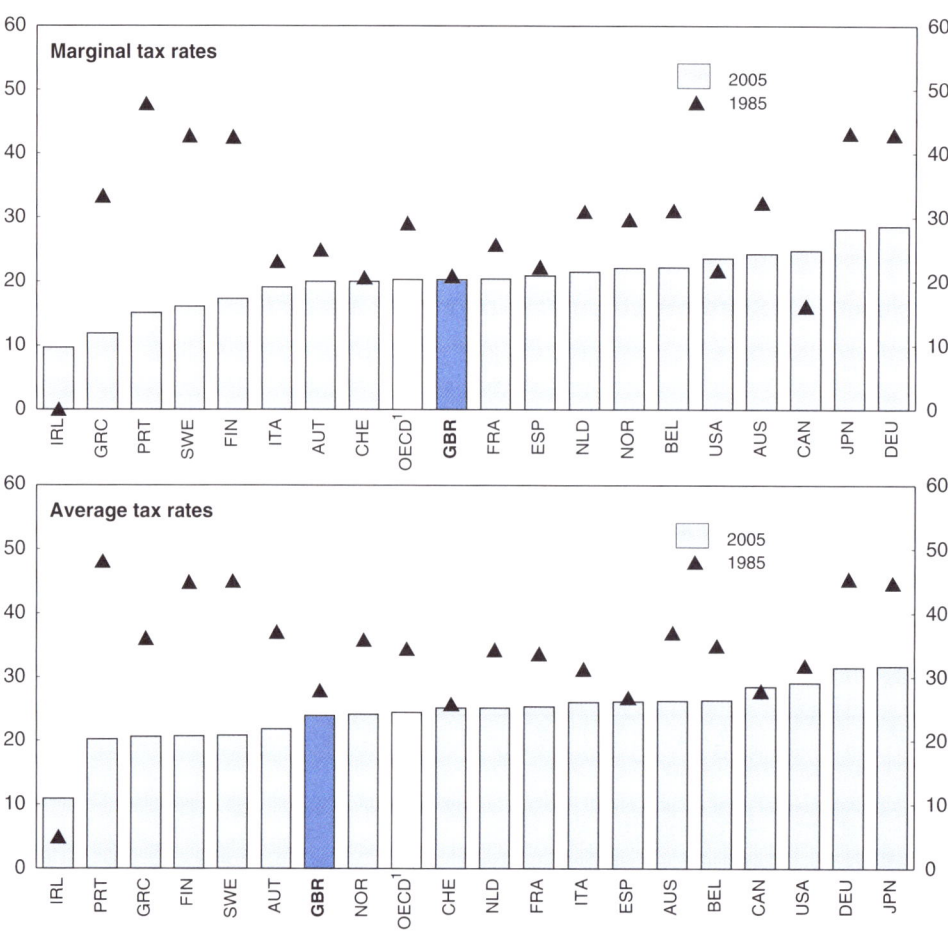

1. Unweighted average of 19 OECD countries.

Source: Institute for Fiscal Studies (2005), *Corporate Tax Rate Data* – online dataset and Devereux, M.P., R. Griffith and A. Klemm (2002), "Corporate Income Tax Reforms and International Tax Competition", *Economic Policy*, Vol. 17, No. 35, Blackwell Publishing.

But by 2006 this figure had slipped to 19%. Nonetheless, the United Kingdom still attracted more projects than any other European country, and its declining share is of a rapidly increasing total. The increasing complexity of the tax system is also seen as a threat to competitiveness. In a World Bank report, the United Kingdom emerged as having the second most lengthy tax code out of the 20 largest economies world wide, and the tax code has more than doubled in length over the past ten years (Table 5.3).[6] On the other hand, while businesses complain loudly about tax complexity (CBI, 2007), it is partly they who are to blame as the UK government has reacted forcefully to aggressive tax planning by businesses. Indeed, Slemrod *et al.* (2007) suggest that tax complexity has increased in recent years mainly because a significant volume of anti-avoidance legislation has been added to the tax code.

The complexity of the tax system contributes to low awareness of incentives and tax reliefs, especially among small enterprises. Surveys suggest that 42% of businesses want simplified tax rules and 34% want a lower administrative burden (PWC, 2006). Another implication is that the corporate tax law can no longer be handled by a single tax advisor, as specialists and sub-specialists are needed. This creates a two-tier market where only

Table 5.2. **Reductions in the statutory corporate tax rate in the European Union**[1]

Per cent

	2002	2006	Change 2002-06	Planned reductions[2]	
				To	By
Germany	38.9	38.9	0	29.8	2008
Spain	35	35	0	30	2008
France	35.4	34.4	−1	–	–
Belgium	40.2	34	−6.2	–	–
Italy	36	33	−3	–	–
Luxembourg	30.4	30.4	0	–	–
United Kingdom	**30**	**30**	**0**	**28**	**2008**
Netherlands	34.5	29.6	−4.9	25.5	2007
Greece	35	29	−6	25	2007
Denmark	30	28	−2	25	2007
Sweden	28	28	0	–	–
Portugal	33	27.5	−5.5	–	–
Finland	29	26	−3	–	–
Austria	34	25	−9	–	–
Ireland	16	12.5	−3.5	–	–
Average EU15	**32**	**29**	**−3**	. .	. .
Malta	35	35	0	–	–
Slovenia	25	25	0	20	2010
Czech Republic	31	24	−7	19	2010
Estonia	26	23	−3	20	2009
Poland	28	19	−9	–	–
Slovak Republic	25	19	−6	–	–
Hungary	18	16	−2	–	–
Romania	. .	16	. .	–	–
Bulgaria	. .	15	. .	12	2007
Latvia	22	15	−7	–	–
Lithuania	15	15	0	–	–
Cyprus[3, 4]	28	10	−18	–	–
Average new member states[5]	**25**	**20**	**−5**	. .	. .

1. Basic combined central and sub-central (statutory) corporate income tax.
2. A hyphen indicates that no reduction is planned.
3. Footnote by Turkey: The information in this document under the heading "Cyprus" relates to the southern part of the Island. There is no single authority representing both Turkish and Greek Cypriot people on the Island. Turkey recognises the Turkish Republic of Northern Cyprus (TRNC). Until a lasting and equitable solution is found within the context of the United Nations, Turkey shall preserve its position concerning the "Cyprus" issue.
4. Footnote by all the European Union Member States of the OECD and the European Commission: The Republic of Cyprus is recognised by all members of the United Nations with the exception of Turkey. The information in this document relates to the area under the effective control of the Government of the Republic of Cyprus.
5. Excluding Bulgaria and Romania.
Source: OECD (2007), *Tax database, www.oecd.org/ctp/taxdatabase*; European Commission (2006), *Structures of the Taxation Systems in the European Union* and national data sources.

some businesses can afford comprehensive tax advice, while for others the cost of advice is greater than the benefit (PWC and the World Bank, 2006).

While the United Kingdom performs badly on the length of tax legislation, its ranking on other measures of tax complexity is much better (Table 5.3). For example, measured by the number of tax payments a business has to make each year the United Kingdom ranks 7th with only seven payments a year. Also the number of hours spent complying with the tax requirements is relatively low compared with the other large economies. On average a business spends 105 hours per year on tax filings, which is the 24th lowest out of 175 countries covered. In 2006, HM Revenue and Customs set up an Administrative Burden Advisory Board

145

Table 5.3. **Tax complexity**

	Length of the tax code[1] (number of pages)	Tax payments[2] (number per year)	Time spent to comply[2] (hours per year)
India	9 000	59	264
United Kingdom	**8 300**	**7**	**105**
Japan	7 200	15	350
United States	5 100	10	325
Italy	3 500	15	360
Canada	2 440	10	119
China[3]	2 000	44	872
Germany	1 700	32	105
Netherlands	1 640	22	250
France	1 300	33	128
Sweden	700	5	122

1. Federal tax legislation only, state and local taxes are excluded.
2. Taxes covered are corporate income tax, value added tax and social security contributions.
3. Includes Hong Kong, China for the length of the tax code.
Source: PricewaterhouseCoopers and the World Bank (2006), Paying Taxes: The Global Picture.

with representatives from the business community to assist it in its project to reduce the administrative burden of the tax system. It specified two targets to cut the administrative burden of its forms and returns (to be reduced by 10%) and its audits and inspections (to be reduced by 15%) for businesses by 2010/11. Budget 2007 announced some further reductions in these areas, and also reductions in wider administrative burdens on business.

How to stay competitive and still raise revenue?

The extent to which globalisation might erode the ability to tax corporate income remains unclear. To date, the share of corporate revenues as a proportion of GDP have held up well, both in the United Kingdom and in other OECD countries (Figure 5.1). However, the pressures on the tax base could intensify. This section considers some of the options that could be taken if this risk were to materialise.

Simplify the tax code

The complexity of the UK system creates two divisions of corporate taxpayers: those who can afford tax lawyers and thereby manage to minimize their tax payments and those who cannot and thereby lose competitiveness. Complexity can also influence firms' decisions on where to locate investment and profits. Tax planning can lead to inefficiencies and may contribute to counter-action by the government leading to greater complexity. Drafting of new tax legislation requires thorough preparation and broad political agreement, so that the probability of later changes is reduced. One model for reform may be the Nordic countries who have changed their corporate tax systems, putting emphasis on simplicity, transparency and tax neutrality. The Swedish tax code is less than a tenth of the UK code in terms of length.

Continue cutting the statutory rate while further broadening the base

There is probably still room to broaden the tax base and lower the rate. HMRC (2007) estimate the overall cost of corporation tax expenditure and relief to be £23 billion in 2006/07,[7] as compared to a tax take of £53 billion. But as corporate tax rates in all countries fall, raising revenue might become harder. Moreover, with much lower corporate tax rates, the self-employed will have increasing incentives to incorporate their businesses thereby lowering overall tax revenues. The implications of globalisation on corporate tax revenues and the need to design a corporate tax system that can serve as a backstop to the personal income tax have led economists to suggest options for more fundamental corporate tax reform. At the same time the tax reform agenda continues to focus on ensuring tax neutrality and minimising distortions to corporate investment and financing decisions.

The design of corporate tax systems affect firms' decisions in three major ways: the government might want to reduce the average effective tax rate to attract and retain companies; the marginal effective tax rate to encourage investment; or the statutory rate to reduce profit shifting. With three objectives, but only two instruments – the rate and the base – designing a better corporate tax system is hard. The challenge is boosted by the need to keep reforms revenue neutral.

Consider options for more fundamental reform

Given the many considerations in designing tax systems, most notably concerning neutrality and equity, there is no consensus on the way forward and the pros and cons of the various options for tax reform need to be assessed.[8] Most choices involve some unpleasant trade-offs or have serious drawbacks:[9]

- Given that it is ultimately individuals who pay tax, a basic question is why corporations should be taxed at all. In principle, it would be better for all taxes to be levied at the individual level.[10] But in a globalised world it is not feasible to fully monitor all cross-border income flows. Taxes on corporations can thus play a useful role, as they provide an easier point of tax collection and can be seen as a withholding tax for final payment by individuals. Corporate taxation may, for instance, be the only way of taxing foreign shareholders of domestic corporations. In principle, rents (pure profits) should be taxed, and in a closed economy, a tax on rents is non-distortionary. But in an open economy, a large fraction of rents may be internationally mobile.

- The United Kingdom is among the handful of OECD countries that tax company profits on a worldwide basis, though double taxation is largely avoided by giving credit for source-based taxation paid. The downside of worldwide taxation is that it provides an incentive for firms to relocate or it may prevent local multinational firms from materialising in the first place. Moreover, firms on the verge of expanding internationally may be discouraged from doing so by the tax costs they would incur. Most other OECD countries operate a dividend exemption system, which exempts foreign source dividend income from domestic tax. While a dividend exemption system would reduce relocation incentives, its drawback is that it encourages the shifting of profits abroad, which would then be allowed to re-enter the country tax free. The government has recently published a paper to consult on this issue (HM Treasury and HMRC, 2007).

- An Allowance for Corporate Equity system provides companies with a deduction of an imputed normal return on their equity from the corporate income tax base, parallel to the deduction for interest on debt. The advantage of this approach is that it avoids tax distortions to real investment and ensures neutrality between debt and equity finance. Moreover, because of the symmetric treatment of debt and equity it eliminates the need for thin capitalisation rules to protect the domestic tax base. With the deduction of an imputed normal return, this tax is a tax on pure profits, thus raising incentives to invest. But the imputed rate of return would need to be set at the right level, while the tax rate would need to be higher, because the tax base is smaller. This may have adverse implications for location decisions and encourage profit shifting. Belgium introduced such a tax in 2006 and Croatia has experimented with it.

● The Comprehensive Business Income Tax, examined by the US Treasury would also ensure neutrality between equity and debt, but it would do so by eliminating the deductibility of interest payments. The ensuing broadening of the tax base would allow a lower corporate tax rate. The lower rate would encourage inward investment and lower incentives for profit shifting through transfer pricing and thin capitalisation. However, such a reform would introduce an interest income tax at source and could lead to a significant increase in the cost of debt finance, which would act as a deterrent to debt-financed inward investment.

● Probably the most radical solution would be to abolish corporate income taxation, while changing the value added tax (VAT) regime and labour taxation in a revenue-neutral manner. Since value added consists of profits and compensation of labour, a tax switch

---

Box 5.5. **The VAT carousel fraud**

The value added tax (VAT) is often considered self-enforcing, because the tax is collected gradually throughout the chain of production and distribution, with refunds of VAT on intermediate inputs provided. However, opportunities for fraud exist, especially for zero-rated goods, such as exports, as businesses can be entitled to net refunds of VAT.

Missing trader intra-community fraud exploits the refund of VAT to exporters as well as the deferred payment of VAT on acquisitions from other EU member states. VAT in the acquiring country is not levied at the border but due at the time of the acquirer's period VAT return, which can lead to a considerable time lag. Goods can thus be exported and imported several times, with VAT refunds claimed repeatedly, while acquisition tax liabilities accumulate but are not paid as the acquiring company disappears before the VAT payment is due. The impact on receipts from missing trader intra-community fraud in 2005/06 was estimated at between £2 billion and £3 billion. The scale of the fraud can also be gleaned from the trade statistics, where the ONS provides adjustments to published trade data. These show a sharp rise in the trade flows associated with fraudulent activity, from £2.4 billion to a staggering £24.8 billion in the first half of 2006. Since then, it has dropped considerably.

The sharp drop in fraud is due mainly to more vigorous investigation principally through targeted pre-repayment verification of suspect VAT repayment claims. But audits and investigations are likely to face limits, because the essence of the fraud is that money is made quickly. Once the money has disappeared into a complex web of transactions, tracing and recovering unjustified VAT refunds becomes time-consuming and costly. Tighter checks on firms seeking to register for VAT or establishing better and quicker information between national tax authorities has also helped, but raises administrative burdens. Another avenue that has been pursued is "reverse charging", by which liability in a business-to-business transaction is placed on the buyer rather than the seller. This eliminates the need for outright refunds. The European authorities allowed reverse charging for mobile phones and computer chips in April 2007. The danger is that fraud will be perpetrated with other goods, not covered by reverse charging. Moreover, reverse charging, by eliminating the gradual accumulation of VAT payments, moves the system closer to a single-stage retail sales tax, raising the risk of revenue losses due to unreported sales to final consumers. Other administrative solutions have been proposed, but all either create other opportunities for fraud or would increase compliance costs. A durable long-term solution may require a fundamental redesign of the VAT treatment of intra-community transactions. Ending VAT zero-rating for trade between EU member states would sharply reduce the scale of refunds (40% of gross VAT receipts are refunded in the United Kingdom) and eliminate some of the most tempting opportunities for missing trader fraud. But such a reform would need agreement by all 27 EU member countries.

Source: Smith (2007) and Bank of England (2006).

could be implemented by increasing the VAT rate and making an offsetting reduction in the taxation of labour income. If the corporate income tax rate were to be abolished, rather than just reduced, several benefits could be achieved. The new tax system would not affect the level of investment, it would be neutral to the sources of finance, and it would not be susceptible to profit shifting nor location choice. But there are also drawbacks: financial services are VAT exempt and their contribution to the corporate tax take has risen, while profits on goods that are exported would be exempt. Moreover, there would be a strong incentive to incorporate. Most importantly perhaps, the VAT rate would have to increase considerably, raising incentives to pursue VAT fraud (Box 5.5).

Summing up

Globalisation and the desire of governments to render the corporate income tax system more efficient have driven down statutory corporate tax rates. As this has been accompanied by base broadening, corporate tax revenue as a share of GDP has not shrunk so far. The United Kingdom was early in this game, but has lost in tax competitiveness as others have moved ahead. Several countries are now planning further tax cuts, suggesting that pressure to reduce statutory tax rates will continue. It will thus be important to continue with a strategy of broadening the base, while cutting the rate. However, there are likely to be limits, because tax competition also plays out on the base. Given the detrimental effect of world-wide taxation on the location of headquarters, there may be merit in moving to a dividend exemption system. And there seems to be considerable room to simplify the tax system.

The degree to which globalisation might undermine the ability to tax corporate income remains uncertain. The location of production is determined by many factors, among which the corporate tax regime is not necessarily the most important. To the extent that globalisation makes it harder to tax mobile factors, there may be room to shift taxation to immobile ones. Property taxation is already high by international standards. Another option would be to raise VAT. The standard VAT rate is relatively low (by European standards) and includes many exemptions and zero and reduced rates. A rough indicator of the tax yield is the ratio of the share of VAT revenues to consumption, divided by the standard rate. This ratio (46.4% in 2003) is below the OECD average (52.9%) and way below that in New Zealand (96.4%) (OECD, 2006). There is thus room to broaden the base; although this would have distributional implications, these would be best addressed through other policies. Once the base has been broadened there may be room to raise the rate later on. A one percentage point increase in the standard VAT rate yields about £4.5 billion in tax revenues. Policy-makers should continue to explore the potential for the more radical reform options discussed above, all of which have merits and drawbacks and have been little tested in other countries.

Box 5.6. **Options for reforming corporate taxation**

- Continue to cut the statutory corporate tax rate and broaden the base.
- Shift taxation to less mobile sources and reduce the corporate tax rate. The VAT base could be broadened and the rate is relatively low.
- Look into the merit of moving to a dividend exemption system.
- Reduce the complexity of the tax code.
- Mull over more radical reform options. All options have advantages and drawbacks and their relative merits would need to be assessed carefully.

Notes

1. Devereux *et al.* (2004) and de Mooij and Nicodème (2007) find that higher profitability and increased size of the corporate sector have also played an important role. There may also be tax base shifting towards corporate taxation, if corporate taxation is lower than personal taxation. It is therefore important to view the tax system as a whole.

2. An exception is Malta which has a statutory rate of 35%, the third highest in the Union.

3. See Zodrow and Mieszkowski (1986) and Wilson (1986).

4. It is possible that firms are more likely to opt to incorporate where the corporate tax is lower. For example, Germany and the United States might have low corporate profits partly because many firms choose other organisational forms that are not subject to corporate taxes (in Germany partnerships and in the US S-corporations).

5. In Figure 5.1 only 19 OECD countries are included and of these 13 are in the EU15 (not including Denmark and Luxembourg). The average statutory rate for the EU13 and the OECD19 is very close.

6. The number on the length of the tax code covers all taxes, not only corporate income tax, but the length of the code is of importance as 84% of all tax payments are remitted by businesses.

7. This is an estimate and consists of £0.5 billion in R&D tax credits, £4.5 billion for the small companies reduced tax rate, £0.3 billion in exemptions for gains on substantial shareholdings, £1.3 billion in structural reliefs for life companies, £6 billion in taper relief and £10 billion in double taxation relief. The latter could, of course, not be removed without putting UK companies at an enormous disadvantage.

8. Moving to a common corporate tax base at the EU level is under scrutiny, while rulings by the European Court of Justice have the potential to undermine tax revenue. As they have an EU-wide dimension they are not discussed here.

9. The options discussed are based on Devereux and Sørensen (2006); Griffith *et al.* (2007); Auerbach *et al.* (2007) and chapter 5 of CESifo (2007).

10. A tax on the income from domestic and foreign capital owned by residents would not affect the location of companies. It would be a tax on savings that would ensure capital export neutrality as the tax treatment of domestic and outbound foreign investment is the same.

References

Adam, S., J. Browne and C. Heady (2007), "Taxation in the UK", draft paper prepared for the IFS Conference on "Reforming the Tax System for the 21st Century: The Mirrlees Review", Cambridge, 12 April, available at: *www.ifs.org.uk/mirrleesreview/publications.php*.

Auerbach, A., M. Devereux and H. Simpson (2007), "Taxing Corporate Income", draft paper prepared for the IFS Conference on "Reforming the Tax System for the 21st Century: The Mirrlees Review", Cambridge, 12 April, available at: *www.ifs.org.uk/mirrleesreview/publications.php*.

Bank of England, (2006), *Inflation Report*, Bank of England, London, August.

CBI (Confederation of British Industry) (2007), "Recommendations for the 2007 Budget", Report by the Confederation of British Industry, March, available at: *www.cbi.org.uk/pdf/budgetrecommendations2007.pdf*.

CESifo (2007), *The EEAG Report on the European Economy 2007*, European Economic Advisory Group at CESifo, Munich.

Devereux, M., R. Griffith and A. Klemm (2004), "How has the UK Corporation Tax Raised so much Revenue", *IFS Working Paper*, No. W04/04, Institute for Fiscal Studies, London.

Devereux, M., B. Lockwood and M. Redoano (2005), "Do Countries Compete over Corporate Tax Rates?", *Working Paper,* Oxford University Centre for Business Taxation.

Devereux, M. and P.B. Sørensen (2006), "The Corporate Income Tax: International Trends and Options for Fundamental Reform", *European Economy – Economic Papers*, No. 264, European Commission, Brussels.

Devereux, M. (2007), "The Impact of Taxation on the Location of Capital, Firms and Profit: A Survey of Empirical Evidence", *Working Papers*, No. WP07/02, Oxford University Centre for Business Taxation.

Elschner, C. et al. (2006), "The Effective Tax Burden on Companies and of Highly Skilled Manpower: Tax Policy Strategies in a Globalised Economy", *Fiscal Studies*, Vol. 27, No. 4, Blackwell Publishing.

Ernst & Young (2006), "European Attractiveness Survey: Team Europe Defends its Goals", available at: *www.ey.com/global/Content.nsf/International/Press_Release_-_European_Attractiveness_Survey_2006*.

Griffith, R., J. Hines and P.B. Sørensen (2007), "International Capital Taxation", draft paper prepared for the IFS Conference on "Reforming the Tax System for the 21st Century: The Mirrlees Review", Cambridge, 12 April, available at: *www.ifs.org.uk/mirrleesreview/publications.php*.

Hawkins, M. et al. (2002), "Budget 2002: Business Taxation Measures", *IFS Briefing Notes*, No. BN24, Institute for Fiscal Studies, London.

HM Treasury and Inland Revenue (2003), "Corporation Tax Reform. A Consultation Document", August, available at: *www.hm-treasury.gov*.

HM Treasury and HMRC (2007), "Taxation of Companies' Foreign Profits: Discussion Document", June, available at: *www.hm-treasury.gov*.

HMRC (HM Revenue and Customs) (2007), "Estimated Costs of the Principal Tax Expenditures and Structural Reliefs", HM Revenue and Customs, April, available at: *www.hmrc.gov.uk/stats/tax_expenditures/table1-5.pdf*.

Krogstrup, S. (2004), "A Synthesis of Recent Development in the Theory of Capital Tax Competition", *EPRU Working Paper Series*, No. 04-02, Economic Policy Research Unit, University of Copenhagen.

de Mooij, R.A. and G. Nicodème (2007), "Corporate Tax Policy, Entrepreneurship and Incorporation in the EU", *European Economy – Economic Papers*, No. 269, European Commission, Brussels.

Nicodème, G. (2006), "Corporate Tax Competition and Coordination in the European Union: What Do We Know? Where Do We Stand?", *European Economy – Economic Papers*, No. 250, European Commission, Brussels.

Nicoletti, G. et al. (2007), "Taxation, Business Environment and FDI Location in OECD Countries", *OECD Economic Studies*, No. 43, Vol. 2006/2, OECD, Paris.

OECD (2005), *Trends in International Migration*, OECD, Paris.

OECD (2006), *Consumption Tax Trends*, OECD, Paris.

OECD (2007), "Tax Effects on Foreign Direct Investment", *OECD Tax Policy Studies*, No. 17, OECD, Paris, forthcoming.

PWC (PricewaterhouseCoopers) (2006), "Enterprise in the UK: Impact of the UK Tax Regime for Private Companies. A PricewaterhouseCoopers Survey", PricewaterhouseCoopers, July.

PWC and the World Bank (2006), "The Increasing Burden of Tax Administration and Compliance", *Paying Taxes: The Global Picture*, PricewaterhouseCoopers.

Slemrod, J., J. Whiting and J. Shaw (2007), "Tax Implementation Issues in the United Kingdom", draft paper prepared for the IFS Conference on "Reforming the Tax System for the 21st Century: The Mirrlees Review", Cambridge, 12 April, available at: *www.ifs.org.uk/mirrleesreview/publications.php*.

Smith, S. (2007), "VAT Fraud and Evasion", *The IFS Green Budget,* Institute for Fiscal Studies and Morgan Stanley, London.

Wilson, J.D. (1986), "A Theory of Interregional Tax Competition", *Journal of Urban Economics*, Vol. 19, No. 3, Elsevier BV.

Zodrow, G.R. and P. Mieszkowski (1986), "Pigou, Tiebout, Property Taxation, and the Underprovision of Local Public Goods", *Journal of Urban Economics*, Vol. 19, No. 3, Elsevier BV.

ISBN 978-92-64-03772-4
OECD Economic Surveys: United Kingdom
© OECD 2007

Glossary

A8	Eight countries that joined the EU in 2004 (Czech Republic, Estonia, Hungary, Latvia, Lithuania, Poland, Slovak Republic, Slovenia)
ACT	Advanced corporation tax
AEN	Additional educational needs
AETR	Average effective tax rate
AR	Average of relatives
CPI	Consumer price index
CVA	Contextual value added
DEL	Departmental expenditure limit
DfES	Department for Education and Skills
DSG	Dedicated schools grant
DTI	Department of Trade and Industry
DWP	Department for Work and Pensions
EMA	Education maintenance allowance
ESA	Employment and support allowance
EU	European Union
EU15	European Union, first 15 member states
FDI	Foreign direct investment
FSM	Free school meals
G7	Group of 7 countries (Canada, France, Germany, Italy, Japan, United Kingdom and United States)
GCSE	General Certificate of Secondary Education
GDP	Gross domestic product
GM	Geometric mean
HICP	Harmonised index of consumer prices
HMRC	HM Revenue and Customs
IALS	International adult literacy survey
ICT	Information and communication technology
IPS	International passenger survey
LA	Local authorities
LFS	Labour force survey
LHA	Local housing allowance
METR	Marginal effective tax rate
MFG	Minimum funding guarantee
MFP	Multifactor productivity
MNE	Multinational enterprise
NAO	National Audit Office
NHS	National Health Service

153

NINo	National insurance number
OFSTED	Office for Standards in Education
ONS	Office for National Statistics
PCA	Personal capability assessment
PFI	Private Finance Initiative
PIAAC	Programme for international assessment of adult competences
PIRLS	Progress in international reading literacy study
PISA	Programme for international student assessment
R&D	Research and development
RA	Ratio of averages
RPI	Retail price index
RPIX	Retail price index excluding mortgage interest payments
RSCA	Revealed symmetric comparative advantage
SEN	Special educational needs
SME	Small and medium-sized enterprises
TFP	Total factor productivity
TIMSS	Trends in international mathematics and science study
VAT	Value added tax
UK	United Kingdom
US	United States
WRS	Worker registration scheme

OECD PUBLICATIONS, 2, rue André-Pascal, 75775 PARIS CEDEX 16
PRINTED IN FRANCE
(10 2007 17 1 P) ISBN 978-92-64-03772-4 – No. 55751 2007